MILTON, POET OF DUALITY

MILTON,
Poet of Duality

A Study of Semiosis in the Poetry and the Prose

R. A. SHOAF

YALE UNIVERSITY PRESS
New Haven   London

Designed by Margaret E.B. Joyner
and set in Janson with Deepdene type.
Printed in the United States of America by
Brun-Brumfield, Inc., Ann Arbor, Michigan.

Library of Congress Cataloging in Publication Data

Shoaf, R. A. (Richard Allen), 1948–
Milton, poet of duality.

Bibliography: p.
Includes index.
1. Milton, John, 1608–1674—Criticism and interpretation. 2. Duality (Logic) in literature. 3. Semiotics
and literature. 4. Monism in literature. I. Title.
PR3592.D82S54   1985   821'.4   84-21903
ISBN 0-300-33343-5 (alk. paper)

The paper in this book meets the guidelines for permanence and
durability of the Committee on Production Guidelines for Book
Longevity of the Council on Library Resources.

10   9   8   7   6   5   4   3   2   1

for

JUDSON BOYCE ALLEN
my friend now half my life

Contents

Milton's Numbers

ONE: Monad, singular, repeatable but not (re)iterable, principle of difference and of generation, without equal, peer, second, or like—God.

TWO: Must itself be two, or divided into

THE DUAL: One + One = One—mating, whole, principle of human creativity, structure of the psyche and of language; Christ, "true image of the Father," and God are the perfect dual.

THE DOUBLE: One + One = Two—duplicity, confusion, division, reiteration, doubt [doub-] (fear), copying, imitation, Narcissus, the failure of self-coincidence—the Devil.

THREE: Trinity, family, beginning of hierarchy and subordination.

FOUR: Tetractys, concord and virtue, "omnium numerorum radix et exordium."

THE WHOLE: Parts in harmony, implying hierarchy and subordination.

SINGULAR: The condition of a whole (N.B. Sometimes *single* must bear this sense).

SINGLE: Incomplete, unwhole(some), deadly, dying—Spenser's Despaire.

PART(NER): A pre-condition of a whole, se*par*ate, equal to or in parity with, one of a pair (which is a whole), a part of is apart from.

PAIR: Two parts or partners, the most basic whole, "the human pair" (im-pair, des-pair, re-pair, pair/pare).

ONE-HALF: The result of doubling the single, the condition of the lost.

RATIO: Human reason, proportionality, that which proportions, adjustment, just, balancing, the image of God in man.

PRODUCT: The unity of a multiple, meaningful, distinct, singular.

AMBIGUITY: Duplicity, the vice of language, two intentions contend for the same semantic space; deceitful and designing, choice and liberty revoked.

POLYSEMY: Multiplicity, the virtue of language, one semantic space produces many intentions; innocent and designed, choice and liberty invoked.

UNISEMY: The end of language.

Preface

The following chapters, twelve in number, involve almost all of Milton's poetry, in English, Latin, and Italian, and a good deal of his prose, especially *Christian Doctrine, Areopagitica,* and the divorce tracts.[1] The first ten chapters form, in effect, a continuous commentary on *Paradise Lost.* The last two extend that commentary to *Paradise Regained* and *Samson Agonistes,* in order to demonstrate their intimate connection with *Paradise Lost,* their similar concern with monism, duality, and the sign. All the chapters are written in as non-specialized a vocabulary as possible and are intended for a general academic audience. If they are frequently informed by contemporary discourse on language and literature, they are equally dependent on "old-fashioned" historical scholarship. Being suspicious of method, I welcome in them any method that delivers insight—but with one hand on the pen, one eye on the next page. Furthermore, and in part because of my suspicion of method, the chapters are deliberately essayistic, since I am trying to generate and defend an entire argument as quickly and as wholly as possible.

That argument, in brief, posits that the dual and the duel (Satan versus Christ, for example) are powerful heuristic tools in the reading of Milton—this because he was a man and a poet deeply concerned with human and divine relationships, with the couples or pairs man and woman, man (or woman) and God. In its attention to numbers, the argument is not a position on, or a study in, numerology; I am not competent in that discipline and am only marginally interested in it. My concern with "Milton's Numbers" is rather with what might be called the being of being alone: we are alone until we are all-one by becoming two—man and wife, friend and friend, worshiper and deity.

My play with words is certainly expendable; it harbors no mystery and claims no right/rite to awe. Rather the wordplay is a sign that signs are multiple in their signification, and this, as Milton clearly saw, is also a sign of sin, the sine qua non of the creation. Hence the crucial occurrences of the word *sign* and of *resign* (which is also *re-sign*) in *Paradise Lost* (fascination with which led to my starting this book long ago): Milton plots the fall into language on the same graph as the fall into sin and finds the curve for much of the way identical. In the end, however, the sign is not sin because it is different from sin (by the grace of one graph, for example) and reproduces itself. With signs, as with human procreation, $1 + 1 = 3$.

To describe the arc of the sign in Milton leads to a covenant with meaning. Meaning, I claim, is the meaning of *Paradise Lost*. This tautology, precisely by being the "same word" (taùtós lógos), exposes the issue at stake: as the same is the same because it is different—that is, not identical (cf. *Christian Doctrine* 1.5, YE 6:275)—so meaning obtains when $1 + 1 = 1$—man and wife, man (or woman) and God, God and Christ, song and singer, sign and signified. The difference within the same and the same within a difference are the motives of meaning. And when their duel becomes a dual, Love, the transcendental of meaning, gets time's number: time becomes meaningful in Love because, like Love, it has so little time. Milton divorced his wife—psychologically, not legally—and wrote tracts on divorce because the time weighed heavy on his hands. Divorce ($1 + 1 = 2$) is meaninglessness (Lovelessness) and thus also, as Milton profoundly understood, the beginning of meaning. God created the world "by his divorcing command," according to Milton (*The Doctrine and Discipline of Divorce*, YE 2:273). And Milton created his poetry by divorcing the past—he was a revolutionary—and by "[making] all things new"—like Christ, he was a son of God. My task in the following pages is to show just how he did it.

Acknowledgments

Every scholar depends on the labors of his colleagues. But a medievalist writing about Milton is necessarily over his head in debt to his colleagues, not to mention at the mercy of their goodwill. Debts of fact and interpretation of the sort normally incurred in the writing of a book of this kind I have acknowledged in my notes. Here I am happy to thank those who in person have suffered my questions and helped me find my way: Marie Boroff, Leslie Brisman, Richard Drake, Lars Engle, Margaret Ferguson, Alastair Fowler, Ken Gross, John Guillory, John Hollander, Leslie Moore, and Fred C. Robinson.

Not least among the colleagues who have helped me is the anonymous reader for Yale University Press. His ten pages, single-spaced, of criticism and commentary on my manuscript contributed more to the book than I can acknowledge in this brief space. Suffice it to say that I will always feel fortunate that a person still unknown to me, a total stranger, should have taken my work as seriously as he did.

In addition to colleagues, my students over the years have contributed to the development of this book. Although I cannot mention them all here, I must single out especially Claire Brown, Michelle Granieri, Matt Leipzig, Brett Millier, Abby Pogrebin, and Michael Rudko.

Although the book was begun and finished in New Haven, parts of it were written, in first draft, in Rome, during my tenure of a fellowship (Younger Humanist) of the National Endowment for the Humanities. It gives me great pleasure to be able to thank the Endowment for the opportunity and the support which it gave me. I am indeed fortunate to have had so much freedom, in every sense of the word, at such a crucial point in my thinking and writing.

The staff and editors of Yale University Press, especially Ellen Graham, have made the production of my book both delightful and instructive. (Horace would have been pleased with them.) My debt to Ms. Graham can never be repaid, and my only consolation is that so many others are in this predicament with me that she must long since have forgiven us all.

Finally, I trust that allowances will be made for so personal a note when I say that the dedication of this book pays homage not only to the greatness of one of America's leading literary scholars but also to his simple human goodness.

MILTON, POET OF DUALITY

Truly it is by continence that we are made as one and regain that unity of self which we lost by falling apart in the search for a variety of pleasures.

—St. Augustine, *Confessions*

A duobus utique bolis diabolus dicitur.

—St. Bernard, *Sermons*

Writing is dangerous from the moment that representation there claims to be presence and the sign of the thing itself. And there is a fatal necessity, inscribed in the very functioning of the sign, that the substitute make one forget the vicariousness of its own function and make itself pass for the plenitude of a speech whose deficiency and infirmity it nevertheless only *supplements*.

—Jacques Derrida, *Of Grammatology*

One can dissolve the entire sign system into a net of fractures. The nature of the sign is to be found in the 'wound' or 'opening' or 'divarication' which constitutes it and annuls it at the same time.

—Umberto Eco, *Semiotics and the Philosophy of Language*

When a part so ptee does duty for the holos we soon grow to use of an allforabit.

—James Joyce, *Finnegan's Wake*

1

The Lexicon of Duality in Paradise Lost

Milton uses the word *sign* twenty-six times in *Paradise Lost* and the word *resign* (which is also *re-sign*) seven times.[1] To my knowledge, no study exists devoted exclusively to these words or to the other, closely related words in the lexicon of duality—*justify, difference, contrary, pair, part, partner, impart,* and so on.[2] Moreover, no study, not even the structuralist or the post-structuralist, undertakes a semiotic analysis of these words, either separately or as a group.[3] And yet the sophistication of Milton's binary oppositions—coupling *sin* and *sign* in the same line (*PL* 2.760), for example[4]—suggests that such an analysis is clearly relevant and that it might produce important results. To be sure, these results would not replace the findings of other studies of signification in Milton's poetry—the typological, for example, or the reader-response-oriented or the psychogenetic[5]—but they would certainly supplement them, adding, in particular, a heightened appreciation of the *textuality* of Milton's verbal repetitions.[6]

In the hope of obtaining such results, I have attempted a semiotic analysis of the lexicon of duality in Milton's poetry. I have arranged the analysis to proceed as inductively as possible. Chapter 1, after a brief history of duality, sorts and defines the other key words in the lexicon and culminates with an analysis of narcissism in sin and the sign. The next nine chapters undertake a reading of *Paradise Lost* as the text which repairs the sign as it also repairs Paradise within us, "happier far" (*PL* 12.587). Chapter 11 follows with a reading of *Paradise Regained* which suggests that the duel between Satan and Jesus produces, by God's design, the dual between Jesus and God. Chapter 12, finally, concludes with a reading of *Samson Agonistes* as the drama of singularizing the self by separating from the world to reunite with God.

Milton's understanding of the sign and its repair emerges from his conception of the difference between duality and dualism. Here then is where we will begin.

The difference between duality and dualism is difference itself: in dualism, difference is really dichotomy—the intelligible world and the sensible world are strictly incommensurate; for duality, however, difference is supplementary—the intelligible and the sensible cannot exist without each other because they cannot exist without the difference between them. It is their difference which unites them, which supplements the meaning of each, making their meaning and meaningfulness possible.

In this many will find a (for some suspiciously) modern idea: difference, and hence opposition, disseminate the elementary structures of language—of meaning—and in fact of all forms of communication.[7] And yet this idea was available, I will argue, to Milton, though terminology and sources for him were different. The most likely of the possible sources, extending back into the Middle Ages and far beyond, is the philosophical principle, to use the version of it Chaucer uses in *Troylus and Criseyde*, that " 'by his contrary is everything declared'."[8] Chaucer's version can be supplemented by many other, similar English and Continental examples.[9] But here it is probably most helpful to cite the clearest and strongest example in Milton's own writing: "That which purifies us is triall, and triall is by what is contrary" (*Areopagitica*, YE 2:515; cf. *PL* 1.366).[10] By his or her contrary is everyone declared. Contraries, or (supplementary) differences, are not only the means to purity but also, as such, the dynamics of meaning itself. We know the meaning of what we have tried and of what has tried us: what we have du*a*led and (yes, of course) du*e*led, we know and understand—it has a meaning for us. And meaning is the meaning, I hope to show, of *Paradise Lost*.

Meaning is the product of duality. And duality is a structure. Dualism, on the other hand, is an -ism—that is, an ideology. And the one must not be confused with the other. Dualism is an ideology Milton strenuously repudiated throughout his career:

> Man is a living being, intrinsically and properly one and individual. He is not double or separable: not, as is commonly thought, produced from and composed of two different and distinct elements, soul and body. On the contrary, the whole man is the soul, and the soul the man: a body, in other words, or individual substance, animated, sensitive, and rational. [*CD* 1.7, YE 6:318]

But if man is "one and individual," he is still dual with the Father because he is created in the image of the Father, " 'to *correspond* with heaven' " (*PL* 7.511); he still participates in a structure of duality, even after the Fall. Indeed, the structure of duality is man's only medium to God after the Fall, for all that is left him of his once pure estate are the ruins of the image of God, or his reason. Man's reason is the fragmented Image of God within him.[11] And this image du*a*ls him with God. Without the ruins of this image, man would be utterly lost, damned. As long as they remain, however, he has some way back to God—back to before that moment when he disobeyed and his original du*a*l with God was changed into a du*e*l with God. The Fall perverted the du*a*l of creation into the du*e*l of disobedience. "Give me the grace to do as you command, and command me to do what you will!" Augustine cries out to God,[12] witnessing in this prayer to the duel between the will of God and the will of man, if also to the hope that God by his grace will transform this du*e*l into a du*a*l again, God *and* man.

But if man refuses grace, insisting instead on the duel, he remains in a state of sin, and almost the first corruption of sin is the perfidious conviction of dualism. Duality perverted by duel-ism leads inevitably to dualism, or the belief in the enmity between body and soul. Original Sin, of course, was an act of disobedience: disobedience transformed the dual between God and man into the duel between them. This is venerable Christian doctrine. Equally venerable is Augustine's teaching that the punishment for this disobedience is disobedience itself:

> In the punishment of that sin the retribution for disobedience is simply disobedience itself. For man's wretchedness is nothing but his own disobedience to himself, so that because he would not do what he could, he now wills to do what he cannot. For in paradise, before his sin, man could not, it is true, do everything; but he could do whatever he wished, just because he did not want to do whatever he could not do. Now, however, as we observe in the offspring of the first man,

and as the Bible witnesses, 'man has become like nothingness.' For
who can list all the multitude of things that a man wishes to do and
cannot, while he is disobedient to himself, that is, while his very mind
and even his lower element, his flesh, do not submit to his will? Even
against his volition his mind is often troubled; and his flesh experiences pain, grows old, and dies, and endures all manner of suffering.
We should not endure all this against our volition if our natural being
were in every way and in every part obedient to our will. [But]
through the justice of God, who is our Lord and master and whom we
refused to serve as his subjects, our flesh, which had been subject to
us, now gives us trouble through its non-compliance, whereas we by
our defiance of God have only succeeded in becoming a nuisance to
ourselves, and not to God. For he does not need our service as we
need the service of our body, so that what we receive is punishment
for ourselves, while what we have done is no punishment for him.
Moreover, the so-called pains of the flesh are really pains of the soul,
experienced in the flesh and from the flesh. [13]

Note that Augustine is not a dualist though Manichaeism is the heresy against which he struggled all his life; [14] rather, he describes that
conflict in the self which the darkened mind of man misinterprets as
dualism. Man in his misery over his disobedience to himself reasons
that there must be enmity between his body and his soul; he ra-
tionalizes fables of warring elements to posit gaps and fissures where,
in fact, there are none, where instead there is only his own tortured
self-coincidence—that union with himself which he can only experience as at best communion with himself, divided from himself by his
very joining with himself. [15] Man's tragedy—(Augustine would say,
his punishment)—is to be one without ever being able to atone. Man's
tragedy is to be one without ever being whole—to be alone and not
atone.

Dualism is the thinking man's way out of this misery. Duality is
the loving man's way out. And if the distinction which I just made is
to escape the stigma of dualism's *dichotomizing*, then it must allow for
the dual, the couple or pair, of the thinking man who is also a loving
man and the loving man who is also a thinking man. It must allow for
what dualism has no faith in—wholeness, the possibility of harmony.
Wholeness, duality, will sometimes, like dualism, insist on sepa-
rateness and division and difference (*chōrismós*); but sometimes, unlike
dualism, it will insist on likeness and union and participation (*méthexis*) and will seek the harmony of the dance (the *perichōrēsis*, the "cir-

cumincession").[16] What it will never do is dichotomize or polarize, for this is to abuse the natural tendency of the reason to divide and distinguish.

Such abuse, however, is precisely dualism's error, however natural.[17] The culmination of this error is Cartesianism, in which the certainty of the *res cogitans* compensates (presumably) for its aloneness over against the *res extensa*.[18] (If Milton in his time is a monist, it is at least in part because he finds such compensation inadequate at best, a mockery at worst—shall I pay out all joy for certainty that I am? That would be heroism only.)[19] Dualism enables the thinking man to hurl his "I am" against the object world, thus to persuade himself that he is his own, obedient to himself. Dualism clears the space for the mastery of technology, which makes all things obedient to the self—except the self.[20]

Loving men, men in whom love disciplines thought, know better. Loving men, the poet and the lunatic, of imagination compact (Plato in spite of himself), all posit couples and coupling—the *coitio* of the knower and the known[21]—dualities which recognize the inevitable— and yes, sometimes tragic—contingency of the whole on its parts and on the participation of the parts, which must be free, cannot be coerced, as Milton's God understands perfectly (*PL* 3.95–111). Loving men understand that precisely because each is (al)one, the only way to be one (whole) is to be two. That Milton is a poet (and a theologian) and not a philosopher is reflected in the fact that he wanted to atone and yet understood that to atone lies not in the power of man.

For man as man is divided from himself by an abyss and a distance he cannot cross, for though they are real, they are never present. The division is the division of difference, of *différance*,[22] the structure of language, of mediation itself, by which man knows himself. And to cross without transgression from this knowledge to the unity of atonement is not possible for flesh until the Word becomes flesh and flesh becomes word, in the re*sign*ation of the self in the autothanatography of the self—the acceptance of division as union, the rejoicing in difference as the same.[23]

Duality, then, recuperated from du*el*-ism, will always resemble du*al*ism, for it is the free play of resemblance itself, unafraid of resemblance, and thus it must embrace separation as well as participation. Twins are no threat to the dual, for they are an occasion of distinction; black and white are no threat to the dual, for they are an occasion of union.[24] Duality never forgets that resemblance is founded on difference and that difference presupposes resemblance, *and* that the paradoxes that say these truths are themselves suspiciously *ratio*nal. Duality, then, will resemble dualism but is finally not dualism, for, as my last sentence shows, it always returns: returning (retroping) is its joy.

All this Milton understood. *Eros* must find *Anteros:*[25]

> But after a while [Eros] darts out the direct rayes of his then most piercing eyesight upon the impostures, and trim disguises that were us'd with him, and discerns that this is not his genuin brother, as he imagin'd, [and then] he has no longer the power to hold fellowship with such a personated mate. For strait his arrows loose their golden heads, and shed their purple feathers, his silk'n breades untwine, and slip their knots and that original and firie vertue giv'n him by Fate, all on a sudden goes out and leaves him undeifi'd, and despoil'd of all his force; till finding *Anteros* at last, he kindles and *repairs* the almost faded ammunition of his Deity by the reflection of a coequal and homogeneal fire. [*DD* 1.6 YE 2:254–55; emphasis added]

And the reason that they must find each other—love and answering love—is that

> there is a hidden efficacie of love and hatred in man as wel as in other kinds, not morall, but naturall, which though not alwayes in the choyce, yet in the successe of mariage wil ever be most predominant [and this] besides daily experience, the author of *Ecclesiasticus. . .* acknowledges. . . *A man,* saith he, *will cleave to his like.* But what might be the cause, whether each ones alloted *Genius* or proper Starre, or whether the supernall influence of Schemes and angular aspects or this elementall *Crasis* here below, whether all these jointly or singly meeting friendly, or unfriendly in either party, I dare not, with the men I am likest to clash, appear so much a Philosopher as to conjecture. The ancient proverb in *Homer* lesse abstruse intitles this worke of leading each like person to his like, peculiarly to God himselfe. . . There is a twofold Seminary or stock in nature, from whence are deriv'd the issues of love and hatred distinctly flowing through the whole masse of created things, and. . . Gods doing ever is to bring the due likenesses and harmonies of his workes together, except when out of two contraries met to their own destruction, he moulds a third existence. [*DD* 1.10 YE 2:271–72]

God, Milton finds in Homer, is he who *tòn ómoîon ágeι . . . ōs tòn ómoîon* (*Od.* 17.218). God is, in short, the ultimate poet, joining like to like.[26] But just so, God will also divide, distinguish, and divorce:

> And certainly those divine meditating words of finding out a meet and like help to man, have in them a consideration of more than the indefinite likenesse of womanhood; nor are they to be made waste paper on, for the dulnesse of Canon divinity: no nor those other allegorick precepts of beneficence fetcht out of the closet of nature to teach us goodnes and compassion in not compelling together unmatchable societies, or if they meet through mischance, by all consequence to dis-joyn them, as God and nature signifies [*sic*] and lectures [*sic*] to us not onely by those recited decrees, but ev'n by the first and last of all his visible works; *when by his divorcing command the world first rose out of Chaos, nor can be renewed again out of confusion but by the separating of unmeet consorts.* [*DD* 1.10, YE 2:272–73; emphasis added]

For in a world that knows sin, both likeness and unlikeness (marriage and divorce) are necessary. Divorce must return before marriage can be, marriage must return before divorce can be. Return, as difference, is the supplement of their very possibility.

Dualism's effort to escape this necessity is as old as civilization itself. Dualism *is* the thinking man's way out. And just so, most thinking men for the past twenty-five centuries have been Platonists. Milton, we know, subjected Platonism, and especially Neoplatonism, to a searching critique, especially in *Paradise Lost.*[27] However, he was more Platonist than anything else—at least in the beginning—and indeed only so could he have become so precisely and brilliantly critical of Platonism.[28] Without Plato and Platonic dualism, Milton could not have become a monist and a poet in the service of Christian duality.

He started then as a Platonist, unquestionably, and was probably attracted also to Neoplatonism. Indeed, Augustine had told him (and all other Christians as well) that the only philosophy qua philosophy a Christian could seriously entertain was Platonism.[29] But however compatible Platonism is with Christianity, one thing is lacking in it, Augustine argues, and it is the most important thing, namely the Incarnation. For the Incarnation is too much likeness for the Platonist and dualist: it is God so like man that he became man, became flesh. This much likeness is repugnant to Athens, to the Greek, to the philosopher who is a dualist, for dualism, especially in its extreme, Manichaean form, insists that the abyss between God and man is uncrossable. To the Christian, however:

> There is no other way in which [Christ] can become ours than by our faith being directed to His flesh. For no man will ever come to Christ as God who despises Him as man; and therefore, if you wish to have any interest in Christ, you must take care, above all things, that you do not disdain His flesh. [30]

To the Christian, this likeness, God and flesh, is the ultimate fusion. [31] And to the Christian poet, it will be the ultimate example of all catachrestic or improper figuration (see chapters 4 and 7 below)—the paradigmatic likening of unlikes that justifies all subsequent metaphor. [32] Ultimately, the Christian poet cannot afford dualism because dualism cannot tolerate metaphor, the likening of unlikes: Plato, remember, dismissed all poets from the Republic. For dualism, such fusion can only be *con*fusion, the stumbling block which the thinking man cannot get around.

The strength of dualism always has been, and always will be its appeal to thought. Thought divides, distinguishes, separates, is discrete. Thought "naturally" knows the subject over against the object. Knowing this (presumably) inescapable dichotomy, thought projects numerous other dichotomies—most significant among them, probably, at least in the long run, the intelligible against the sensible.

It is the merit of the philosophical writings of Jacques Derrida to have shown how all such dualisms and dichotomies logocentrically inscribe their own doom: you cannot have the intelligible without the sensible, the Name-of-the-Father without castration, the *pharmakon*/healer without the *pharmakon*/poison, etc. The difference (*différance*) between them—the between-ness, say [33]—grants them their being: the non-presence of the one is the guarantor of the presence of the other, but the non-presence is therefore present. [34] But even such a critique as Derrida's cannot finally nullify the appeal of dualism: man will always be more ready to imagine mythic forces of good and evil or light and dark battling it out on eternity's stage than to admit that "within himself / The danger lies, yet lies within his power" (*PL* 9.348–49). Man will always prefer to see double, so to speak, than to hear on(e)ly. [35]

The appeal of dualism has been great more or less throughout

Western History, but it was acute in the Renaissance.[36] This we know and can measure through the efforts of Renaissance men to transcend it—for transcendence, when it suceeds, always retains what is transcended.[37] Consider, for example, the following effort by Sir Thomas Browne:

> That we are the breath and similitude of God, it is indisputable, and upon record of Holy Scripture; but to call ourselves a microcosm, or little world, I thought it only a pleasant trope of rhetoric, till my near judgement and second thoughts told me there was a real truth therein: for first we are a rude mass, and in the rank of creatures, which only are, and have a dull kind of being not yet privileged with life, or preferred to sense or reason; next we live the life of plants, the life of animals, the life of men, and at last the life of spirits, running on in one mysterious nature those five kinds of existences, which comprehend the creatures, not only of the world, but of the universe; thus is man that great and true *Amphibium*, whose nature is disposed to live not only like other creatures in divers elements, but in *divided and distinguished worlds*, for though there be but one to sense, there are two to reason; the one visible, the other invisible.[38]

This is ultimately dualism—the effort at transcendence fails—for division and distinction and unlikeness emerge to depress the tendency to likeness, to return (as likeness); but still duality, we feel, is the tendency of Browne's argument: man is the likeness that would *dual* with the various parts of creation. Or again, consider these famous lines by George Herbert:

> Man is all symmetry,
> Full of proportions, one limb to another,
>   And all to all the world besides:
>   Each part may call the farthest, brother:
> For head with foot hath private amity,
>   And both with moons and tides.
>
>   Nothing hath got so far,
> But man hath caught and kept it, as his prey.
>   His eyes dismount the highest star:
>   He is in little all the sphere.
> Herbs gladly cure our flesh, because that they
>   Find their acquaintance there.[39]

Here, the effort at transcendence is much more nearly successful, owing to the greater density of the figuration in the poetry, and we feel duality emerging from the strains of dualism: man is the likeness that *does* dual with the various parts of the creation. And yet the figures exhibit their excess, as all figures do, and the words *caught, prey,* and *dismount* imply the duel between man and creation which is the principal motive of dualism. In this poem unity is not yet whole.

Finally, consider a philosopher, a thinking man as such, Nicolas Cusanus, to whom Cassirer devotes so much attention.[40] His celebrated notion of "coincidentia oppositorum," the foundation of what he praises as "docta ignorantia," tells the tale: Cusanus uses dualism to overcome dualism. In Cassirer's words:

> The basic character of that 'copulative theology' sought by Cusanus lies in this reconciliation of mind and nature, of intellect and sense. With complete consciousness of method, he now opposes this to all theology that is merely 'disjunctive,' negating, and divisive.[41]

In this way, to be sure, Cusanus can be said to anticipate the structure of duality, especially in his "copulative theology": "mediatio Christi . . . est copula hujus coincidentiae, ascensus hominis interioris in Deum, et Dei in Hominem."[42] But to anticipate duality, he must presume dualism, even the radical dualism of Plato himself.[43]

Thus we arrive at the contradictoriness so determinative for Renaissance epistemology (whose analogue in Renaissance poetics is, of course, *paradoxa epidemica*).[44] Attracted by dualism because they were Platonists, Renaissance men were also suspicious of it because they were Christians. Faced with such a dilemma, Milton probably thought it best to turn his back on it, to become a monist.[45] As a monist who was also a poet, he could concentrate on the dual as a structure and ignore it as an -ism—an ideology or a philosophy. He was, as monist and poet, free to look for likeness and unlikeness alike.

But this freedom brought with it, still brings with it, grave responsibilities. Most grave among them perhaps is the responsibility of *ratio*nality itself, of proportioning.[46] For if the poet, like God, is ever bringing like to like, then equally he must ever be on guard against confusing like and unlike, for confusion, as we will see, is the Devil's work. In short, he must divide to join, distinguish to unite, sever to suture—and be himself *severe.* Again like God, he must "dispart" to join like to like (*PL* 7.24–41); he must imitate the *lógos tomeús* described by Philo Judaeus, "the 'Logos as cutter' who produces 'creation by dichotomy' but is the 'joiner of the universe' as well".[47] Should he fail to be sufficiently severe, the poet will produce only monsters of confusion—he will indeed be of the Devil's party. Should he be too severe, however, and utterly dichotomize the parts of creation, he will produce no poem, no metaphor, at all, but only a treatise of the *cogito*, immune from the world and its uncertainty—and again he will be of the Devil's party—for ultimately such severity as this presumes that man can be as singular and as one and as alone as God himself (*PL* 8.403–07), which is precisely to confuse man with God.

If Milton, writing in the seventeeth century, resembles Cartesian man—seeking distinctions, gradations, precision everywhere—it is because, yes, he is a *ratio*nalist,[48] but a Christian, not a Cartesian, rationalist, seeking not "clear and distinct" ideas but the differences of the myriad parts of the plenitude. If Milton, writing in the late seventeenth century, resembles a Baroque artist—seeking strange and wondrous combinations in similes, metaphors, syntax, and meter—it is because he is a man of imagination, sensitive to the *ir-ratio*nal, but a man of the prophetic imagination,[49] seeking not the bizarre for its own sake but the mysterious articulations of the unities of the plenitude. In short, when Milton is Cartesian, it is to chasten the Baroque within him; and when he is Baroque, it is to humanize the Cartesian within him. He proportions the two within him, justifies and adjusts them within him, to repair himself to prepare himself to return to God.

Now that duality has been differentiated—not dichotomized—from dualism, our next task is to sort the lexicon of duality in *Paradise Lost* itself. And the first word to be sorted is the justification of the poem itself, or *justify*. Perhaps no line of *Paradise Lost* is so famous, so common an element of our cultural deposit, as line 26 of Book 1: "And justify the ways of God to men." This word asserts the strategy of difference and duality in the poem and thus prepares for the later articulation of the structure of signification, itself the prescription of the argument for the repair of the sign on the way to the meaning of meaning.

The verb to *justify* obviously evokes the senses of difference and duality (*OED*, J:643–44, 5 and 9). One does not "justify" A to B unless there is some "distance and distaste" (*PL* 9.9) and, implicitly, some misunderstanding between them. Hence it follows that one justifies in order to eliminate or reduce or correct the distance, the disagreement, and the misunderstanding. One justifies, in fact, to equalize the opposing parties (to transform duel into dual). "To equalize," as *Paradise Lost* will again and again insist, is not "to render identical"— that is the effort and the desire of Satan, and after him, of Eve fallen (see *PL* 10.144–56)—rather, it is to adjust to one another parties that are ontologically unequal, God and man. It is to re-establish equity, or proper proportionality, or meaningful duality, between the Creator and his creature in the dimension of understanding.

Two intimately related issues surface at this point. One is so immediate that it is almost invisible. For if Milton seeks "to justify the ways of God to men," to re-establish equity between the Creator and his creature in the dimension of understanding, he must presume, necessarily, that God's ways are intelligible to man, that man can understand them. No justification is possible without prior understanding. Man must still possess, then, some basic likeness to the Divine, on account of which and through which he can perceive and understand the ways of the Divine, because of which he is still dual with God. This basic likeness, we recall, is the ruins of the image of God in man after the Fall (Gen. 1:26).

At the same time, however, past finding are the ways of God (Rom. 11:33). Obviously man cannot understand, and Milton does not presume that he can understand, the full mystery and the as yet unaccomplished providence of God's ways. At some point, understanding must resign its task to faith. And faith *can* understand the ways of God, Milton would affirm, although in a different way from that of reason or intelligence. Exactly where, at what threshold, understanding resigns its task to faith is a question answerable only in the case of an individual person. Suffice it, then, to note here that Milton provokes the issue of reason versus faith in the very word *justify*.[50] Faith is at issue throughout the poem.

If Milton is God's advocate, he who justifies his ways to men, man in his turn needs his own advocate or mediator (see *PL* 11.22–38), namely Christ, his faith in whom justifies him before the Father. And, in fact, it is this need and, more important, the one who fulfills it, the Logos, which obviously inspire Milton's assumption of the role of advocate or mediator. Milton is to God as Christ is to man and God. For if Christ justified men to God, he also necessarily justified and justifies God to men. And the way he justified God to men is crucial to understanding Milton's strategy: "And the Word was made flesh, and dwelt among men" (John 1:1). If the Word of God was made flesh and dwelt among men, he also, necessarily, spoke to men, even as Milton is speaking to men in *Paradise Lost*. Christ justified God—he represented God, advocated his "cause," was his vicar, mediated him—through speech. He was himself the Word and used words. Thus even only to listen to him was, and is, to practice at least as much faith as assumes that his words mean at least what convention suggests they mean. Christ justified God in just that way which invokes and provokes faith. So too Milton: to justify God by words is to justify by faith, and Milton uses *justify* even predicated of God to insist on exactly this.

As is evident, I am using the word *faith* in an unusual way. In fact, I am presuming carefully graded degrees of faith: one degree (theological faith) believes in the resurrected and living Christ; another, lesser degree (verbal faith) believes in, or at least for the moment suspends disbelief in, the words a speaker is speaking. However, these degrees of faith are connected, if graded, and it is possible, I am arguing, to pass from the one to the other—that is, verbal faith can become theological faith.

Verbal faith, of course, is faith in mediation, and just so, should it become theological faith, it becomes also, indeed has become, faith in the Mediator. Hence—and this is the second issue to surface at this point—as man is justified by faith in the Mediator, so Milton can justify God's ways to men only by faith, his and his reader's, in the Mediator. If Milton is analogous to Christ—and his faith underwrites this analogy—then he is mediating God to men; and his words are analogous to the Word, the Logos. Milton's language, by the very attempt at justification, or the reestablishment of equity between God and men, serves as the mediator, the advocate, the equalizer. Not that the language *is*, but that it serves *as*, the mediator where *as* articulates the structure—differential and dual—of signification, the signification both to be and being redeemed.[51] The language as the mediator is different from, but *like*, *the* Mediator: it duals the Mediator. Thus, when the reader puts his faith in Milton's language, which he must do in order to read the poem, it is *as if* he puts his faith in the Mediator. But such an action is to justify himself before God; but to be justified before God the reader must have had God and his ways justified to him. *If* the reader is justified, God's ways must have been justified; *if* God's ways are justified, the reader is justified. Fictionally—as if-ly—to read *Paradise Lost* is to be justified and to fulfill Milton's intention of justifying the ways of God to men. Concede only as much as *as if*, have only as much faith as a willing suspension of disbelief, and you grant Milton his premise, that faith is the minimal pre-requisite of signification. You cannot enter into any activity of signification, such as reading, without faith in signs. Grant Milton's premise—give him only the structure of (your) faith—and he can and will return you, if you will, to "a Paradise within thee, happier far" (*PL* 12.587), for the mediator needs only faith to redeem the sign.

One question obviously cries out to be answered: Why bother? Why bother justifying the ways of God to men? And a related question: Why bother, even "as if-ly," reading *Paradise Lost?*

Behind these questions, motivating them, lies a more basic, more troubling, and possibly more human question: Why does Milton repeat the story told in Genesis? This question leads to the next item in the lexicon of duality to be sorted—namely, repetition. In one regard, the answer to the question is simply that Milton repeats the story so as not to duplicate it.[52] Satan duplicates: he thinks, and hopes to make " 'all *like* himself rebellious' " (*PL* 7.138–39; emphasis added). He also "reiterate[s]" (*PL* 1.214): his final justification for seducing Eve is " 'others to make *such* / *As I* ' " (*PL* 9.127–28; emphasis added), and when she becomes such as he—that is fallen—she does not fear "to iterate," Milton is careful to repeat, "her former trespass" (*PL* 9.1005–06). She is Satan's duplicate and his toy. Milton, on the other hand, who *does* fear iteration and the ensuing bondage, repeats the story told in Genesis—duals it and, when necesary, duels it—so as to be original and therefore free. All this in contrast to Satan, who seeks originality without repetition and ends up in reiteration without originality: " 'Ever to do ill our sole delight, / As being the contrary to his high will / Whom we resist' " (*PL* 1.160–62). Who contradicts must reiterate.

To *repeat*, however, is to "seek again," or, as in *re-petition*, to "petition again" (*OED* R:462, branch II, 4), and this is why Milton, who does not want to contradict, repeats the story told in Genesis. He prays again, or prays anew, in the re-petition which is his poem and which is in his poem, and he prays again or prays anew, because the only way to justify the ways of God to men is to repeat them.

Milton, I am arguing, exploits faith to transform credibility into *credo.* Just to read *Paradise Lost* is to enter into justice. The whole experience of *Paradise Lost* is of a *ratio*nal process (which includes human emotion) of *adjustment:* on the one hand, adjustment of matters divine to human comprehension—this, of course, is the celebrated notion of accommodation, which posits the duality of heaven and earth (*PL* 5.468–503, 574–76 especially; 7.511, 557; 8.67) such that exchange of terms in similes relating heaven and earth is possible;[53] on the other hand, adjustment of human reason to the modality of comprehension, or the re-*pair* of the reason (*ratio*) which is the image of God in man, such that it resembles God again—is in his likeness again (Gen. 2:6). In effect, then, we, the readers, in repeating the poem by reading it, also *pair* it (adjust to it), even as the poem *pairs* (and repeats) Scripture in order that we might together *repair* the *impairment* of justice wrought by the Fall.

After justification, faith, and repetition, *pair* and its reflexes, along with *part*ner, constitute the next most important group of words in Milton's argument. We should never lose sight of the following facts: Adam and Eve are a *pair,* "the loveliest pair" (*PL* 4.321, 366; see also 5.227; 8.58 esp; 9.127; 11.105). They live in Par(*pair*)adise. Only as a *pair* are they fully and completely human (whole). When they are no longer a *pair* but are a *part*—though not, as we shall see, se*para*te— they are *impaired* by Satan.[54] Satan is able to im*pair* them, and im-*pair* them, in part because Adam believes Eve is " 'beyond com*pare*' " (*PL* 9.227–28) when, in fact, only Christ is "beyond com*pare*" (*PL* 3.138). When they beg God's forgiveness for their sin, they "re*pair*" (*PL* 10.1087) for this purpose to the place at which he first judged them, where the verb *repair* is also obviously *re-pair*, connoting their joining themselves again to God.[55] Finally, because of their fall, hereafter " 'objects divine / Must needs *impair* and weary human sense' " (*PL* 12.9–10; emphasis added).

All these facts are implicit in Adam's first words to Eve in the poem: " 'Sole *partner* and sole *part* of all these joys'." To be a partner, Eve must also be *a part,* and if a part she must also be *apart,* a condition much to the liking of Satan who eventually exploits it. In a sense, the whole of Milton's argument resides in this one line: the dual in the line reflects the ontological duality of man in the *pair* male and female, and

that duality or pair is continuous with and analogous to, not identical
with, the duality which is structural in signification—an entity is
named *as* (and thus paired *with*) a sign, and a sign is paired *with* or
dualed *by* what it signifies, and all these dualities or pairs are instances
of justification, or adjustment, of one person or thing to another.
Duality, Milton understands perfectly, is structural in human life.
Indeed, human beings began in and from duality. Not only were
they created in the image of God (Gen. 2:7; see also *PL* 7.519–20),
thus dualing him, but they were also—and this is equally important—created " 'to repair his [God's] numbers. . . impaired [by Satan's seduction of " 'well nigh half / The angelic name' "]' " (*PL* 9.144,
142; see also 7.152–53: " 'I [God] can repair / That detriment' ").
Man repairs (or, we might say, re-adjusts) the numbers of created
beings; Satan's rebellion was a depletion of the just number of beings.
The significance of Satan's remarking this repair lies mainly in the
fact that only he can believe that is God impaired. Raphael had earlier
wondered: " 'Who can impair thee [God]?' " (*PL* 7.608). Obviously,
the answer is no one. And yet Satan thought to impair God and
believes that he did so—believing as a consequence that " 'peace is
despaired " (*PL* 1.660; emphasis added)—and all this because, when
God exalted Christ, "with envy against the son of God / [He, Satan]
could not bear / Through pride that sight, and thought himself im-
paired" (*PL* 5.662–65; emphasis added). Thinking himself impaired,
Satan thought to impair God, and did so, though in a sense contrary
to his will and beyond his present understanding, since he im-paired
God by ceasing his own pairing with God as one of God's creatures—
and, as a result, is now "visibly impaired" (*PL* 4.850). Rather than be
apart from and thus creatively *a part of* God, he sought, and forever
seeks, to *part* God *from* God's own identity, so as himself, "affecting
all equality" (*PL* 5.763), to usurp God's place (*PL* 4.961), which, were
he to succeed at it, would completely eliminate one (id)entity from
creation. In other words, rather than be two, and thus one (a whole),
he chose, and still chooses, to be one alone—in God's place, forgetting that God, unlike him (*PL* 6.341), is "matchless" (*PL* 4.41). He
thus became half or less, always single—" 'Divided empire with
heaven's king I hold' " (*PL* 4.111). Whereas, before the Fall, he and
Beelzebub " 'were one' " (*PL* 5.677–78), now he and all the fallen
angels are forever deprived of such intimacy—they are beyond repair. But because of his (and Adam and Eve's) sin, everyone and

everything else must be repaired. This fundamental adjustment Milton's poem would further: as we pair the poem by reading it, the poem repairs us, to God.

We pair the poem, of course, when we repeat it through reading; we and the poem then form a pair—we become mates. And our pairing is thus a repairing of communication. What this means exactly I want now to demonstrate by a reading of the text in which Milton's trope of pairing originates—that is, Book 1 of *The Faerie Queene*.

In canto vii of Book 1, Arthur proposes to help Una by listening to her story: " 'Found never helpe, who never would his hurts impart,' " he tells her in stanza 40, and the word *impart* is our first access to Milton's reading of this (and the related episode of Despaire's speech to Redcrosse Knight in canto ix). Una replies:

'O but . . . great griefe will not be tould,
    And can more easily be thought, then said.'
'Right so,' quoth he, 'but he, that never would,
    Could never: will to might gives greatest aid.'
'But griefe,' quoth she, 'does greater grow displaid,
    If then it find not helpe, and breedes despaire.'
'Despaire breedes not,' quoth he, 'where faith is staid.'
'No faith so fast,' quoth she, 'but flesh does paire.'
'Flesh may empaire,' quoth he, 'but reason can repaire.'

His goodly reason, and well guided speach
    So deepe did settle in her gratious thought,
    That her perswaded to disclose the breach,
    Which love and fortune in her heart had wrought. . .
                                    [1.vii.41 and 42].

This is extraordinary and moving poetry. Here I want only to isolate the data crucial to Milton's reading of it. Most important is the play on the word *pair*, which proliferates into *des-pair*, *em-paire*, and *re-paire*, where the latter has precisely the heft Milton seeks in his own trope. Una must "impart" her story to Arthur, which is also, the context makes clear, to impart herself with Arthur, and thus become a partner with him, thereby forming a unity which can "disclose the *breach*," or rupture of unity, which she has suffered. Clearly Spenser implies, and Milton heard him imply, that Una (unity, one-ness) is not truly one unless she is two, or im-parted to and with Arthur. And just so, *des-pair* is the destruction of the pairing which makes unity (and joy) both conceivable and obtainable.

The opposite of *despair*, Christianity argues, and thus its antidote almost as if by a sympathetic magic, is faith, which for Spenser and Milton alike is the structure of pairing in the special sense we are considering here. (Faith, therefore, let us note, resembles despair insofar as it is a kind of pairing.) Still, though faith is the antidote, Una objects that " 'No faith [is] so fast but flesh does paire'." Obviously, *paire* here must mean "damage" or "ruin"; this much is clear from Arthur's response: " 'Flesh may *empaire* but reason can repaire' " (emphasis added). However, we can see quite clearly that if *paire* means "empaire," Spenser also succeeded in writing *both paire* and *empaire;* and this, I take it, is the point—both senses rather than just one. Flesh *paires* in the sense of "ruins," yes, just as Una insists, for it is weak and helpless, but flesh also paires in the sense of "partners," and *did it not*, there would be no "re-paire" by *re*ason. The flesh pairs and also pares the spirit, and this duality can *ruin* faith, for "the spirit is willing but the flesh is weak" (Matt. 26:41), and yet, if the flesh did not partner, or paire, the spirit, the spirit could not, in the world as we have it, communicate its intent. Without the flesh pairing, the spirit cannot ask the other to have faith in it, cannot communicate. And so it is that the very possibility of faith is also the possibility of despair: the pairing of faith can become despairing of faith. When, finally, Arthur responds to Una that " 'reason can repaire'," he eliminates the possibility of despair—as it were the shadow of the possibility of faith—but presumes the latter, because there must be pairing before there can be re-pairing. Reason must presume the pairing of the flesh before it can repair the flesh and the spirit; and Spenser insists on reason (twice) in this passage, because reason, as we can hear in English, *re*peats: rather than unilaterally or instantly acting in a situation, reason repeats the situation in the mind—as we might say, reflects upon it—and then reacts to it.

Reason repairs the pairing of the flesh, and thus persuades Una "to disclose the breach, / Which love and fortune in her heart had wrought." This is exciting language. Normally we assume that the thing to do with a breach is to close it; and obviously Spenser assumes that Arthur will help Una to just that end. However, he also insists, brilliantly, that before closure, disclosure: we cannot close until and unless we disclose—that is, we must perform the opposite of our intention before we can achieve our intention. Just as we cannot repair unless we are paired (in the sense of both damaged and partnered), so we cannot close, or heal, until we disclose, or make a breach *to* the breach. We must repeat the wound to heal the wound—(think of the surgeon's knife)—we must repair the wound with a wound. Not thus to repeat, not thus to repair, is to des-pair:

> The Knight was much enmovèd with his [Despaire's] speach,
>> That as a swords point through his hart did perse,
>> And in his conscience made *a secret breach*,
>> Well knowing true all, that he did reherse,
>> And to his fresh remembrance did reverse
>> The ugly vew of his deformèd crimes,
>> That all his manly powres it did disperse,
>> As he were charmèd with inchaunted rimes,
> That oftentimes he quakt, and fainted oftentimes.
>
>   [1.ix.48; emphasis added]

The words of Despaire make a "*secret* breach": they do not disclose to close, they do not repeat the wound to heal the wound, they do not repair the wound with a wound, they do not open to close—rather, they close (*secret*) to open, they pair only in the sense of *to damage*, they wound only to wound. The words of Despaire are *not* truly dual: they are viciously single-minded (*des*pair—that is, not-pair). Arthur's words, on the other hand, are truly dual: they pair in order to repair, they damage—yes, it does hurt Una to have to answer Arthur's words with her words—*and* they make a partner of her—Una and Arthur enter into partnership for communication. Whereas Arthur's speech, which is also a sword ("*well guided*. . . / So deepe did [it] settle in her gratious thought" [1.vii. 42; emphasis added]), repeats so as to liberate Una's memory from the iterative (the iteration and reiteration of her grief), the sword of Despaire's speech cuts memory off from the new and different, burdening "*fresh* remembrance"— that is, present memory—with old crimes, and does so by reversing, where *reverse* is the nullification of repetition, since it merely does the verse again. *Repetition* is "praying again," but *reversal* is merely "return"; and where, as in reversal/return, there is no difference, there is no true repetition, only reiteration: thus, *repraying* repeats "repetition," but *return* reiterates "reversal." In the one, there is real difference, and hence repetition; in the other, only a phenomenal difference, and hence reiteration. And it is reiteration with which Despaire wishes to confront Redcrosse Knight, for, as Spenser well knew, despair is the experience of relentless reiteration which all too often culminates in suicide. Despaire, as Spenser observes with chilling point, a "thousand times" (1.ix.54) has tried (in vain) to kill himself. The despairing human being can see no alternative, no difference—can see rather only his misery and grief reiterate themselves and the self reiterate itself in the face of its misery and grief. So bound in and to reiteration, the only alternative apparent is the awesome difference of death—self-slaughter—which, since no one knows what death is, may simply turn out to reiterate the life being abandoned.

Recrosse Knight escapes self-slaughter (which, let us note, is murder in which the one who kills reiterates the one who dies), but Satan does not. And, in a sense, if we stop to think about it, Satan's sin *was* suicide. Like Spenser's Despaire, Satan is murderously single in his rhetoric and behavior: he is, we might say, a monomaniac. (And in this he is also a parody of Christ, who " 'dares be *singularly* good' " [*PR* 3.57], but more on this in Chapter 11). In his monomaniacal singularity, Satan has severed himself from God and thus killed the brightest of the archangels, himself. Milton has a brilliant way of suggesting that Satan is a suicide while still acknowledging the obvious fact that though ruined (*PL* 1.593), he is not literally dead. It consists in a subtle but powerful quotation, like many others we will observe, of Dante—in this case of *Inferno* 13, the story of Piero delle Vigne.

This particular moment is one of the most famous in all three canticles of the *Commedia*. My only concern at present, however, a very narrow one, is the image of the torn tree limb effusing speech (*Inf.* 13.22–108).[56] This stunning and oft-repeated image derives, of course, from Virgil, from whom Ariosto, Tasso, and Spenser imitate it,[57] but significantly, in Virgil it is not the branches or the stalks of the plant which speak—rather, the speech issues from the mound, or *tumulus* (*Aeneid* 3.40). It is in Dante that the branches or limbs speak, and after him, of course, in Ariosto, Tasso, and Spenser. From the branch of Piero which he has torn, Dante says, "usciva insieme / Parole e sangue" (came out words and blood together [*Inf.* 13.43–44]). It is this line, I believe, to which Milton alludes so as to suggest that Satan is a suicide.

In Book 1 of *Paradise Lost* (lines 612–16), as the fallen angels gather around Satan to hear his first speech to them after the Fall, Milton likens them to blasted trees:

> As when heaven's fire
> Hath scathed the forest oaks, or mountain pines,
> With singed top their stately growth though bare
> Stands on the blasted heath.

The punctuation, which leaves the simile a freestanding syntactic unit,[58] also therefore leaves open the possibility of its reference *forward* as well as backward; in other words, Satan can also resemble a blasted tree as he prepares to speak. I feel sure that this dual reference is intentional, for it enables Milton to go on to suggest a likeness between Piero delle Vigne and Satan. He writes, just before Satan begins to address the fallen angels, that

> Thrice he essayed, and thrice in spite of scorn,
> Tears such as angels weep, burst forth: at last
> *Words interwove with sighs found out their way.*[59]
>   [*PL* 1.619–21; emphasis added]

Sighs, of course, are not blood, and the allusion must be reckoned a distant one. But if distant, it is nonetheless audible, especially between the Italian *insieme* and the English *interwove*, and it invites us to understand that Satan was, albeit in a very special sense, a suicide, now hardening, as it were, with the hardness of a tree trunk.

Unlike Satan, Redcrosse Knight is not a suicide, in any sense. He is saved from this fate by the timely aid of Una's speech (*FQ* 1.ix.52– 54): she re-pairs him, exhorting him to turn his back on Despaire. To complete the process of repairing him, she conducts him to the House of Holiness, where he is treated by Fidelia, who is "able, with her words [of Scripture] to kill, / And raise againe to life the hart, that she did thrill" (*FQ* 1.x.19). This couplet, I take it, concludes the extended metaphor of speech as a sword ("thrill"), and in doing so, also finishes one seam in Spenser's understanding of duality and pairing. If Arthur's speech is dual, fully exploiting mutability, and if Despaire's speech is monomaniacal, Fidelia's is both. It is single—"the letter killeth" (2 Cor. 3:6)—in that it insists on the identity, the non-contra-dictoriness of the Law, which is everywhere and always identical; yet it is also dual, pairing and re-pairing—"but the spirit giveth life" (2 Cor. 3:6))—in that it *again* raises, or *re*raises, the heart to life (it re-peats or re-pairs life), thus insisting on difference, newness (the Pauline "novus homo"), and, perhaps most important, con*vers*ion, the opponent of re*vers*al. Note, this much said, that the prosopopoeia,

Fidelia, means *faith*, and then recall our earlier insistence that faith and despair nearly resemble each other in that each is a kind of pairing, and you will grasp Spenser's intent: faith alone repairs despair (re-pairs the pair des-pair destroys). Moreover, faith repairs despair precisely because faith repeats (resembles) despair:

> The faithfull knight now grew in litle space,
> By hearing her [Fidelia], and by her sisters lore,
> To such perfection of all heavenly grace,
> That wretched world he gan for to abhore,
> And *mortal life gan loathe,* as thing forlore,
> *Greeved with remembrance of his wicked wayes*
> *And prickt with anguish of his sinnes so sore,*
> *That He desirde to end his wretched dayes:*
> So much the dart of sinfull guilt the soule dismayes.
>
> [FQ 1.x.21; emphasis added]

Faith, like Despaire, burdens present memory with the weight of old crimes (cf. 1.ix.48), and this letter kills–Redcrosse Knight desires to commit suicide. He does not do it, however, because Fidelia and her sister Speranza comfort him:

> But wise Speranza gave him comfort sweet,
> And taught him how to take assured hold
> Upon her silver anchor, as was meet
> Else had his sins so great, and manifold
> Made him forget all that Fidelia told. . .   [FQ 1.x.22.]

To forget, of course, would be to forfeit the hope of repair: one must remember to repair, although memory must not be permitted to consume the present in reiteration of the past. If one remembers in faith, this will not happen, but still, remembering in faith will always bring one near to despair, for faith repeats despair so as to repair despair—as the surgeon wounds to heal a wound.

Ultimately, Spenser's metaphor of speech as a sword, and thus also his understanding of pairing, goes back to Hebrews 4:11:

> For the word of God is living and effectual and more piercing than any two-edged sword and reaching unto the division of the soul and the spirit, of the joints also and the marrow; and is a discerner of the thoughts and intents of the heart.

The importance of this verse is, I assume, obvious, but I would call special attention to the word *two-edged* and the subsequent emphasis on *division*, for these words contribute most, I think, to Spenser's combination of pairing with the sword image.[60] Clearly too, the words of Arthur and Fidelia are analogous to the word of God, and it is not difficult to figure the words of Despaire as a perversion of that word. We can conclude finally from Spenser's recourse to this verse his conviction that the word of God and, by analogy, the words of a faithful Christian, will repair fallen man. And that implication, we are about to see, is one which Milton not only inferred but also made explicit in his own lexicon of duality.

It is in his treatise *Of Education* that Milton makes Spenser's implication explicit:

> The end, then, of learning is *to repair* the ruins of our first parents by regaining to know God aright, and out of that knowledge to love Him, to imitate Him, to be like Him, as we may the nearest by possessing our souls of true virtue, which, being united to the heavenly grace of faith, makes up the highest perfection. [YE 2:366–67; emphasis added]

We now know what, and how much, education must have meant to Milton when he conceives of it as "repair." And since *Paradise Lost* is an educative poem (just like *The Fairie Queene*)—it could not be anything else and "justify the ways of God to men"—we can fully appreciate its emphasis on pairing and the related concepts. *Paradise Lost* would *repair* us and *re-pair* us to God; it would make us again two, and therefore truly one.

This mystery, that to be one we must be two,[61] also resides in and spurs the poem's insistence on the sign. *Sign* is the last word in the lexicon of duality to be sorted at the present time, and once it has been defined and described, the reading of *Paradise Lost* can get under way. Milton, as I have noted, uses the word *sign* in *Paradise Lost* twenty-six times, *resign* (*re-sign*) seven times. The most important occurrence for our purposes is the third one, which in effect defines it for the remainder of the poem. Sin describes for Satan her birth and appellation and recalls for him his reaction to her:

> 'back they [the host of heaven] recoiled afraid
> At first, and called me sin, and for a *sign*
> Portentous held me; but familiar grown,

> I pleased, and with attractive graces won
> The most averse, thee chiefly, who full oft
> Thyself in me thy perfect image viewing
> Becamst enamored.'   [*PL* 2.759–65]

This third occurrence of the word *sign* shadows all its other occurrences with the memory of its simultaneity with *Sin*. The *sign*, this
moment suggests, would be *sin* were it not for the *g*. This is not
intended to be flip. It is meant to suggest what I think the poem
premises, that all signs emerge from sin. This does not mean, I hasten
to say, that all signs are sinful—obviously, they are not (see, for
example, *PL* 7.339–41)—but that sin is the pre-condition—eventually, I will argue, the pretext—of the sign.

How and why this should be so, Milton makes clear in the very
next step of Sin's narrative:

> 'I pleased, and with attractive graces won
> The most averse, thee chiefly, who full oft
> Thyself in me thy perfect image viewing
> Becamst enamored.'   [*PL* 2.762–65]

She describes, of course, the gesture of Narcissus.[62] Most eerie and
debilitating in narcissism is the phenomenon of false or pseudo-du-
ality or -difference. In narcissism, one for the moment appears two—
Milton captures as much in the illusory dual "*Thyself* in me *thy perfect
image* viewing," where "thyself" and "thy perfect image" appear two
and different but are really one and identical. Further, the illusion of
one as two confers upon the one, the narcissist, a parody of identity,
since identity demands that each be two in order to be one. Satan is a
parody of him*self*.

Sin (who is followed by a sign) is a mirror for Satan and his (and
everyman's) narcissism.[63] Sin is thus properly defined as a corruption
of difference, or, very strictly speaking, of apartness. Hence, for
example, she is "double-formed" (*PL* 2.741)—Milton's response, of
course, to Spenser's Duessa. Rather than a singular, different or apart
from other singulars with whom she might dual as well as duel, Sin is
a mixture, a duplicity, of woman and monster which can never unite
in a meaningful singular, which can never dual, only duel—hence her
daughter, Discord (*PL* 10.707). She is a confusion of parts that can
never be apart from, to form parts of, a whole creature or creation.

But in the culture which Milton inherited, creation is differentiation, the Creator se*para*ting his creation from himself, so that it ulti-

mately stands or falls apart from him.[64] Milton himself takes this position in Raphael's discourse on creation. God "*'diffuse*[s] / His good to worlds and ages infinite'" (*PL* 7.190–91),[65] and, moreover,

> [He] conglobed
> *Like things to like*, the rest to several place
> *Disparted*, and between spun out the Air,
> And earth self-balanced on her centre hung.
> [*PL* 7.239–42; emphasis added. Cf. *PL* 3.710]

Then, too, as we have seen, Milton uses this argument in *The Doctrine and Discipline of Divorce*, where it is of fundamental importance also for understanding the relationship between marriage and metaphor.[66] Here, we recall, Milton inflects the theory that creation is differentiation with the trope of divorce:

> by all consequence to dis-joyn them [unmatchable societies], as God and nature signifies and lectures to us not onely by those recited decrees, but ev'n by the first and last of all his visible works: when by his divorcing command the world first rose out of Chaos, nor can be renew'd again out of confusion but by the separating of unmeet consorts. [*DD* 1.10, YE 2:273]

Creation, to infer Milton's major premise, must be the marriage, harmonious and mutually beneficial, of distinct elements—meet consorts, to adapt his words—which, for all that they are married, retain their distinctness (are not confused); on this definition and its implications, more in due course. For the present, it is necessary to add only that, in the same treatise, Milton also introduces a crucial definition of divorce, one which directly anticipates the Son's creation of the world in *Paradise Lost*, Book 7:

> divorce, which like a divine touch in one moment heals all; and like the word of God, in one instant hushes outrageous tempests into a sudden stilnesse and peacefull calm. [*DD* 2.17, YE 2:333]

Next to these extraordinary words, we must set those which Raphael quotes in Book 7:

> 'Silence, ye troubled waves, and thou deep, peace,'
> Said then the omnific Word, 'your discord end.'   [*PL* 7.216–17]

Immediately we see, beyond any possible confusion, that creation for Milton is differentiation, distinction, or, most strictly, divorce, and that the opposite of creation is confusion. Rarely, I suppose, have a man's personal life and his theology, especially his theology of creation, so nearly coincided.

And yet, it will be objected, is this not to let dualism return, through the back door, as it were? Surely divorce is dichotomy and dichotomizing? My answer to both questions is yes. Because duality differs from dualism, and thus from divorce and dichotomy etc., it does, it must, resemble dualism, and hence divorce and dichotomy. Dualing without difference and opposition is impossible; this is why it can so easily degenerate into dueling; and when it has degenerated into dueling, if reconciliation is not possible, then divorce (dichotomy) is the only alternative, lamentable as that may be. But the difference and opposition of duality are different from the dichotomy of dualism, because dualism *starts* from dichotomy, from the presumption of incommensurability between this world and the next, God and man, and so on, whereas duality starts from unity, the presumption of the articulated whole, where "all is in all."[67] Duality, in short, is a structure in the service of monism. Dualism, on the other hand, is an ideology opposed to monism. And if Milton is so concerned with difference, distinction, separation, and severity, it is not because he subscribes to dualism, but because he is in search of unity and must therefore be ever on guard against joining "unmeet consorts," incompatible realities. Milton severs (is severe) because he seeks to fuse; he is a monist seeking the whole of unity. Satan severs (Eve from Adam, for example) because he seeks to *con*fuse (Eve with himself, all creation "such as he"); he is a dualist seeking the unity of all in the (w)hole of his own desire. Thus Milton, as many have observed, nearly resembles Satan, but in the end he differs from Satan *because* he resembles Satan, duals with him, as well as duels with him. The resemblance is this, that Milton, like Satan, desires originality; the difference is this, that Milton, unlike Satan, desires to be *an* original, not *the* original.

Creation, then, we have learned, is the union of meet consorts. The opposite of creation is the confusion of parts which might otherwise and elsewhere be meet consorts. And we can readily agree that narcissism is confusion, for in narcissism there is no true separation, since the other is identical with the self,[68] and there *are* no parts for the creation of a whole—the whole in fact is reduced to identity with the part. Or we might say, equally appropriate to the present concern, that in narcissism, *copia* degenerates into a mere copy.

Ovid is careful, in his account of Narcissus, to stress the psychic economics of narcissism—as did Freud after him—and he especially emphasizes the word *copia*.[69] When Echo pursues Narcissus, the boy, greedy of himself, exclaims: " 'Ante emoriar quam sit tibi *copia nostri*' " (*Meta*. 3.391; emphasis added). But when, later, he lies dying by the pool, he laments " 'inopem me *copia* fecit' " (*Meta*. 3.466; emphasis added). He who would not share his copia earlier, now finds it festering within him, slowly destroying him. Rather than give of it and thus reproduce himself, Narcissus hoarded his copia, which now "produces" (in what is actually a parody of production—see chapter 6 below) only a copy of himself. Narcissism impoverishes the copia of the self to a mere copy of the self, for the part pretending to be (the) whole can re-produce only itself, a copy of itself. And the copy is the defeat of difference, the triumph of confusion.

Through the imagery of narcissism, Milton is recognizing that sin is the illusion and confusion in which one attempts to be one without ever becoming two or different from itself, merely copying itself endlessly instead. (And this, if we stop to reflect on it, is precisely pride, the chief of sins and hence the loneliest.) Sin is always a frustration of difference: in the sin of lust, for example, the difference of the other's body is only an illusion to the lustful, for the lustful wants the other's body *as* his or her own and reduces it to his or her own, thereby confusing it with his or her own.

Since signification also originates in and through difference (Saussure's argument), every sign necessarily emerges from non-differentiation or the frustration of difference. This differentiation Milton is obliged to acknowledge as deriving from sin, if he believes that creation is differentiation; it is as if chaos had escaped its proper place and infiltrated creation, since there can be no place for non-differentiation (chaos) in creation *unless* sin has already perverted or corrupted creation—into precisely the illusion of difference, or the "pair" Sin and Satan, for example. The non-differentiation from which signs emerge is a pretext invented by Sin (and Satan), and hence Milton's coupling of *Sin* and *sign* in the same breath.[70] But even as we admit as much, we are forced to recognize that the same non-differentiation is also the pretext for the whole creation. Sin is the occasion of creation. Nothing would have been created had Sin not entered the cosmos (*o felix culpa!*).[71] God created the world, "conglobing like to like [by] disparting," for man, whom he created to repair the numbers of the fallen angels (*PL* 9.144). Sin or self-love—that is, narcissism—is always an option of creation, or else it is no creation at all, only the mechanical reproduction of robots. Without the option of self-love, a *creature* is impossible: a creature that cannot change its love is not a creature, and hence the precision of Milton's words: "'God made thee perfect, *not immutable*'" (*PL* 5.524; emphasis added. See also 5.236–37).

Such is Milton's integrity that he will not shrink from even the most shocking consequences of his theology, whose essence is "'Sufficient to have stood, though free to fall'" (*PL* 3.99). We must be no less bold. We must recognize and admit, for example, that because all signs are post-sin, there is no prior innocence or prior guilt of the sign. The sign always brings with it the option of non-differentiation: hence the apple, for example—"'the only sign of [their] obedience left'" (*PL* 4.428)—brings with it the option of transgression, in the event of which non-differentiation between man and God results or as Milton has God put it, "'*like one of us* man is become / To know both good and evil'" (*PL* 11.84–85; emphasis added).

The only exceptions to this rule are signs—to us only imaginable—which have ceased signifying, which have become unisemous. These are, on the one hand, the signs of the damned, which have been reduced to the singleness of indices, and, on the other, the sign who is Christ, the Logos, who is the fullest because the emptiest sign, the end of language. Non-differentiation is not an option for these signs, though for opposite reasons (see chapter 11 below on the unisemy of Christ). It is not an option for the signs of the damned—these signs do not signify though they may point to or point out—for they are already eternally differentiated in and by the original option of non-differentiation, or Satan's attempt to be God. These signs are single as a result of the eternal singleness—and hence loneliness—of their users; they are no longer capable of duality.

From which we may infer that a sign is neither innocent nor guilty except as the one who uses it is innocent or guilty. In other words, a sign is always an option.[72] And from this it follows that signs in *Paradise Lost* are to be considered instruments, in some measure contingent on the intentionality of their user or maker. Milton posits—indeed, as a Protestant he must—a subjectivity which subjects signs to its discrete intention. From this it follows that the redemption of the sign is inconceivable apart from the redemption of the individual. But the redemption of the individual entails his repair and his re-pair to God. So, also, the redemption of the sign entails its repair and, most important, its re-pair to the thing it signifies. When the sign *Paradise* is re-paired (and let us not forget to hear *pairing* in Paradise) to the individual conscience, and the individual "possess[es] / A paradise within [him], happier far" (*PL* 12.586–87), then that sign, like the individual, is redeemed.[73] When the individual Christian subjects himself in good conscience to the arbitrariness of the sign, so that the free play of signification is liberated, that individual's faith is sufficient to justify him. His faith then enables him to discover in apartness followed by union the same creativity,[74] though on a lesser scale, as God did when he made the heavens and the earth, "conglobing like to like [by] disparting."

2

Surprised by Signs:
Mediation in Dante and Milton

In "Crazy Jane Talks with the Bishop," Yeats has Jane tell the Bishop:

> 'Fair and foul are near of kin,
> And fair needs foul . . .
>
> 'A woman can be proud and stiff
> When on love intent,
> But Love has pitched his mansion in
> The place of excrement,
> For nothing can be sole or whole
> That has not been rent.'[1]

We say yes, this is our experience of participation, of the being apart because of which—but also by means of which—we seek to be whole. And yet, the experience of participation was not always so. Man was once innocent of participation, though by no means ignorant of it, even as participation itself was innocent. *Paradise Lost* narrates that moment of innocence, its loss, and its eventual repair.

And the course of the narrative can be run by means of the signpost (post-sin) *sign*. The sign is the significance of *Paradise Lost*. In *Paradise Lost* we are also surprised by signs.

For example, before the Fall, Adam tells Eve:

> 'for well thou knowest
> God hath pronounced it death to taste that Tree,
> The only sign of our obedience left
> Among so many signs of power and rule
> Conferred upon us.'   [*PL* 4.426–30]

[30]

The apple too is a sign. Moreover, it is a completely arbitrary sign. God has said so—there is no other motivation for this sign—God has said it shall be an apple. Why? Why a tree? Why an apple? Why not a stream?—from which it is death to drink? Or a cavern?—whose inner recess it is death to see? On the one hand, Milton's point is the majesty and sovereignty of God's will: it is simply God's right to pronounce it so. But on the other hand, his point is the one I am arguing: Adam and Eve freely and in good conscience dual with this sign, they subject themselves to it; they obey this completely arbitrary sign, and as long as they obey, they are blessed, at one with God—with the further consequence that they thus assure the free play of signification, whose most immediate result is that they see all around them other "signs of power and rule / *Conferred* upon" them, where the word *conferred* also insists on the arbitrary will of God. For, if the power and rule are conferred, they can also be removed; and, presumably, the signs, in the event of removal, will arbitrarily change their significance—if one of the signs of power and rule before the Fall is nakedness, for example, signifying the absence of shame in the presence of a just self-love (*PL* 4.312–18), then after the Fall, this sign will, in fact, signify its opposite, or the presence of shame in the absence of a just self-love (*PL* 9.1091–98). However, such a re-versal (re-turn) will not occur as long as the dual is whole. For, as long as the dual is whole, the verse, "the (present) absence of shame signifies the (absent) presence of a just self-love," is true and trustworthy: the verse does not have to be reiterated, *in reverse*. As long as Adam and Eve obey, they do not die (cf. the locutions: "I almost died of shame," "I was mortified with shame"); rather, they live by the arbitrary (will-full) submission to God's will (*arbitrium*).

But after the Fall, Adam and Eve must suffer the arbitrary rather than freely will it. In the classic Augustinian formulation, they must suffer the will itself (its will-full-ness, also its will-fall-ness): because they would not will the will of another, otherness wills the will of man. And nowhere do they (or we) suffer this willfulness more grievously than in the arbitrariness of the sign, for, after the Fall, signs have a will of their own:

> Nature first gave *signs*, imprest
> On bird, beast, air, air suddenly eclipsed
> After short blush of morn; nigh in her sight
> The bird of Jove, stoopt from his very tower,

> Two birds of grayest plume before him drove:
> Down from a hill the beast that reigns in woods,
> First hunter then, pursued a gentle brace,
> Goodliest of all the forest, hart and hind;
> Direct to the Eastern gate was bent thir flight.
> Adam observed, and with his eye the chase
> Pursuing, not unmoved to Eve thus spake:
> 'O Eve, some furder change awaits us nigh,
> Which Heaven by these mute *signs* in nature shows,
> Forerunners of his purpose, or to warn
> Us haply too secure of our discharge
> From penalty.'   [*PL* 11.182–97; emphasis added]

Besides being "mute," which is disturbing enough, these signs are also unexpected, eerie, and uninterpretable beyond a certain point, and this because they were once *different* in significance—"the beast that reigns in woods" was "*first* hunter then"—and their earlier significance—as when the lion did not signify the hunter—has now vanished to be replaced by a significance inscrutable in part (hence Adam's anxious questions in lines 201–07). The lion, in short, proves an arbitrary sign. So now does the whole creation:

> 'Yet doubt not but in valley and in plain
> God is as here, and will be found alike
> Present, and of his presence many a sign
> Still following thee, still compassing thee round
> With goodness and paternal love, his face
> Express, and of his steps the track divine.'   [*PL* 11.349–54]

All quite reassuring—until we (as well as Adam) realize that the signs could be anything or precisely nothing. Note the curious emphasis on the effects of the signs: they follow (behind and past), they encompass (here and present), they lead (there, "his steps," and future). But if their effects are so evident, they themselves, the signs, are unclear, not even named. Nor could they be in a fallen world in which the arbitrariness of signs is not subject to man's control.

If the apple too is a sign, it is even more than that, the sign of signs. Not only is it the sign that signs are the case in Paradise (objective genitive); it is also the sign distinctive of signs (subjective genitive). It is the sign that signifies signifying, how signs work. This we can understand, as Milton did, with Dante's help.

In *Paradiso*, canto 26, Adam explains to the pilgrim Dante the nature of human language and the cause of his fall from Paradise:

> 'Or, figliuol mio, non il gustar del legno
> fu per sé la cagion di tanto essilio
> ma solamente il trapassar del segno.'   [*Pd.* 26.115–17]

['Now know, my son, that the tasting of the tree was not in itself the cause of so long an exile but solely the overpassing of the bound']

Obviously Dante's position here differs in a number of particulars from Milton's, although I am inclined to believe that Milton's "to taste that Tree" owes at least as much to Dante's "il gustar del legno," (even if the latter mentions the notion only to negate it) as it does to Scripture. Be that as it may, most important for a purchase on Milton's understanding of the sign is Dante's *il trapassar del segno*, which translates not only as "the going beyond the boundary, or marker," but also as "the transgression of the sign." From Dante's position Adam's sin consisted in a misuse—let us call it that for the moment—of the sign. It is crucial to define this misuse as carefully as we can, because Dante's position and Milton's are remarkably alike.

Mediation is the issue. Before the Fall, there was a limit, marked by a medium (the apple); this medium, obeying the structure of mediation, interrupted that which it mediated—death (the knowledge of good and evil). As long as Adam obeyed and did not transgress the sign, evil remained mediated, known only through the sign and not experientially—that is, in the flesh, which knowledge is death. Experientially, all Adam knew was good, for God had created only good. Hence, Milton could have Adam say:

> 'Evil into the mind of god or man
> May come and go, so unapproved, and leave
> No spot or blame behind.'   [*PL* 5.117–19]

Mediated, evil may be understood, without having to be experienced. But when Adam fell and transgressed the sign, he obliterated the medium which had blocked, or interrupted, death. Or, as Milton puts it, in lines momentous for his poetics as well as his theology:

>   each the other viewing,
> Soon found their eyes how opened, and their minds
> How darkened; *innocence, that as a veil*
> *Had shadowed them from knowing ill*, was gone,
> Just confidence, and native righteousness
> And honour from about them, naked left
> To guilty *shame he covered, but his robe*
> *Uncovered more.*   [*PL* 9.1052–59; emphasis added]

Before the Fall, mediation, a "veil," had "shadowed" Adam and Eve "from knowing ill." A shadow interrupts the light, and that which is in shadow can be understood to be protected from the light (the sun, for example), which, although normally beneficial, may, under certain conditions, prove harmful. Innocence, like a veil, had protected Adam and eve from the harmful effects of "knowing ill." In other words, they had known ill (*PL* 5.117–19), but innocence had shadowed them from any harmful effects of such knowledge. This knowledge, like the sun, in itself was good, "so unapproved," but if ever proved—if, so to speak, Adam and Eve ever stood directly in its "light" (unmediated)—the effects would be—and, as we know, were—disastrous.

At the same time, *shadowed* has not only this primary meaning, but also carries with it the connotation of *image*.[2] Milton is suggesting that the veil was also an image or sign: before the Fall, there was only one image or sign which *covered*, all others (being good) *uncovering* their Maker and his goodness—as it were, letting the sunshine in. After the Fall, however, Adam and Eve were left naked, naked within, so much so that Christ their

>   inward nakedness, much more
> Opprobrious, with his robe of righteousness
> Arraying covered from his Father's sight.   [*PL* 10.221–23]

Note that Christ and his righteousness effectively take the place of innocence, the veil and the image. On this, more later. For now, consider only that, naked within, Adam and Eve, before Christ's merciful act, are covered with that which *uncovers*, namely shame.

The sense of Milton's words is something like this. If shame covers a person with a blush, say, that blush uncovers the thoughts or the motives or, as we might say, the repressions which that person is experiencing inwardly at that moment.[3] Shame is a sign which uncovers even as it covers; it is a sign with a certain inevitable surplus, saying more than the sayer can say.[4] In this way, Milton is suggesting that, after the Fall, every sign is subject to the dialectic of covering and uncovering—every sign is afflicted with a certain surplus of meaning. Hence, for example, if signs cover an event with an explanation, they also uncover the biases of the reporter; or, if signs uncover some hidden truth, they also cover it with their mediation of that hitherto hidden truth—and therefore some of its original occultation may remain. Milton is thus adumbrating a post-lapsarian poetics, and in this poetics it is understood that the sign obscures as much as it reveals.

And the sign is vitiated in this way because, when Adam obliterated the medium which "had shadowed them from knowing ill," he in effect reversed the polarity of mediation. Evil is no longer mediated (the veil is gone), and man knows evil experientially—he dies. On the other hand, good is now mediated (everywhere veiled), not known or, rather, known only partially by experience, because it reaches man or emerges from him only *through* or *with* evil, which is its medium, its veil, covering it and uncovering it and often doing both at the same time. In short, "knowledge of good [is now] *bought* dear by *knowing ill*" (*PL* 4.222), where the word *bought*, insisting on exchange as well as change, also insists on confusion.

Milton recognizes this pernicious confusion also, in a brilliant passage of *Areopagitica* in which he deploys an image of twins:

> It was from out the rind of one apple tasted, that the knowledge of good and evil, *as two twins cleaving together*, leaped forth into the world. And perhaps this is that doom which Adam fell into of knowing good and evil, that is to say, of knowing good by evil. [YE 2:514; emphasis added]

The familial inflection which the image of twins adds to the relationship between good and evil is most important in the long run for the various sets of twins it evokes: Jacob and Esau, Eteocles and Polyneices, Castor and Pollux, and so on. Within each pair, there was competition for dominion and power, and the victor, when there was a victor, did not escape unscathed. The struggle between good and evil, Milton thus suggests, cannot, before the Day of Judgment, issue in the unambiguous triumph of the good—human affairs are too complicated for that.

But if particular sets of twins are important to Milton's position, twinship itself is also significant. Twins are, as it were, a biological confusion and, however superficially, also an illusion: twins for the moment look like one but really are two. Analogously, good and evil, Milton implies, are an experiential confusion (which, I assume, no one would deny) and, in one sense anyway, an illusion. This is basically the Augustinian sense in which evil is considered to be a corruption or deficiency of the good.[5] In this sense, evil is the good distorted or partially vitiated, and as such, evil can *look like* good, double for it, mimic it; it is this condition—one which we have all suffered at some time or another—which probably motivated Milton's image initially. It is when evil looks like good, as one twin looks like the other, that it most treacherously covers and uncovers what it mediates—now, by its apparent identity with it, *covering* the real good; now, by its real difference from it, *uncovering* only part of the real good, and that perhaps the least important part at any given moment.

From this position we can take the full measure of Milton's boldness when he claims, in the character of Michael:

'Since [Adam's] original lapse, true liberty
Is lost, which always with right reason dwells
Twinned, and from her hath no dividual being.'
[*PL* 12.83–85; emphasis added]

The twins liberty and reason are for Milton the redemption of twinship: they are the case of identity in duality. Liberty has "no dividual being" from its twin reason—but not because it has no being of its own, rather because its own being and reason's own being are dual, distinct but undivided (see the discussion of Shakespeare's "The Phoenix and the Turtle" in chapter 7). Still, after the Fall the twins are sundered, and "true liberty is lost" because right reason is corrupted (as we have already seen). And the corruption of these twins, in effect, is the corruption of twinship, of duality, as Milton understands it, for if the twins liberty and reason fail, become sundered and confused, then all twins and twinship fail; duality falls into dualism or, worse, duplicity, and the capacity of a free understanding to discern—to see in right relation to each other the many parts of a unified whole—is vitiated. A corrupted reason cannot choose freely; it can only see the whole according to the part that compels it the most—Eros, for example, according to the genitalia (cf. *PL* 12.86–90, the next part of Michael's speech). One of the twins infects the other, and twinship itself becomes a disease, the disease of confusion, duplicity, reiteration.

With the twins liberty and reason corrupted, their being unnaturally divided, the reason cannot discern the good from the evil that looks like it, twins it. The image of twins goes back, I am suggesting, to a fundamental Augustinian position. But that position itself originates, as Milton well knew, in the most basic datum of the creation, namely that "it was good" (Gen. 1:10). If evil can look like good, that is because there is only good—now more, now less, vitiated. God created nothing but good, and the only way man can experience evil—that is, know evil experientially—is to know original good as subsequent evil, to know it mediated by evil; or, as Milton puts it most directly, "We do not even know good except through evil" (*CD* 1.10, YE 6:352).

At this point, we may cast the argument to good advantage, in terms of media as covering and uncovering. Before the Fall, good was a medium, a sign and a source of signs which *un*covered only, manifesting the Maker; evil, on the other hand, was mediated, covered (by the one sign) to be uncovered. After the Fall, evil is a medium, which covers and uncovers indiscriminately or confusedly. Already in "Draft IV" of his projected tragedy "Adam Unparadized," Milton had written:

> Man next and Eve having by this time been seduced by the serpent appears *confusedly covered* with leaves conscience in a shape accuses him. [Ed. Fowler, p. 421; emphasis added]

After the Fall, covering is confused. Evil, the covering which had held it in check removed, has itself become a covering. Evil after the Fall has become both an obscure sign and a sign of obscurity which now mediates the good, which is no longer the only medium. To have gone beyond the bound, to have transgressed the sign, then, must have been to rend the veil with which the good had covered "knowing ill"—we may think of it as a literal rending of the v-e-i-l into the shreds of e-v-i-l (this is also a confusion) so that Adam and Eve can no longer l-i-v-e in Paradise. It must have been to refuse the necessity by which one, and only one, sign mediated by covering to uncover. And the punishment: precisely evil mixed in with, or confused with good—the universal necessity, in short, of endless mediation in which all signs cover and uncover indiscriminately. Adam loosed upon the world mere mediation, which obscures as much as it reveals.

In a world in which good is the medium and evil is mediated, mediation is constant and one. In such a world, all can agree that the good is good and the evil evil, since mediation is *un*ambiguous, *un*obscure. In a world in which the polarity of mediation has been reversed, however, in which evil is the medium and good is mediated, mediation is inconstant (mutable) and multiple. In such a world, none can agree on the good, since good is perceived *as*—mediated *as* and *by*—any one of the myriad species of evil in which it is confused or by which it is veiled. And if some few should happen to agree on the good, it will always be to the (potentially disastrous) exclusion of some other good obscured for the moment by evil in some form or other. In such a world, in short, mediation is ambiguous, multivalent, and without control. In a world in which the good of gold is mediated by either prodigality (desire defective) or avarice (desire excessive), the good of gold cannot be experienced (cf. Dante *Purg.* 22.25–54); at best it can only be imagined and partially perceived in, say, the figure of a truly liberal prince, which itself is a covering uncovering the bias of a Western capitalistic outlook.

This description, although only an approximation of Dante's meaning inflected by only a part of Milton's meaning, does help us, nonetheless, to understand Dante's subsequent emphasis on the arbitrary in language—"piacere," "s'abbella," "l'usa mortali come fronda"— and on the mutable.[6] For the one arbitrary sign in the garden which Adam refused to obey, we, his sons and daughters, have and have had a nearly infinite succession of arbitrary signs. And in their arbitrariness, partiality, ambiguity, and obscurity, they have distorted and will continue to distort the good.

If we turn from Dante's position to consider Milton for a moment, we can see how the one poet helps us to understand the other. They both, in fact, seek to explain God's prohibition of the fruit of the Tree in terms of signs, and signs in terms of God's prohibition. They seek this explanation because of the question of obedience. To obey is necessarily to have faith: one must trust whom one obeys. Faith (or its absence) is nowhere more certainly or clearly manifest than in signs and the use of signs, since the structure of signification is precisely faith. This is, presumably, I think both poets would agree, why God instituted the Tree as a boundary or limit or sign. If Adam and Eve had believed his word "In the day ye eat thereof ye shall die" (Gen. 2:17), if they had had faith in his word, then that faith would have been visible in their attitude toward the Tree. The very premise of Eden and man's sojourn there, in short, is signification, the sign, and, as Milton clearly saw, also sin, since sin is the pre-condition or occasion of creation itself.

If both poets agree on the necessity of the sign to any account of God's prohibition and man's disobedience, they also agree on the most important effect of the one arbitrary sign, or the absolute trustworthiness of *all* other signs: this is the implication, by contraries, in Dante's emphasis on the arbitrariness and mutability—hence untrustworthiness—of signs after the Fall; and it is explicit in Milton's lines "The only sign of our obedience left / Among so many signs of power and rule / Conferred upon us," where the sense is, I take it, that because God left only one sign of obedience among all others, all the others are possible and, as possible, true and trustworthy—they let the sunshine in.

Dante's phrase "il trapassar del segno" helps us to grasp Milton's understanding of signs before the Fall. It also helps us, and we will follow up on this in the next chapter, to see the full measure of his conviction that, after the Fall, faith's free submission to the arbitrariness of the sign is the only possible means (medium) to redemption, the redemption of both the individual and the sign. If narcissism (perverted self-love) is the corruption of difference, and thus the ruin of mediation in confusion, the rectification of narcissism and the redemption of the sign will lie in resignation (re-sign-ation) of the self to the ultimate difference, the Holy Other. Such resignation makes of the self a trope, a metaphor, by wedding it again (after the divorce of sin) to God its author. This marriage, which is meaning, is the meaning of Milton's poem: it is the dual of his duel with the tradition.

3

Resigning / Re-sign-ing and the Trope

Before the Fall, obedience was simple. Then there was only one sign to which to submit and only one law to obey; since the Fall, however, there has been an infinitude of signs demanding faith or credit and a welter of laws demanding obedience. Faith and obedience have become difficult, for the sign may deceive and the law may be unjust. And who wants to be deceived? Who wants to suffer injustice? Yet all must run just these risks.

Or perhaps not. Perhaps there is an alternative to these risks. There is one sign left in the world that is like "the only sign of our obedience"—namely Christ, or the Word of God. Christ replaces the Tree—or, more accurately, serves in our fallen world in the capacity in which the Tree served in the unfallen world. Note, incidentally, that this is why both Dante and Milton, insist on the Tree—"il gustar del legno" and "to taste that Tree"—because Christ on the Tree of the Cross supplants that other fruit on the Tree of the Knowledge of Good and Evil. [1] And does so precisely because he is the Mediator, or, as Milton puts it in the opening of Book 11, after Adam and Eve have prayed for forgiveness (*PL* 10.1097–1104) and as Christ pleads with God on their behalf:

> 'Now therefore bend thine ear
> To supplication, hear his sighs though mute;
> Unskilful with what words to pray, let mee
> *Interpret* for him, mee his Advocate
> And propitiation.'   [*PL* 11.30–34; emphasis added]

The Word of God mediates between man and God, he *inter-prets* man to God, and the prefix makes the point: he is *between* man and God, and being between man and God, He fulfills, although to a different end, the function which the apple or the Tree fulfilled, of interrupting that which he mediates—in this case, the vision of God which otherwise could appear only as wrath and judgment to the fallen pair. (In this regard, consider again *PL* 10.221–23: "But inward nakedness much more / Opprobrious, with his robe of righteousness, / Arraying [he] covered from his Father's sight.") Paradoxically, the Fall interpolated a new word in the text of creation, a word which can "re-sign" (*PL* 12.301) men to a "Paradise within, happier far," or, equally valid, *recover* for them such a Paradise (cf. *PR* 1.3).

Like that other sign in the garden, this Word, Christ, if he is obeyed, if he is credited, if faith is placed in him, stands surety for the trustworthiness of all other signs. But trustworthiness is different in a fallen world from what it was before, even as faith in Christ is different from, and more difficult than, faith in that other sign before the Fall. Faith in the Word of God is faith in the invisible (Heb. 11:1), and the trustworthiness of signs is now the trustworthiness of that which must change and therefore may decay or improve. In short, space and time (distance and deferral), having been vitiated by sin (confusion), now "design" the world.

Through space and in time, men and women must now "resign" the world. They will resign the world if they re-sign it: if they restore to the world, by their free submission, its significatory status (let all signs uncover, not cover) so that the world is no longer an end in itself, loved for itself exclusively, but a *means* to an other world (thus meaningful). In that act, they give up the world, resign it, and ready themselves for that other world ("Paradise within, happier far"). Such re-sign-ation requires enormous labor. Space and time force men who fear, understandably, the pain of distance and deferral, to acquiesce in their de-sign. Nothing seems more natural to the natural man than the de-sign of *this* world, in which things and activities (gold, for example, and sex) become ends in themselves, not signs, no longer signifying other than themselves, thus handing over to oblivion (apparently) the thought and the reality of death. But so to behave is, in fact, to acquiesce in distance and deferral, since it throws off and delays death, the inevitable; and thus, so to behave is ironically to endure pain, though not the pain one thought one was avoiding and may for the moment have avoided, but rather the pain of self-deception and inauthenticity. To distance and defer the pain of mortality, to acquiesce in space and time, is to forget the eternality of Being, its structural futurity; to deceive oneself into forgetting death, which is the very possibility of life, is to endure pain as grievous and as cruel as the pain of the cancer; it is to refuse to live significantly when, in fact, he who has chosen to live significantly may even endure the cancer, since his past, his having-been, because significant, will survive his present agony and deliver him to the future of the remembrance of others.[2]

Eve, after the Fall, wishes to forget death and thus forget Being, since Being has now become immense labor. Adam, "his more attentive mind / *Laboring*" (*PL* 10.1011–12; emphasis added) corrects her; and as he does so, he re-signs the world and happens thus, by prevenient grace (*PL* 11.3), upon the way of free submission to the arbitrariness of signs. At first blush, my argument must seem perverse, since, of course, Eve wants to commit suicide (*PL* 10.1001–06), thus (apparently) to hasten death, to resign the world, to accept the pain she has helped to cause. But Adam, however laboriously, succeeds in understanding that Eve's desire is actually " 'contumacy [which] will provoke the Highest / *To make death in us live*" ' (*PL* 10.1027–28; emphasis added). Contrary to its appearance as a desire for death, Eve's desire is a desire for life: her act would be *for* life, since the end of suicide *is* life, however perversely. Thus God would make death in them live, because where there is life, even the desire for life, there must be death; or rather, more precisely, God would make death in them live, because they would have *chosen* that death go on living by clinging suicidally to life. God would have simply acknowledged their free choice. If, on the other hand, they wish to choose life, then they must desire death; the only way to escape death is to desire death; the only way to escape death is to desire it freely enough to accept it. And this Adam can see is *not* what Eve is doing:

> 'Eve, thy contempt of life and pleasure seems
> To argue in thee something more sublime
> And excellent than what thy mind contemns;
> But self-destruction therefore sought, refutes
> That excellence thought in thee, and implies,

> Not thy contempt, *but anguish and regret*
> *For loss of life and pleasure overloved.'*

[*PL* 10.1013–19; emphasis added]

Eve, in short, actually desires the de-sign of space and time—this world, this life—out of an unconscious, and quite understandable, fear of the distance and deferral which death entails.

To this desire Adam opposes the desire for death. Adam desires death as the term which gives life significance. Adam desires " 'to pass commodiously this life, sustained / By him with many comforts, till we end / In dust, our *final rest and native home*' " (*PL* 10.1083–85; emphasis added). Because he freely accepts that dust (death) is his "final rest and native home," Adam has life, significant life, and may have it abundantly. Because he is thus willing to resign life to death, Adam is able to re-sign it. But it works the other way round, too: because he is willing to re-sign life, to give it the significance of death, Adam is able to resign it.[3] This free submission of the will to death, the seemingly most arbitrary, capricious, and meaningless event in the world, this free immolation of the will in the Will of God, Milton conveys through the moment of Adam's first fashioning of (implying free subjection to) an arbitrary sign:

> 'What better can we do, than to the place
> Repairing where he judged us, prostrate fall
> Before him reverent, and there confess
> Humbly our faults, and pardon beg, with tears
> Watering the ground, and with our sighs the Air
> Frequenting, sent from hearts contrite, in sign
> Of sorrow unfeigned, and humiliation meek.'   [*PL* 10.1086–92]

Commentary on this remarkable passage should begin with the extraordinary word *unfeigned*: if the sorrow is "unfeigned," it follows that it *might have been* feigned, it might have been a fiction invented by a malicious and deceitful will; in which case, the sign would have been false, signifying the opposite of what it evidently meant; hence, by saying "sorrow unfeigned," Adam in effect accepts responsibility for the sign, what it means, and that he intends it one way and not the other. So to accept responsibility is to concede the arbitrariness of this and all other signs—tears and sighs might be affectations of the hypo-crite. Furthermore, it is to subject the self to the sign, saying in effect: I cannot control arbitrary signs, the fact that they might signify even the opposite of what they appear to mean, but I can at this moment, in this instance, affirm my own will that these signs mean what I intend them to mean. And just so, Milton repeats Adam's decision to fashion his sign, repeats it verbatim six lines later (at Book 10, lines 1090–1104), so as to prove, to demonstrate, that Adam meant what he said, that his intention was true, his sorrow indeed unfeigned, and thus his sign trustworthy if also arbitrary.

This need to prove, of course, is evidence of the Fall (see chapter 10 below), since before the Fall, there could have been no question but that intention and deed would coincide. In fact, if and when they fail to coincide, their failure is precisely proof of the presence of the Adversary, Satan, who sets things *apart* (such as intention and deed). Further evidence of the Fall lies in the fact that the proof is by way of verbatim repetition: as it might be in a legal case, where exact demonstration of the evidence is crucial, Milton here repeats the evidence of Adam's true intention, trustworthy sign. Verbatim repetition, then, is itself evidence, evidence of the spatio-temporal gap between intention and deed.

This repetition, it is important to note, is not reiteration (see the analysis of Spenser's Despaire in chapter 1 above). Rather, it is verbatim repetition with the one, crucial difference of tense change, signifying elapsed time—reiteration, quite to the contrary, represses time. The second time the verbs *fell*, *confessed*, and *begged* occur, they are in the past tense, so as to indicate that what was future in Adam's present has in fact become part of his past, and therefore endures as long as memory endures. Hence, although the repetition is fallen, it is not damned.[4]

As much is true of the repetition which Adam and Eve actually (within the fiction, actually) perform—Milton repeats their repetition, their repetition in deed of Adam's intention in thought—and it is crucial to see that their repetition is a praying again, a re-petition (see especially *PL* 11.10), a seeking again of what was already sought in the intention to seek it. As such a seeking again, the repetition is a re-pair of the self, or a dualing anew with God which answers to that new dualing of intention and arbitrary sign which generates a present significance. Milton articulates as much with the participle *repairing* in "What better can we do, than to the place / Repairing'." The lines can be read at least two ways: "to the place going" is the obvious and necessary sense; but, because of the syntax of "What better can we

do, than," the phrase "to the place" does not necessarily need to be
followed by a verb—the sense of "going" to the place is clearly implied in " 'What better can we do, than *to* the place' "—and thus
"repairing" can, without conflicting with the obvious sense, have also
its other sense; and the lines can then read " 'What better can we do,
than [go] to the place / Repairing [ourselves to God]'."

In this reading, the lines offer up Milton's meaning to us. By
repairing to the place "where [Christ] judged us" (*PL* 10.1087) and
thus also re-pairing themselves to him, Adam and Eve join again, dual
themselves again with, the Mediator. And it is this re-pair, this duality, of the self and (if I may) "the only sign of its atonement left"
which makes possible the subsequent pairing, or dualing, of intention
and arbitrary sign (" 'in sign of sorrow unfeigned' "). Because Adam
and Eve re-pair themselves to Christ, they are able to subject themselves to a sign—are able, in short, to signify.[5]

Without Christ, there is no significance. With him, there is not
only significance but also a variety of significations, the most important of these being metaphor, or the trope. But before we turn to
consider *improper* signification, such as metaphor, we need to remark
on what might be easily overlooked, namely the absence or invis-
ibility, of Christ the Mediator when Adam and Eve re-pair to him in
the place where he judged them. Adam and Eve place their faith in the
invisible Mediator who will never again be visible to them the way he
was before the Fall. And if their faith is faith in the invisible, it is also
faith in things hoped for (such as forgiveness—cf. Heb. 11:1). It is
very much a re-signed faith, resigned to death (distance and deferral)
and therefore re-signing the world. Moreover, the signs to which
Adam and Eve, because of their faith, are now able to subject themselves, so as to re-sign the world, are not only arbitrary, having no
necessary connection with what they signify, but also mutable, capable of changing connections so as to signify something else (for better
or worse). It is because of this mutability, of course, that Adam (and
Milton) must repeat their discourses. We are at this point finally
equipped to grasp the implication of Adam's lament after the Fall,
that " 'in our faces [are] evident the signs / Of foul concupiscence' "
(*PL* 9.1077–78): for their faces to yield such signs, their *eyes* must have
changed (must have suffered the consequences of the Fall), and the
signs in their faces which before the Fall signified "sweet reluctant
amorous delay" (*PL* 4.311) or "the Rites / Mysterious of connubial

love" (*PL* 4.742–43) now signify the opposite to their eyes, or concupiscence—identical faces, identical signs but (O Hell) how
changed, *not* the *same*.[6]

Against change itself, there is, of course, no remedy for fallen man
except the "final remedy" of the final change, death:

> 'I provided Death; so Death becomes
> *His final remedy*, and after life
> Tried in sharp tribulation, and refined
> By faith and faithful works, to second life,
> Wakt in the renovation of the just,
> *Resigns* him up with Heaven and Earth renewed.'
>
> [*PL* 11.61–66: emphasis added]

Death "resigns [man] up" and re-signs man up to second life after man
resigns and re-signs this world, by faith, in this life. Milton, like
Dante, is ever accurate. Death *signs* man again when it introduces him
to the new life: death is the threshold to new significance, and hence it
re-signs man for that significance. And if death is "the final remedy,"
the renewing re-sign-ation, then it is also necessarily a good.[7] And if
death is good, then change is, or at least can be, good, too.

Milton will articulate both these propositions in the metaphor of
death as fruition. Thus, as he argues the good of death, he brilliantly
manages to argue it where the good of change, itself the genre of
death, is demonstrable—that is, in a metaphor. He posits, in effect,
that if the good of death is knowable in metaphor, then in metaphor
somehow is the good of death—that is, of change. And this position is
possible because in metaphor, obviously, lies the good of renovation
or renewal (species of change). Insofar as metaphor *renews* language
and perception, it is a change (of which death is a species) which is
good, useful, and creative. Thus, to argue the good of death in a
metaphor is—profoundly Miltonic, this—to argue the good of death
or change in and through the good of death or change. Or, actually to
use the metaphor, the renovation (by metaphor) of death (tenor) in
fruition (vehicle) is the fruition of death in renovation (through
language).

Metaphor, like Christ the Mediator and the Word of God, is the event of the death which *is*, in order that life might flourish. Put most generally, metaphor is the language event in which the *proper* sense of a word or a phrase *dies*, in order that an *improper*, often surprising as well as unpredicted, sense might *rise* from that death into life (which, strictly speaking, is the new life of the proper sense).[8] We can see this generality applied in the passage we have been considering: "with tears / Watering the ground" (*PL* 10.1089–90). This, of course, is a horticultural trope, or metaphor, and it is, so to speak, a sub-trope of the larger figure in the poem structured around fruit. To see its crucial extension in Milton's (and Christianity's) comprehension of death, we must turn next to book 11, where Michael tells Adam:

> 'So mayst thou live, till *like ripe* Fruit thou *drop*
> Into thy mother's lap, or be with ease
> *Gathered*, not harshly *pluckt, for death mature.*'
>
> [*PL* 11.535–37; emphasis added]

The very death in the metaphor of "fruit" and of "drop," "gathered," "pluckt," and "mature" in the proper sense, so as to be improperly predicated of Adam, is that death for new life which the metaphor asserts to be, in conjunction with God's recent decree (*PL* 11.61–66), Adam's future and his hope. Structurally, the metaphor *is* what Adam can expect: he will die, his old significance will die, into a new significance, a new life.

But Adam can expect this change, this good if obviously difficult change, only if he leads a pure and upright life—" 'if thou well observe / The rule of not too much' " (*PL* 11.530–31). He must himself be fertile—"By their fruits ye shall know them" (Matt. 7:16)—if he would eventually become a part of the earth's fertility. Or, say, if he would enjoy a "Paradise within," he must be capable of being a garden—he must be, so to speak, arable land. So much is the motive, I suspect, for the particular trope "with tears / Watering the ground" (*PL* 10.1089–90). As Adam and Eve prepare to bring forth fruits of repentance, their tears watering the ground also suggest fertilization of their inner selves; and this suggestion is realized, made explicit, only moments later, in Book 11, when Christ addresses God: " 'See Father, what first fruits on earth are sprung / From thy implanted grace in man.' " (*PL* 11.22–23) It is as if the "ground" had been both within man and outside him ("on earth"); and, of course, in a real sense, it is, since man himself is earth or ground. In the close connection between these two scenes, then, Milton argues that Adam and Eve do become arable, their tears watering the ground of themselves as well as the earth, so that, eventually, they may "'like ripe fruit . . .drop / Into [their] mother's lap'."

This argument, in itself compelling, has extraordinary precedent, I would like to suggest now, in Milton's poetry and elsewhere as well. For, already as early as Sonnet III (1629?), in a notably Dantesque vocabulary, Milton imagines the "arable self," and, perhaps even more important, he also suggests the very close connection between this trope and the mutability of language which is responsible for tropes themselves.

Sonnet III and the other Italian sonnets, as Carey notes,[9] are love poems, and this is noteworthy chiefly because they are written in the language of love, Italian, which, after the great medieval *fin'amors* poets, especially Petrarch, must be the aspiration of any poet who would write about love. Indeed, so much is this the case that the language of love may be a higher and more significant aspiration than love itself. And this, I believe, was the case with the young Milton (probably only twenty-one years old at the time), more in love with Italian and Italian poetry than with any particular young woman.[10] How I arrive at this hypothesis can be gathered quickly from the text of the canzone which follows Sonnet III:

> Canzon dirotti, e tu per me rispondi.
> Dice mia Donna, e'l suo dir, è il mio cuore
> Questa è lingua di cui si vanta Amore.
>
> [Canzone, I will tell you, and you can answer for me. My lady says—
> and her word is my heart—'This is the language on which Love
> prides himself'. [Carey trans., pp. 93–94]

The last line is forceful enough: Italian *is* love's language. But the previous line may in fact be even more important: the heart of the poet is his lady's word or speech, not the lady herself, which does tend to suggest a poet's, rather than a lover's, priorities.

If Milton is writing about his love for, and gradual acquisition of, Italian, then the text of Sonnet 3 becomes as exciting as it is intriguing:

Qual in colle aspro, al imbrunir di sera
   L'avezza giovinetta pastorella
   Va bagnando l'herbetta strana e bella
   Che mal si spande a disusata spera
Fuor di sua natia alma primavera,
   Cosi amor meco insù la lingua snella
   Desta il fior novo di strania favella,
   Mentre io di te, vezzosamente altera,
Canto, dal mio buon popol non inteso
   E'l bel Tamigi cangio col bel Arno.
   Amor lo volse, ed io a l'altrui peso
Seppi ch'Amor cosa mai volse indarno.
Deh! foss'il mio cuor lento e'l duro seno
   A chi pianta dal ciel si buon terreno.

As on some rugged mountain at dusk a young shepherdess, used to
the climate herself, waters an exotic little plant which can hardly
spread its leaves in such unfamiliar surroundings, far from the mild
springtime which gave it life, so on my nimble tongue love raises up
the new flower of a foreign language as I sing to you, charming in
your pride, and exchange the beautiful Thames for the beautiful
Arno (without my worthy fellow-countrymen understanding me at
all). Love willed it, and I knew at other people's expense that Love
never willed anything in vain. Ah that my sluggish heart and stony
breast were as good a soil for him who sows his seed from heaven!
[Carey trans., pp. 92–93]

Obviously, the last couplet is relevant to the horticultural imagery of
Paradise Lost: a sluggish heart and a stony breast are no fit ground for a
"Paradise within." But this obvious relevance intensifies when we
realize that Milton is practically quoting Dante, *Purgatorio,* canto 30,
lines 115–20:

'Questi fu tal ne la sua vita nova,
   Virtuälmente, ch'ogni abito destro
   Fatto averebbe in lui mirabil prova.
Ma tanto più maligno e più silvestro
   Si fa 'l terren col mal seme e non colto,
   Quant' elli ha più del buon vigor terrestro.'

['This man was such in his new life, virtually, that every right disposition would have made marvelous proof in him. But so much the
more rank and wild becomes the land, ill-sown and untilled, as it has
more of good strength of soil.']

The context is Beatrice's chastisement of Dante for his apostasy, his turning from her and from God when she died; because of this apostasy he became, in effect, a wood or forest. Dante employs this trope here, I have argued elsewhere,[11] because of its rich exegetical heritage: the Fathers of the Church, especially Augustine and Ambrose, are strongly attracted to the trope of a man as a garden or forest for their arguments about the effects of the Fall on the image of God in man. Milton was probably aware of this exegetical heritage,[12] and even if he was not, he could certainly have seen the basic point in *Purgatorio*, canto 30: if a man is not upright and pure, he cannot be arable land for God's seed sown from Heaven.[13] Already in this early sonnet, then, Adam's "Paradise within" and "fruit of ripe old age" have firm, living roots.

But the matter does not stop there. If Milton laments that his heart and breast are not "buon terreno," he is led to do so by the quite contrary condition of his tongue, so adaptable ("snella") that love can cause the "fior" of Tuscan Italian (one of whose centers is, of course, *Fior*enze) to grow there ("destare"). It is, in other words, relatively easy to change ("cangio") languages, much easier, in fact, than to change hearts, in the sense of repentance and conversion. Hence the feeling behind "Deh!" If growing the "Paradise within" were as easy as growing the flower of Tuscan Italian on the tongue, if the heart and breast were "si buon terreno" as the tongue (which is nevertheless itself, by implication, "aspro"), then salvation would be much nearer to hand than regrettably it is. If the heart and breast enjoyed the tongue's capacity to change and to exchange one language and another, then they would be more arable and fertile for their Maker's seed. If Milton's heart and breast, for example, could exchange their sluggishness and stoniness for zeal and humility (that is, "buon terreno") as easily and as meaningfully as the tongue—that is to say, language—can exchange arability and the self, then Milton could enjoy the Paradise within. As the tongue can exchange English for Italian, so language can exchange the sense of a self *able* to receive God's grace and will with the sense of fertile land actually receiving seed and growing a crop of edible fruit. This exchange, which is a trope, is the fertility of language, itself a trope. And this fertility, this trope, is the change and exchange the self must undergo to become capable of the Paradise within and of the fruit of a ripe old age. When the heart and breast (of Milton, Adam, Eve, Everyman) become as convertible to zeal and humility as "cuor" and "seno" are to "buon terreno," or as the English tongue is to the Italian—when they become, in short, words, and thus repaired to the Word—then the self will at last be arable, ready for the one "chi pianta dal ciel."

This degree of convertibility in the self could be nothing less than the death of the self; the self would have to will the will of another (as words always obey the will of another to some degree). Such self-emptying, or *kenosis* (Phil. 2:6; see also chapter 11 below), is not possible to the human as human, and yet it is demanded of him. So much so that if a man flees from it, he can do so only by filling himself with the things of this world, and these, since they can never satisfy the appetite for felicity innate to man, will only continue to accumulate until they burden the soul, weight it down, with death. This exhaustion is the final lot of the avaricious. As Milton knew from St. Paul, "all avarice is the service of idols" (Eph. 5:5), since the avaricious, in trying to fill the need for God with the things of this world, in effect transmute these things into substitutes for God, or idols; therefore, necessarily, all avarice is also a falsification of the things of this world. Moreover, in turning to the things of this world to turn them into his deity, one who is avaricious also falsifies conversion (turning) itself, for he never really turns from himself; instead, he turns into himself, and he turns the things of this world into himself, too. This false turning is a counterfeit conversion: it looks like conversion but is actually perversion. Such counterfeit conversion is a particularly abhorrent crime, since it parodies and deforms the soul's talent to fill itself (endlessly) with God.

The most powerful indictment of this crime in Western poetry is found in Dante's account of the punishment of Master Adam of Brescia, the counterfeiter or false coiner, whose hydropsy and concomitant weight figure the ponderous evil of avarice (*Inf.* 30.49–57). And since Milton in Sonnet 3 is concerned with precisely the difficulty of conversion (lines 13–14), and thus necessarily with the temptation to false conversion, he takes his rhyme scheme from *Inferno*, canto 30, at just the moment (lines 10–12) when he insists on the absolute demand Love makes of him to change ("cangio"):

> E'l bel Tamigio cangio col bel Arno.
> Amor lo volse, ed io a l'altrui peso
> Seppi ch'Amor cosa mai volse indarno.

Milton is here quoting from Adam's description of his grievous thirst:

> 'Ed ora, lasso! un gocciol d'acqua bramo.
> Li ruscelletti che de' verdi colli
>   Del Casentin discendon giuso in Arno,
>   Faccendo i lor canali freddi e molli,
> Sempre mi stanno innanzi, e non *indarno*—
>   Ché l'imagine lor vie più m'asciuga
>   Che 'l male ond'io nel volto mi discarno.'
>
> [*Inf.* 30.63–69; emphasis added]
>
> ['and now, alas! I crave one drop of water! The little brooks that from
> the green hills of Casentino run down into the Arno, making their
> channels cool and moist, are always before me and not in vain, for the
> image of them parches me far more than the malady that wastes my
> features.']

We can be the more certain that he is quoting from this speech in that
the phrase "a l'altrui peso," while it can be translated "at other people's expense,"[14] also reads "at others' *weight*," where *weight* ("peso")
describes precisely the condition of Master Adam.

The latter, in the passage from *Inferno*, is telling Dante and Virgil
that the *image* of water parches him, which is also to tell them in effect
that he, the falsifier of images, suffers from a *false* image, since it is
contrary to the property of water to parch. Images of water should
refresh, as does water itself; but for the damned, they can only parch;
they are *real* images but not *true* to that which they image, since they
falsify it.[15] Hence Dante's word *indarno*, rhyming with *Arno* in
Milton's poem, is crucial: the images of water are always in front of
Master Adam and "not in vain," although they are false, because they
are Love's punishment of the falsifier, and Love, as Milton says, "cosa
mai volse indarno." By means of this carefully considered quotation,
Milton is acknowledging to himself and to his readers that conversion
must be true and complete, just as Love wills it. On the one hand, his
Italian must be "dal [suo] buon popol *non inteso*" (line 9; emphasis
added) if it is to be true Italian—as "altera," in fact, as is his lady—not
mixed, that is, with any lingering traces of English, or his "cangio" is
false. On the other hand, but similarly, his heart and breast must
become completely arable, or again, his "cangio," his conversion, is
false. And if false, then he himself must sink beneath the weight of
Master Adam—the old Adam, falsifier because falsified by Satan.

Hence, again, the feeling behind "Deh!" Milton does desire a true and complete conversion. And yet the weight of the old Adam, the old man (Rom. 6:6; Eph. 4:22) is so great that by himself no man can empty himself. For that he must turn to the New Adam, whose "burden is light" (Matt. 11:30), who is true because he is the Truth. And he is the Truth because he died to be the Word: he exchanged himself for the Word. He did the Father's will, obedient unto death. He let God speak him, and never falsified him whose image he is.

And this sacrifice (exchange) Milton articulates with the same trope of fruit and trees:

> 'See Father, what *first fruits* on Earth are sprung
> From thy *implanted* Grace in Man, these sighs
> And Prayers, which in this golden censer, mixt
> With incense, I thy priest before thee bring,
> *Fruits* of more pleasing savor from thy seed
> *Sown* with contrition in his heart, than those
> Which his own hand *manuring* all the trees
> Of Paradise could have product, ere fallen
> From innocence. Now therefore bend thine ear
> To supplication, hear his sighs though mute.
> Unskillful with what words to pray, let *mee*
> Interpret for him, *mee his Advocate*
> And propitiation, all his works on *mee*
> Good or not good *ingraft*, *my merit those*
> Shall perfect, and for these my death shall pay.
> Accept *me*, and in *mee* from these receive
> The smell of peace toward mankind.'
>
> [*PL* 11.22–38; emphasis added]

Christ the Mediator, the High Priest, interprets for Adam mute. He is the Word Adam and Eve can address to God (see especially *PL* 11.16–21). But before they can produce this Word, this fruit, they must themselves become more like the Word—that is to say, in the trope which Milton has chosen for such conversion, they must become more arable. To this end, after the description of their prayer, as Book 11 opens, we are told—what Sonnett III would lead us to expect—that

>   from the mercy-seat above
> Prevenient grace descending had removed
> The stony from their hearts, and made new flesh
> Regenerate grow instead.   [*PL* 11.2–5]

Adam and Eve become "buon terreno," not only by the watering of their tears, but also by the clearing away of the stony from their hearts: gone is the "duro seno" of Sonnet 3. Thus prepared, they can receive the " 'seed / Sown with contrition' " from the one "chi pianta dal ciel." Clearly, Milton is translating the Dantesque vocabulary of Sonnet III in the scenes of Adam and Eve's repentance and forgiveness; and the translated text informs us that Adam and Eve become more nearly one with the Word (though, of course, not fully the Word yet) by becoming good soil in which He can grow. They are thus superior to Deucalion and Pyrrha (*PL* 11.10–14) who repeopled the world from the bones of their ancient mother, or the stones of the earth (*Meta.* 1.313–415), because they are now more like the earth itself than its bones; they are productive—arable, not stony—as only the earth can be productive. And they produce (*PL* 11.29) within their hearts (*PL* 11.27) not stones but the tree (Christ) on whom God can, and will, "ingraft" their "good" and "not good." Because they now "live in [him] transplanted' " (*PL* 3.292), he is growing in them: they are all parts of the same plant (cf. John 15:5). And thus "supplanted" indeed is the Devil now (*PL* 10.513), since the "second root" (*PL* 3.288), who is the root of all good (cf. 1 Tim.6:10), is growing in the hearts of Adam and Eve. And as he, the Word, grows in their hearts, he translates (transplants) their hearts into the Word: he interprets for them. He is the tree (a trope) in growing which Adam and Eve become capable of being tropes, or ripe fruit, to be " 'gathered, not harshly pluckt, for death mature' " (*PL* 11.537). Without this tree, there is no trope. This tree replaces the tree of mediation that grew in the Garden, and by his "dearest mediation" (*PL* 3.266), he crosses on man's behalf from flesh to word; and this crossing is the supreme translation, the change ("cangio") that makes change meaningful.

Milton anticipates this change—to show, I think, how and how much love is necessary for the translation from flesh into Word—in the character of Eve *before* she and Adam pray together for forgiveness. Five times in his speech, Christ repeats the first-person objective pronoun (a *ploce*).[16] This emphasis on "mee" is a repetition of Eve's similar emphasis (six times) in her speech to Adam before her lament recommending suicide:

'On *me* exercise not
Thy hatred for this misery befallen,
On *me* already lost, *mee* than thyself
More miserable; both have sin'd, but thou
Against God only, I against God and thee,
And to the place of judgment will return,
There with my cries importune Heaven, that all
The sentence from thy head removed may light
On *me, sole cause to thee of all this woe,*
Mee, Mee only just object of his ire.'

[*PL* 10.927–36; emphasis added]

For me, this repetition is one of the most beautiful moments in all English poetry. If Eve continued the Fall initiated by Satan, she initiates the return to God completed by Christ. So Milton acknowledges the ultimate irrelevance of all misogyny. His reasoning is somewhat as follows. Christ is Eve, in the sense that the Maker contains and *is* the creature he makes; but Eve also is Christ—made by him, she "possesses" him in some way, to some extent. And this before grace has made the self newly arable. Hence, however distorted by remorse and self-loathing and suicidal despair, the Christ in her, the Word of God in her, can speak, and does speak, Christ-like. Eve's love for Adam gives the Word to Eve, although she must become arable before the Word can also grow in her. Her willingness, mixed with whatever confusion and self-loathing, to *inter*cede on Adam's behalf, to take upon herself all the punishment and thereby propitiate God, *mediating* his wrath to Adam (by blocking and deferring it), such that Adam will know it but not suffer it—this willingness to die for Adam is Christ in her, is the Word in her, though operating, as it were, only through the stony.

Eve, to be sure, will go on the express her desire for suicide (*PL* 10.1000–02), because of the stony in her heart, and Adam will have to chasten and subdue this desire. Even so, she has already, Milton insists, the capacity and the will to change—to translate herself by sacrifice—into the Word. This willingness of Eve—I will now take a liberty justified, I hope, by its outcome—to dual for Adam, to take his place (vicariously), even though—no, precisely because—she is *not* Adam, is evidence of the redeeming and the redeemable in her. To take the place of another in this context is to sacrifice oneself for

another. It is not to usurp the privilege of another—that is what Eve
wanted to do when Satan seduced her. It is rather to give oneself up,
to hand oneself over, on behalf of another. This vicariousness, the
structure of mutuality, is the love necessary for the translation from
flesh into Word, and, as such, it is the foundation of Christianity, the
founding decision of Christ—his love for men. *His* willingness to dual
for Adam and Eve, when he does in fact dual for Eve (repeating
"me"), manifests his sacrificial role, which his love persuades Him to
assume. And this is why, of course, Milton presents him, in the
speech in which he duals for Eve, in the role of the *Priest*—" 'in this
golden censer, mixt / With incense, I thy Priest before thee bring' "
(*PL* 11.24–25).

   If Christ the priest and Eve dual for others—and here I continue
with the liberty I am taking—we may infer what is obvious in another
context, that the Word / word duals for an other (the thing or what it
signifies); and from this I would like further to infer that the structure
of language is mutuality, and the structure of prophetic language the
most intense degree of mutuality, or sacrifice.

   I can imagine many objections to this conclusion, but I would
exclude immediately the objection that I am claiming that language is
somehow mysteriously Christian; on the contrary, I would claim
only that Christ perfectly understood language, its vicariousness or
mutuality or sacrificiality—and this, in large part, because he was a
Jew. We are not all Christians or all Jews, *but* we *are* all language-
users; and it is this which grounds my argument—whereas, of
course, it is this *and* Christianity which ground Milton's argument.
   Another objection which is likely to arise is more difficult to meet
and dismiss. Someone might counter: Are you not merely lapsing
into the old and outmoded notion of substitutability?—the notion
that a word should be adequate to the thing? Are you not suddenly
forgetting all that Saussurian and post-Saussurian theory have taught
us?—especially that the free play of the signifier, especially the signifier in the text of fiction, *produces* meaning, and thus that the signifier is not merely to be (or, at least *ought* not merely to be) consumed
as the substitute for a pre-scripted (and pre-digested) meaning, there-
upon immediately to be forgotten, handed over to oblivion?[17] Surely

you are forgetting the summons with which the great texts serve us: deconstruct and produce!

No, I am not. I know and accept that this is the summons I receive from *Finnegan's Wake*, say, or *The Sound and the Fury*. But it is *not*, I believe, the summons served by *Paradise Lost*. And this because, more than any other text I know except the *Commedia*, *Paradise Lost* is *intended*: it is prophetic, the poem of a prophet. Milton has a meaning to convey. He intends to "assert Eternal Providence" (*PL* 1.25). Therefore, this intention must be recovered—though not, I agree, by substituting it for the poem. Contrariwise, to deconstruct his text would necessarily be to transgress his intention, if not his text. I do *not* say that it cannot be done or ought not to be done, only that if it is done, it *must* transgress the prophetic intention.[18] And that intention, to put it briefly, is the intention of the Word.

I am *not* lapsing into the old and outmoded notion of substitutability for the very good reason that if Milton intends a meaning, and he certainly does, that meaning is vicariousness or mutuality; the meaning he intends is meaning itself, understood as other than, and different from, substitutability. Vicariousness (or meaning) is not substitutability where the substitute is always understood to be expendable, disposable, if and when the "real product" should turn up. No, the meaning of *Paradise Lost* is not expendability, least of all its own expendability. *Paradise Lost* is not a substitute for anything. It is the real product, although at the same time, it is not an end in itself, for a real product (see *PR* 1.150 and chapter 11 below) is always the unity of a multiple, a whole, in which the members of the whole coinhere in their individuality and thus can participate in the production of yet more and yet other wholes.[19]

And meaning is the most real product men can produce, for meaning is the whole in which the individuality of the members is the most discrete while the integrity of the whole is the most complete. Meaning is meaningful precisely because it is the coinherence of individuals in a whole and not the incoherence of the many in a random one. The condition of meaning and meaningfulness in our post-lapsarian world obtains most nearly perfectly in the duality of God and man: the product of God plus man is meaning, or, as John perfectly intuited, the Word. And the meaning of *Paradise Lost* is meaning, we may conclude, because *Paradise Lost*, which attempts "to justify the ways of God to men" and to "assert Eternal Providence," duals (and as we shall see, duels) the Word of God.[20] *Paradise Lost* is the product of Milton plus God.

Ultimately. Proximately, of course, *Paradise Lost* is the product of Milton and his muse: "Urania . . . / The *meaning*, not the *Name* I call" (*PL* 7.195; emphasis added).[21] He calls on the meaning and not on the name, of course, because the name is only a convention, variable with time and place and idiom. The meaning, however, is not a convention and not variable, though neither is it an eternal prescript antedating Milton like an an essence on deposit. No, the meaning is precisely the product of Milton *and* his muse. It is, in other words, the duality coinhering in the whole—and this whole which makes the meaning is, I am arguing furthermore, itself the product of sacrifice, Milton's sacrifice of himself to God:

> He who would not be frustrate of his hope to write well hereafter in laudable things, ought him selfe to bee a true Poem, that is, a composition, and patterne of the best and honorablest things. ["An Apology Against a Pamphlet, YE 1:890]

Milton and the poem "assert eternal Providence" because they are "joined to" (*ad-serere*) Eternal Providence, paired to it because offered up to it.[22] Or, at least, that is their intention. And such was Milton's intention from at least as early as "Elegia Sexta" (1629), in which he wrote:

> let this poet live frugally, like the philosopher from Samos . . . In addition his youth must be chaste and free from crime, his morals strict and his hand unstained. He must be like you, priest, when, bathed in holy water and gleaming in your sacred vestment. . . . For the poet is sacred to the gods: he is their priest: his innermost heart and his mouth are both full of love. [Carey trans. pp. 118–19]

If Milton intended to make of himself a sacrifice, he also had the courage—which is to say, he was human enough—to recognize and admit that he (and his poem) might not live up to the demand:

> Mee of these
> Nor skilled nor studious, higher Argument
> Remains, sufficient of itself to raise
> That name [Heroic name], unless an age too late,
>   or cold

> Climate, of Years damp my *intended* wing
> Deprest, *and much they may, if all be mine,*
> *Not hers who brings it nightly to my ear.*   [*PL* 9.41–47; emphasis added]

It is an impressive moment. If you want to be one, be two. And Milton and his muse *are* two, are paired; they dual each other and thus communicate, make meaning—they are the means, each to the other. And this Milton proves by the very outcry of doubt, for *doub*t is double as Spenser had already shown Milton.[23] Doubt implies the presence of that which is doubted. This implication can be, and often is, very threatening, but it can also be comforting—it depends, of course, on *who* is implied as one's dual by one's doubt. In the present case, the doubt is comforting, for clearly, all can *not* be Milton's since she, the Muse, is present in the doubt.[24] Here, doubt is in effect duality, for it inhibits any ruinous singleness of voice. And if Milton and his muse thus communicate—his words and hers form a whole—that in turn is proof that he and his poem have sacrificed themselves to Eternal Providence—his words and God's also form a whole—for the Muse is, as we know from the beginning, "heavenly" (*PL* 1.6). And Milton is resigned (and re-signed) to her.

4

Rhymes and Puns

Milton and *Paradise Lost* are holy, sacred.[1] They are the products of sacrifice. But even if Milton makes of himself a voluntary sacrifice, and of his poem also a voluntary sacrifice, such sacrifice still originates in violence. As the Greek words, *témnō* and *témenos*, make clear, sacrifice is "a cutting off" and "a separating by cutting off." In the case of the poem, this sacrificial violence is the violence of predication, definition, distinction—in short, of precision (which itself, of course, is *cutting* since *caedere*, the etymon of *-cision*, means "to cut"). To be precise in his argument to justify the ways of God to men, to be severe in his understanding of the ways of God, to be accurate in his characterization of how it is with men, Milton must cut, chisel, hone language; he must sacrifice all the techniques of rhetoric and epic writing, as well as all the positions of theology, Catholic or Protestant, to his own pure vision (to be p*u*re he must p*a*re); he must practice violence and submit to violence, and he must therefore constantly risk falling into the abyss of confusion. The only thing that distinguishes Milton's sacrifice from violence is love. The sacrifice practiced by perverted self-love, however—by narcissism—always perpetrates violence, and this violence is never precise, never severe, but always issues in confusion. So much Milton makes clear in the moment of Adam's post-lapsarian pun.

After Eve has sacrificed Adam, "fondly overcome with female charm" (*PL* 9.999), to her own desire and he has eaten of the fruit, he begins "to dalliance [to] move [her]":

> 'Eve, now I see thou art exact of taste,
> And elegant, of sapience no small part,
> Since to each meaning savour we apply,
> And palate call judicious.'   [*PL* 9.1016–20]

Much is readied in the word *dalliance*, of course: we know that what follows will be frivolous, not severe, and we also know that frivolity at *this* moment is tasteless. Adam's *dalliance* is a frivolous pun on *sapience*, which, however, for all its frivolity from *his* point of view, from ours sounds heavy with the Fall itself—it is the d(e)-alliance of the Fall (cf. *PL* 2.819 for the same pun)—especially if, as readers of Milton, we remember Comus tempting the Lady just before her brothers rescue her: " 'Be wise, and taste . . . ' " (*C* 812)—of course, if the Lady tastes (*sapio, -ere*), she is not wise (*sapient*). In the word *sapience*, Adam has confused the sense "taste" and the sense "wisdom" or "judiciousness," to each of which "savour we apply," where the sense "knowledge" (*savoir*) is replete, beyond Adam's knowing, with the crime he and Eve have just committed. The word *sapience* is now evidence of the Fall.

The obvious question to ask at this point is, Why does Milton figure the effects of the Fall in a pun?[2] Or, the same question from a different perspective, What is it about a pun that makes it a figure for the effects of the Fall? Geoffrey Hartman offers a helpful clue:

> You can define a pun as two meanings competing for the same phonemic space or as one sound bringing forth semantic twins, but, however you look at it, it's a crowded situation. Either there is too much sound for the sense or too much sense for the sound.[3]

A pun, like twins, (see chapter 2 above) is a moment of confusion, and confusion is the prime effect of the Fall:

> This death consists, first, in the loss or at least the extensive darkening of that right reason, whose function it was to discern the chief good, and which was, as it were, the life of the understanding. [*CD* 1. 12, YE 6:395]

Confusion, the inability to discern the prime good, is the effect of the Fall because the source or cause of the Fall is pride, or the desire to know as God knows—to be God. God knows instantaneously and infinitely, without the labor of discerning, of distinguishing, of taking the steps of reasoning, without the patience (and therefore also the impatience) of waiting for thought to complete itself *in time*. Adam and Eve eat the apple to speed up the process of their im*prove*ment (*PL* 5.498) to godhead: if the serpent became man-like (so fast) by eating of the fruit, then Eve reasons that she will become God-like (equally fast) by eating of it too. She and Adam will hasten the process by which they *prove* to be gods, knowing instantaneously and infinitely. But they are deceived, by themselves as well as the Devil; they can know only discursively (*PL* 5.488) and experientially, they can know only in time. Hence, when they eat the apple, they can know as God knows only humanly, in time. They can have, in short, only time's version of God's knowing; and what they get for their trouble, therefore, is the pun—Adam becomes a *pun*theist as his *pun*ishment. He gets for his "affected godhead" the simulacrum of divine knowledge: the simultaneity (of meanings) in a pun is time's version of eternity's instantaneity of knowing—its *adam*bration of that instantaneity. Adam *puns* when he falls because what he gets in the Fall is exactly what he asks for—he is not, as Milton insists, deceived. He gets *human* godhead, the human knowing as God knows, but only *as* God knows.

It is Boethius who argues that God sees time like space: he sees past, present, and future all at once, just as the human eye sees multiple objects in space at once.[4] Unlike the ear, which must wait to hear information, the eye sees information, not instantaneously to be sure, but much, much faster than the ear hears it. By analogy with this condition of man's perception, Boethius tries to explain predestination and God's foreknowledge by suggesting that God sees time all at once, in "an eternal present." The simulacrum of such omniscience, then, would be precisely that knowing in which multiple information is perceived in a single unit—a pun (or a metaphor).

A pun spatializes time. In the pun, time, measured in the word, is converted to space so as to contain many data (at least two) at once. Pun (and metaphor) are an overcoming of time (one version of the sin of pride). In a pun or metaphor, the simultaneity of meanings gives us a feeling of the access of power (the overcoming of time): we feel we know more, faster, than we feel we do in ordinary discourse.[5] We experience this feeling most profoundly, of course, in metaphor, the highest degree of fusion of meanings:

Figures of speech may be characterized by overspecified ends and indeterminate middles . . . this structure may explain the shifting relations of concrete and abstract in poetics, and . . . the very elision or subsuming of middle terms allows, if it does not actually compel, interpretation. I mean that the strength of the end terms depends on our seeing the elided members of the chain . . . the more clearly we see them, the stronger the metaphor which collapses that chain, makes a mental bang, and speeds the mind by freeing it from over-elaboration and the toil of consecutiveness. A great verbal figure gives us the second wind of inspiration; it makes us sure, after all, of overtaking the tortoise.[6]

In metaphor we feel we know as God knows (if only by a hare)—hence the suspicion of metaphor which all institutions have always felt. But whether in metaphor or pun (the simplest degree of metaphor), this fusion (we *feel* we *know*) can all too easily become *con*fusion (feeling knowing, feeling *as* knowing): the sounds or senses or both can become mixed, and the mixture can (and usually does) confuse us.

But so what? someone will object. We want feeling knowing, we want the Wordsworthian "feeling intellect" (*The Prelude* 14.226), we want the power of metaphor (even if it is only metaphoric power). And if the price we must pay is the risk of confusion, so be it. And I agree, because I too am a fallen man. I too want to avoid the sacrifice (témnō) in signification, in all communication (mutuality). In ordinary discourse, I must sacrifice my mind to individual, discrete words, cut it up among them as they in turn cut up and cut off the reality I understand, so as to share (portion) it with others. This is the structure of signification: sacrifice, the cutting up and the cutting off of the self and the real. And I, like most men, will welcome any alternative to this labor, this suffering, this trial. Puns and metaphors are welcome relief from ratiocination.

But they can only be relief, a vacation from discourse. For, if we speak always only in puns and metaphors, we shall never be pure: we shall always be "affecting godhead," mixing our immanence—I did *not* say eminence, though, of course, I did—with the transcendent by means of the simulacrum of divine knowing, simultaneity masking as instantaneity. We shall always be impure mixtures of god and man, and who of us thus impure can pretend to be another man's god? Rather than affect such pride, we must be humble before the necessi-

ty of sacrifice, purify ourselves by the trial that is by contraries,
sorting and separating and cutting out the meanings that are heard in
the word (and that herd in the word).

Or so at least the Puritan poet. The Puritan poet would have us
and language be pure. But the Puritan poet, especially Milton,
knows—unlike the Cartesian science of the seventeenth century
which wanted a perfect adequation between one word and one
thing—that men and women and words, because never full, frequently fall, decline in cases and number and time. And so it is that
the Puritan poet will not purify words by attempting a perfectly
mathematical language; rather, he will purify them and us by deploy-
ing all the resources in language of fusion (and therefore also, necessarily, of potential *con*fusion) so as to provoke and invoke the power of
discernment, the power of choice, that we might try ourselves in his
text.[7] He will unite so as to sever, sever so as to unite (and ask us to do
the same), precisely because it is a fallen world in which no perfect
mathesis is possible and in which sacrifice therefore is ultimately
necessary.

The readiest example of Milton's sacrificial technique, this technique
of severance, is what I call the severed rhyme. Milton, we know,
scorns rhyme as "the jingling sound of *like* endings"—as, in other
words, confusion (in sound). Just so, by true sacrifice in technique, he
cuts between the confusion of rhyming words and his own carefully
crafted line, in which "the sense [is] variously drawn out from one
verse into another."[8] In this, his technique resembles the work of
sacraments, in which "[the sign] is *severed* from a common to an holy
use."[9] Moreover, when he does rhyme, he cuts between the otherwise
connected couplet so as to distinguish the rhyme both as atypical of
his text and atypical in itself. For example, in what are to my knowledge the first five severed rhymes (two in the second passage) in
Paradise Lost, Milton writes:

> 'But what if he . . .
>
> . . . .
>
> Have left us this our spirit and strength *entire*
> Strongly to suffer and support our pains,
> That we may so suffice his vengeful *ire*,
> Or do him mightier service as his thralls

By right of war, whatever his business be
Here in the heart of hell to work in *fire*.'
[*PL* 1.143, 146–51; emphasis added]

       Thither let us *tend*
[and]
. . . .
Consult how we may henceforth most *offend*
Our enemy, our own loss how *repair*,
How overcome this dire calamity,
What reinforcement we may gain from hope,
If not what resolution from *despair*.
[*PL* 1.183, 187–91; emphasis added]

Beyond compare the Son of God was seen
Most glorious, in him all his Father shone
Substantially expressed, and in his *face*
Divine compassion visibly appeared,
Love without end, and without measure *grace*.
[*PL* 3.138–42; emphasis added]

She as a veil down to the slender waist
Her unadorned golden tresses wore
Disheveled, but in wanton ringlets waved
As the vine curls her tendrils, which implied
Subjection, but required with gentle *sway*,
And by her yielded, by him best received,
Yielded with coy submission, modest pride,
And sweet reluctant amorous *delay*.   [*PL* 4.304–11; emphasis added]

The second and third severed rhymes in *Paradise Lost* belong to Satan, the *author* of confusion. As telling is the third rhyme itself: repair / despair. After all we have learned from Spenser, and all we have learned of what Milton learned from Spenser, we can hardly fail to appreciate the ironies of this rhyme. Satan, who tried to "impair" God, only to wind up literally "impairing" (unpairing himself from) God, commits a rhyme (an act of confusion) on the word (-pair) that inscribes his own error. He rhymes on what he cannot do, repair.

The next two severed rhymes are hardly less significant than the first three, although their function, of course, is different. They serve to further and to strengthen the close relationship between Christ and Eve which Milton posits, and which he affirms as the transformation and redemption of Eve. Furthermore, the rhyme in the introductory portrait of Eve also serves to characterize her as potentially confused and as a potential source of confusion, and this is the confusion, to complete the connection between Eve and Christ, which Christ will eventually undo and sort out, since, as the Word made flesh, he is ultimately the opposite of (but therefore similar to) confusion (hence the rhyme Milton predicates of him, which serves to distinguish him from Satan—the Word does *not* further confuse confusion). But in addition to these ideological resonances, and more pertinent to our present concern, which is Milton's technique, these severed rhymes instance Milton's sacrifice of the technique of rhyme to his own more severe technique. Rhyme may enter his poem only as a victim of a more sublime technique.

If Milton is severe with rhymes (and, as we shall see, with puns), he is thus the contrary of Adam, who was " 'not enough severe, / It seems, in [Eve's] restraint' " (*PL* 9.1169–70). Had Adam been more severe, he would have severed Eve from her dueling insistence on parting (severing) from his side.[10] But, as he says, to have done more than he did " 'had been force, / And force upon free will hath here no place' " (*PL* 9.1173–74).

Similarly, Milton is the contrary of Eve, who was "not enough severe" in her resistance to the serpent. In the seduction scene, Eve is both author and reader, and none too successful as either. Her "authority" is suggested in a number of ways: for example, in the word *elegant*, when, in a fitting prelude to his tasteless pun, Adam flatters her—" 'Eve, now I see thou art exact of taste, / And elegant' "; as Fowler notes, it is "a word that would normally be applied to literary taste."[11] But perhaps the most important suggestion of her authority is at the same time the suggestion as to why it is impure, "not enough severe." After the serpent's exordium of flattery, Milton comments: "So glozed the tempter, and his *proem* tuned" (*PL* 9.549; emphasis added). Satan is beginning the poem which earns him the title "author of all ill." And, just so, when he has finished the first part of his poem of seduction, Eve takes up the work: "pausing a while, thus to her self she *mused*" (*PL* 9.744). Eve, "not unamazed," (*PL* 9.552) is not unamused either; she is her own muse, she amuses herself, only to "amaze" (*PL* 9.889) Adam and, Medusa-like, to turn him to stone— "astonied [he] stood and blank" (*PL* 9.890). "Not severe enough," Eve does not cut between amazement and amusement, and so the one leads "naturally" into the other, as Satan hoped and expected they would. Eve in falling becomes a poet, filling in for Satan.

Thus Milton traces poetry back to an origin in the Fall—an origin, that is, in confusion—which would be an origin in perverted sacrifice (Satan's sacrifice of Adam and Eve to his own ambition for revenge); and this origin, in turn, would suggest that the purgation and redemption of art consist in replacing perverted sacrifice with true sacrifice. Eventually, each of us must say what he or she means. So each will be defined, determinate, and named. He who would be all can only fall ill.

So it was with Satan, as he realizes too late, and realizes by distinguishing the parts of a pun. Ordinarily, Satan is a hack, hacking apart words and meanings and truth, only to reunite them according to his own perverse sense of the (w)hole. For example, when he declares that God " 'tempted our attempt and wrought our fall' " (*PL* 1.642), *tempted* swallows *attempt*, as he, by a rhetorical sleight of hand, makes God the rebel angel. Temptation is possible originally only in and through a fallen creature—God tempts only after the Fall and tempts only men (Gen. 22:1, for example). Therefore, if God tempted the rebel angels' attempt, he was, and is, according to Satan's diabolic logic, no better than they, and they are no worse than he (this latter, obviously, a very important consequence for Satan the politician). Satan achieves this confusion by refusing the pun (the distinctions in the pun) to fuse (and confuse) the senses of *tempt* and *attempt:* to express it typographically, it is as if he had claimed that their (at)tempt is the same as God's tempt(ation)—their sin, as it were, was merely to prefix *at* to what God had already started. But this is to ruin two useful words at once—it is, of course, to do a good deal more than that. And the ruin is hackwork: the difference between *tempt* and *attempt* is hacked away, and the two words come too close together. Drawn into each other's orbit, as it were, their mutual gravitational fields cause them to collapse inward and implode. And where once there were two good words (duality in tension), there is now (in Hell) only hackwork.

Once in the poem, briefly, however, Satan is more than a hack, almost a poet. In the famous dramatic soliloquy which opens Book 4 of *Paradise Lost*, Satan acknowledges and confesses the two meanings of *owe*, one of which would have saved his life: " '[I] understood not that a grateful mind / By owing owes not, but still pays, at once / Indebted and discharged' " (*PL* 4.55–57). Satan, in his fit of remorse, recognizes the two senses of *owe*, which, earlier, in his fit of rebellion, he had so confused that the option of "to acknowledge as one's own" (*OED* O: I, 1C) was eliminated, completely silenced, by the sense "to be under obligation to repay" (*OED* O: II, 2). Satan makes a distinction—he du*a*ls rather than du*e*ls—and understands, though only for an instant, the truth. Rather than confuse, he separates, and is thus able to unite with the truth. But he flees from such union, lest the truth make him free.

And he would divorce Eve from the truth, too, to enslave her to himself. Hence his ploy, not play, with the word *part* in the seduction scene. Here, he sees to it that Eve does not, as in a moment of weakness he did, distinguish the meanings in a pun.

If *fruit* constitutes the master trope of *Paradise Lost*, *part* constitutes the master pun. To be sure, its similar *pair* cannot be separated from it far, but still, *part* does not really have a peer. Its two senses—"belonging to," as part of, and "separated," as apart from—so often duel in the poem, especially when they should dual, that finally, knowing how to separate them and when to unite them is itself a fairly reliable measure of how pure we have become through our trials in the poem.

But Eve is sadly impure when her moment of trial comes:

'What can your knowledge hurt him, or this tree
Impart against his will if all be his?
Or is it envy, and can envy dwell
In heavenly breasts? These, these and many more
Causes *import* your need of this fair fruit.
Goddess humane, reach then, and freely taste.'

[*PL* 9.727–32; emphasis added]

We hear the pun, of course; we hear it by distinguishing the parts of the word *impart*. And we answer Satan's question, as Eve should have done: "Why, the Tree can im-part": the Tree can make parts where before there were none. Indeed, it can make a part (im-part) against

God's will precisely because all is his; if Eve worships the Tree, she turns this part of his creation into the whole, God himself, and thus "makes it against him." Just so, later, "intent . . . *wholly* on her taste" (*PL* 9.786; emphasis added) she can go on to exclaim:

> 'O sovereign, virtuous, precious of all trees
> In Paradise, of operation blest
> To sapience, hitherto obscured, infamed,
> And thy fair fruit let hang, as to no end
> Created; but henceforth my early care,
> Not without song, each morning, and due praise
> Shall tend thee.'   [*PL* 9.795–801]

She has made the Tree into God when in fact it is God's (she has destroyed the genitive), and this replacement of the whole by the part, of the owner by the owned, becomes henceforth the type of all man's sins: replacement of the Creator with the creature. Replacement, substitution, becomes the structure of sin—but only because it *was* the structure of obedience. If man replaced his will with God's in one respect, the sign of the apple, the rest of creation replaced itself with man, substituting itself for man—in short, served man. But when man sinned, replacement, substitution, became utterly arbitrary, and now when creation replaces itself with man, the sense is usually that it substitutes man for itself (reversal), consuming man in its own process. And if man tries to avenge himself, living well, as they say, he only reverses the horrible trend and consumes the creation.

When the part im-parts against the whole, death alone can result, for the source of life (the whole) has been cut off, abandoned. This Satan knows and in his envy seeks against Adam and Eve. And when Death arrives in the Garden, he arrives as the parody of the whole: his " 'vast unhidebound corpse' " (*PL* 10.601) "that shape had none / Distinguishable in member" (*PL* 2.667–68) contains everything only by being nothing, the opposite of Being—to him " 'alike is hell, Paradise, and Heaven' " (*PL* 10.598). To ensure that Adam and Eve suffer death, this hole that parodies the whole, Satan must silence, mute, the duality in *impart;* the doubleness of which he is the author must not be allowed to be heard monistically (on[e]ly) as duality, of which God is the author; if Eve were at one with God, she would hear the pun and choose (and choosing, go free). But through Satan's efforts,

she is not at one with God, she is at one with him, Satan, or doubleness, and this is to be divided with and within herself. Hence, she
cannot hear the pun; and to make doubly sure that she does not hear
it, Satan muffles it by three lines later doubling it—mimicking it—
with a copy, *import*. The double, *import*, interferes with and tends to
replace *impart*, making it difficult for Eve to concentrate on *impart's*
partiality. In short, the double helps to confuse her, and thus to
continue and enhance that massive confusion Satan is here and now
perpetrating. In the next line, he will call her "goddess humane." And
then, convinced by this contradiction in terms, she eats the apple; and
with this act, Milton will write, she "knew not eating death" (*PL*
9.792), where the four words are *syntactically* what the pun is *seman-
tically*—the confusion of senses (she did not know she was eating
death; she did not know (sense: "connaître") death who eats (cf. *PL*
10.597, 609). Eve's fall (im*port*ation) into (*part*ial) knowledge is complete with this *re*pletion.

Once we have heard and understood the pun here, in Satan's
seduction of Eve, we hear it reverberate throughout the poem. Eve,
fallen, will wonder:

> 'But to Adam in what sort
> Shall I appear? Shall I to him make known
> As yet my change, and give him to *partake*
> Full happiness with me . . . '   [*PL* 9.816–19; emphasis added]

In addition to the bitter irony in " '*part*ake / *Full* " (where, incidentally, the enjambement almost by itself generates the irony), we hear
the pun part-ache (so near to the heart-ache of fallen love), and we feel
the ache of a part which can only appear in a "sort"—sorted, fated,
doomed, pitifully disguised (doubled). Indeed, now we have

> No more of talk where God or angel guest
> With man, as with his friend, familiar used
> To sit indulgent, and with him *partake*
> Rural repast . . .   [*PL* 9.1–4; emphasis added]

Now, our fallen but open ears must hear that "the parting angel" (*PL*
9.276), not only departed, but also parted Adam and Eve:

> 'Offspring of heaven and earth, and all earth's lord,
>   That such an enemy we have, who seeks
>   Our ruin, both by thee informed I learn,

And from *the parting angel* overheard
As in a shady nook I stood behind.'

[*PL* 9.273–77; emphasis added]

And hearing this, we must decide (choose) what it means. [12] Now we remember that when Satan accosted Eve in her sleep, he " 'even to [her] mouth of that same fruit held *part* / Which he had plucked' " (*PL* 5.83–84; emphasis added); and we know that the evil lay as much in the part as in the fruit plucked. [13] Now, when Adam puns, we shudder to hear " 'I see thou art exact of taste, / And elegant, of sapience no small *part*" (*PL* 9.1016–17; emphasis added), since we are also hearing the partitioning—in a sense, dismemberment—of Wisdom himself, the Word of God, the Son of Man. [14]

When Satan in his seduction of Eve hears her, "yet sinless" (*PL* 9.659), explain the prohibition on the Tree, "with show of zeal and love / To man, and indignation at his wrong, / [He n]ew *part* puts on" (*PL* 9.665–67; emphasis added). And when Christ judges Adam, he will condemn him for " 'resign[ing]' " (*PL* 10.148) to Eve " '[his] *part* / And person' " (*PL* 10.155–56; emphasis added). In the play God had authored, Adam and Eve had their parts, as did Satan. [15] And so indeed, each had to impersonate himself or herself—nothing created but what it is dual. And yet, so long as each obeyed, he or she did *not* have to impersonate another—did not have to double, mimic, copy. There was a difference, a difference between dualing and doubling. But when man fell, he fell into impersonation, because the Fall itself, Christ makes clear, was impersonation, doubling, copying, substitution, reiteration. And therefore, by the logic of the dual (the Logos of the One), man's redemption will be by substitution, substitution with a difference, or the sacrifice of the Word.

5

The Nightingale:
Sacrifice Perverted

For a poet, such as the Puritan poet Milton, who is redeemed by the option of Option himself (the Word), the pun, being a result of the Fall, is an occasion of trial "which purifies us." The real poet, who is not a hack, responds to duality, and especially the duality which has been ruined to doubleness or confusion in puns, with precision: that is to say, he cuts between (does *not* hack), he sorts and separates out the contending senses, as far as is possible (the work can never be finished), so as to maximize the option, the choice (which also is reason), the freedom, with which the pun challenges him and his readers. Milton's puns, then, are severe, cut off from the jocular or trivial, because for him the trial of confusion, in which contraries must be clarified and sorted out, is no laughing matter. And the same absence of frivolous humor in the man himself may be traced to the personal sacrifice which precedes and grounds the sacrifices of technique. So as to purge and redeem art from confusion, Milton makes of himself also a sacrifice, a pleasing sacrifice (Rom. 12:1). Moreover, the instruments of his immolation, which cut him off from other men—revolutionary zeal, prophetic fervor, blindness—are not laughing matters either.

Since we understand by means of contraries, we will see the meaning, the difference, of Milton's (and ultimately also of Christ's) sacrifices best if we first see their contrary or opposite, the perverse sacrifice perpetrated by Evil. Such is the sacrifice of Philomela the nightingale, the bird to which Milton assimilated himself throughout his career.[1]

A sacrifice can die, and Milton and his poem are sacrifices because they too must die if they are to have meaning. But this is as much as to say that Milton is human and his poem a human artifact: only the human—that is, the mortal—can die; and of humans and mortality only is meaning made. This much said, we can see, what is startling only at first, that Milton and his poem are a sacrifice in order to be human. If humanity consists in mutuality, or the supra-bestial will to share the self—"Do unto others as you would have them do unto you" (Matt. 7:12)—then the highest degree of humanity will be the highest degree of mutuality, or sacrifice—"No greater love hath a man than this, that he lay down his life for another" (John 15:13). To be fully human, and therefore most Christ-like, a man must be willing to sacrifice himself for another. As a sacrifice, his death will be meaningful and will make meaning.

Still, sacrifice is near kin to butchery, and mutuality is frequently perverted into catastrophe: the human always risks lapsing back into the animal. Hence, Milton must exorcise the alternative of mere violence from his poem, and this he does through the trope of the nightingale (*PL* 3.38–40; cf. *PL* 4.600–04, 5.39–41). As Dante does so often, Milton overcomes an impasse or escapes a difficulty by transuming it, making it work toward his own ultimate achievement.[2] In this case, Milton adapts Ovid's account of Procne, Philomela, and Tereus (*Meta.* 6.424–674) to be his figure of sacrifice perverted, and assimilates himself to the victim of sacrifice—Philomela, the nightingale—so as to exorcise from his text the kind of victim he must *not* be if his poem is to have the meaning of meaning.

As early as 1629, Milton gives evidence of figuring himself as the nightingale, and by "Il Penseroso" (1639?), the figure has assumed the importance it will have throughout the rest of his career.[3]

Come pensive nun .   .   .
. . . .
And the mute Silence hist along,
'Less Philomel will deign a song,
In her sweetest, saddest plight,
Smoothing the rugged brow of night,
While Cynthia checks her dragon yoke,
Gently o'er the accustomed oak,
Sweet bird that shunn'st the noise of folly,
Most musical, most melancholy!

Thee chauntress oft the woods among,
I woo to hear thy even-song,
And missing thee, I walk unseen
On the dry smooth-shaven green.
                    [lines 31, 55–66; Carey ed., pp. 141–42]

Philomel is the bird of night (the *night*ingale) who does not mix with
the "noise of folly." Hers is the "sweetest, saddest plight," and by
that plight she is separated, set apart, the superlatives suggesting her
uniqueness. Moreover, she is "most musical," the bird of harmony,
which is the proportioning of parts. She is, in short, the bird of the
bard, and as such Milton makes her his own. He "woo[s] to hear [her]
even-song," not only because it is the song of evening but also because
it is *even*—just, proportioned, balanced, harmonious.[4] And should he
miss her, he "walk[s] unseen," for together they are (all) one but apart
he is alone.

Of all Philomel's distinctions, the beginning is sacrifice; she is a
victim, and a victim, moreover, of confusion. Milton attaches such
significance to her because she figures the very suffering he endures.[5]
To be sure, Eve can be seen as Philomel, raped in the garden by
Satan, but Milton's allusions to the nightingale, I believe, at least
cumulatively, emphasize the relation between her and himself more
than that between her and Eve. And this, finally, because Ovid's
fable, Milton's source, is a tale of textual production.

It must be admitted that part of the enduring, if morbid, attraction of
the story of Procne, Philomela, and Tereus is the graphic savagery
with which Ovid narrates it.[6] But the greater attraction of the story is
its relation to the book of the poem in which it occurs, a book carefully
devoted to human creativity of a variety of sorts, especially as it is
contrasted to the creativity of the gods. The book opens with the story
of the contest between Arachne and Minerva (Athena) and closes with
Boreas's wooing of Orithyia; in between are the stories of Niobe and
her children, the Lydian peasants (who became frogs), Marsyas, Pel-
ops (briefly sketched in), and Procne, Philomela, and Tereus. Moreover, the preceding book closes with the story of the contest between
the Muses and the Pierides (who became magpies), which is narrated
to Minerva, who then opens Book 6 with her account of Arachne. The
following book, Book 7, opens with Ovid's version of the voyage of

the Argo, a story in which Medea figures prominently from the beginning. Throughout this stretch of the *Metamorphoses*, the violence of the gods—indeed their savagery—repeatedly occupies Ovid's attention; and if Book 7 opens with an account of one of the most violent women in classical fable, Ovid's strategy is explicable, in part at least, by her direct descent from the Sun, whose violence (as, for example, with Marsyas) is frequent and inordinate.

Human creativity, these books suggest through their emphasis on the violence of the gods, whether artistic or reproductive, is a threat to the gods, predominantly because it can, and often does, elevate humans to a status nearly equal to that of the gods. Human creativity is an almost literal transgression of the limits separating men and gods; so much is clear in Niobe's boast:

> 'Tutam me copia fecit.
> Maior sum quam cui possit Fortuna nocere.'
>
> [*Meta* 6.194–95]

['My very abundance has made me safe. I am too great for Fortune to harm']

Only the gods are impervious to Fortune's outrageous slings and arrows, but Niobe claims that she is greater than anyone whom Fortune can harm; and therefore, obviously, she claims that she is at least equal to the gods. For which presumption she is cruelly and mercilessly punished. When the gods finish with her, "nihil est in imagine vivum" ("there is nothing left alive in the image" [*Meta* 6.305]: in other words, turned to marble (*Meta* 6.312), Niobe is reduced to an artifact (*imago*) such as a human would create, which is not only not alive, but is also such bad art that it does not even afford the illusion of life or verisimilitude. Niobe is punished, in short, with and in a parody, or even a mockery, of human creativity, sculpture. And yet Ovid himself has a way of overcoming the gods, though his transgression is a good deal subtler than Niobe's. The last item he reports of her reads:

> ibi fixa cacumine montis
> Liquitur et lacrimis etiam nunc marmora manant.
>
> [*Meta.* 6.311–12]

[There set on a mountain's peak, she weeps, and even to this day tears trickle from the marble.]

If the human artifact is ridiculed by the violent mockery of the gods, the human still expresses (ex-presses) itself. If Niobe's tongue hardens to stone (*Meta.* 6.306–07), her silence does not inhibit her (human) capacity to make a meaningful sign. The gods win, they belittle human creativity; but they do not succeed in totally eliminating the human—the stone weeps.

In these books of the *Metamorphoses*, then, human creativity is understood to confuse men and gods—Pallas Athena can find no flaw in Arachne's tapestry, it so surpasses hers—and such confusion is a grave menace to the gods—Athena beats Arachne on the forehead with her shuttle and then transforms the helpless girl into a spider. This emphasis on confusion continues throughout Book 6 and is, I will argue, the principal concern of Ovid's account of the metamorphosis of Procne, Philomela, and Tereus. Human creativity, especially artistic creativity, Ovid understands, not only from time to time generates confusion between men and gods, but also, when it originates in violence like the violence of the gods, generates confusion, even chaos, in the community of men. He implies, it seems to me, that human creativity, especially artistic creativity, should not vie with divine creativity, not even nor most importantly because the gods are immortal and inaccessible, but also and crucially because mortals and mortal art are capable of a more human and more humane end.

Whether this is precisely the implication Milton derived from Book 6 of the *Metamorphoses* or not, he certainly, as we shall see, understood and made use of the various figures of confusion in the story of Procne, Philomela, and Tereus. To begin with, he could not have failed to notice that Ovid repeatedly returns to two concerns that are also two of his own deep anxieties, blindness and silence.[7] And the first of these, we should hasten to observe, is also a condition of Milton's very existence.

Almost from the very beginning, Ovid calls attention to the blindness of the sighted. The Thracians celebrate the marriage of Procne and Tereus and the birth of Itys, and Ovid exclaims: "Usque adeo latet utilitas" ("Even so is our true advantage hidden" [*Meta.* 6.438]). Similarly, when Tereus beseeches Pandion to send Philomela with him, his sudden lust for her fuels his powers of persuasion—"Facundum faciebat amor" ("Love made him eloquent" [*Meta.* 6.469])—and Ovid laments:

> Pro superi, quantum mortalia pectora *caecae*
> *Noctis* habent! ipso sceleris molimine Tereus
> Creditur esse pius laudemque a crimine sumit.
>
> [*Meta.* 6.472–74; emphasis added]

> [Ye gods, what blind night rules in the hearts of men! In the very act of pushing on his shameful plan Tereus gets credit for a kind heart and wins praise from wickedness.]

Finally and gruesomely, as Procne feeds Tereus the unspeakable banquet,

> inque suam viscera congerit aluum.
> *Tantaque nox animi est:* 'Itym huc accersite' dixit.
>
> [*Meta.* 6:651–52; emphasis added]

> [and [he] gorges himself with flesh of his own flesh. And in the utter blindness of his understanding he cries: 'Go, call me Itys hither.']

Obviously such blindness as this Milton abhors and desires to avoid; indeed, he relies on his physical blindness to purge and protect him from this inner blindness.

Even more insistent is Ovid's emphasis on silence, and this emphasis is crucial to Milton's strategy. Silence enters Ovid's narrative as the sequel to Philomela's rape. Tereus, to silence her, cuts her tongue out; and the scene obviously evokes a sacrifice:

> quo fuit accinctus, vagina liberat ensem
> arreptam coma fixis post terga lacertis
> vincla pati cogit. Iugulum Philomela parabat.
>
> [*Meta.* 6.551–53.]

> [he drew his sword which was hanging by his side in its sheath, caught her by the hair, and twisting her arms behind her back, he bound them fast. Philomela gladly offered her throat.]

Philomela offers Tereus her throat in a gesture reminiscent of the way a priest would prepare the throat of a victim.[8] If the scene is a parody of a sacrifice, this is only to underscore the savagery of Tereus. And in such a perverted sacrifice, Philomela is reduced to silence. In this condition, she seeks revenge—vengeance, we should observe, may be the form of sacrifice perverted—and Ovid writes, in profoundly suggestive language:

> Os mutum facti *caret indice.* Grande doloris
> Ingenium est miserisque venit sollertia rebus.
> Stamina barbarica suspendit callida tela
> Purpureasque notas filis intexuit albis,
> *Indicium sceleris.* . . .
> Fortunaque suae carmen miserabile *legit* [sc. Procne]
> *Et* (mirum potuisse) *silet* dolor ora repressit
> Verbaque quaerenti satis indignantia linguae
> Defuerunt nec flere vacat. . . .
>
> [*Meta.* 6.574–78, 582–85; emphasis added]

[speechless lips can give no token of her wrongs. But grief has sharp wits, and in trouble cunning comes. She hangs a Thracian web on her loom, and skillfully weaving purple signs on a white background, she thus tells the story of her wrongs. . . . [Procne] reads the pitiable tale of her misfortune, and (a miracle that she could!) says not a word. Grief chokes the words that rise to her lips, and her questing tongue can find no words strong enough to express her outraged feelings. Here is no room for tears.]

Note especially the emphasis on *index:* Philomela, who can no longer speak, must "point"—cf. *Meta.* 6.609: "pro voce manus fuit" ("in place of a voice, there was her hand")—and she must point through her artwork, the tapestry, which is a displaced text (*intexuit*).[9] This displaced text mutates into a song (*carmen*) which Procne "legit et silet," becoming thus the twin or the copy of her sister. Silence spreads, is a contagion. Moreover, language fails, lacking words of sufficient indignation. In sum, Ovid appears to suggest that the sacrifice (perverted) of Philomela produces silence, which produces texts which produce silence. More on this in a moment.

The contagion of silence continues to spread: Tereus's house is "nefandum" ("unspeakable"—*Meta.* 6.601), and Procne declares, " 'In omne *nefas* ego me, germana, paravi' " (" 'I am prepared for any crime, my sister' " [*Meta.* 6.618; emphasis added]). But, as this latter example suggests, the silence is fluent; it is somehow both silence and speech—it is silence always on the verge of speech (ne-fas). And this bizarre hybrid erupts when

Dissimulare nequit crudelia gaudia Progne;
Iamque suae cupiens exsistere nuntia cladis:
'Intus habes quem poscis' it.

[*Meta.* 6.653–55]

[Procne cannot hide her cruel joy, and eager to be the messenger of
her bloody news, she says: 'You have, within, him whom you want.']

When her husband has eaten her son, Procne can speak; and then she
speaks a horrific pun, "'Intus habes'."

These examples should suffice to demonstrate the consistency
and the insistence of Ovid's strategy. Moreover, the last example adds
what I take to be the target of this strategy: confusion, the abolition of
difference. Blindness, and especially silence (which is also speech),
inscribe a discourse on the confusion or destructive commingling of
persons and things which is the engine of the horror in the tale of
Procne, Philomela, and Tereus. Immediately after her rape, Philomela rages at Tereus:

'*Omnia turbasti* paelex ego facta sororis,
Tu *geminus* coniunx, hostis mihi debita poena.'

[*Meta.* 6.537–38; emphasis added]

['You have confused all natural relations: I have become a concubine,
my sister's rival, you, a husband to both. Now Procne must be my
enemy.]

Later, Procne, after she has read the tapestry,

fasque nefasque
Confusura ruit poenaeque in imagine tota est.

[*Meta.* 6.585–86; emphasis added]

[she hurries on to confound right and wrong, her whole soul bent on
the thought of vengeance.]

Moreover, she later declares that "'scelus est pietas in coniuge
Tereo'" ("'faithfulness to such a husband as Tereus is a crime'"
[*Meta.* 6.635]), and this, "pietas" as "scelus," is an instance of the
confusion which Ovid is observing. Finally, there is the most
gruesome and barbarous instance of confusion: Itys the son ingested
by and in Tereus the father. And this confusion, as I have already
noted, is named in the text by a pun—"'Intus habes quem poscis'"—

which is the confusion of two senses in one word or phrase. Ovid's text, then, is an exploration of the fatal effects of the destruction of difference caused by the blindness of sight and the voice of silence.

Milton's deployment of Ovid's text is brilliant. In the opening lines of Book 3 of *Paradise Lost*, near the end of the invocation, he writes:

> Then feed on thoughts, that voluntary move
> Harmonious numbers; as the wakeful bird
> Sings darkling, and in the shadiest covert hid
> Tunes her nocturnal note.   [*PL* 3.37–40]

He inflects the allusion twice, each time at a crucial juncture. The first occasion is when he recounts how Adam and Eve first retire to sleep in the garden:

> Now came still evening on, and twilight grey
> Had in her sober livery all things clad;
> Silence accompanied, for beast and bird,
> They to their grassy couch, these to their nests
> Were slunk, all but the wakeful nightingale;
> She all night long her amorous descant sung;
> *Silence was pleased* . . .   [*PL* 4.598–604]

The second is Satan's first attempt to seduce Eve, as she dreams; she reports his words to her thus to Adam:

>   'Now is the pleasant time,
> The cool, the silent, save where silence yields
> To the night-warbling bird, that now awake
> Tunes sweetest his love-laboured song . . .'   [*PL* 5.38–41]

In these three passages, we can measure the extent and the effects of Milton's assimilation of himself to Philomela.

Note first the obvious and crucial distinction between the second and third passages: in the second, the nightingale is feminine, in the third, masculine. Moreover, Milton uses the same predicate of the bird in both passages—namely, "tunes"—probably to signal the intended comparison. Next, note that in all three passages, the nightingale is wakeful and alert when others are asleep. Probably the best word to describe the bird and Milton alike is vigilant. Moreover, not only is the nightingale wakeful, but also, in the first passage, she sings in the dark, is hidden, and night—with all its associations of darkness, mystery, and fear—is predicated of her "note" (which is "nocturnal"). Clearly, obscurity is her habitat; after all, she is the *nightingale*. But there is more than ornithology to Milton's words. The poet too emerges from "shadiest covert"—that is, from the hiddenness of imagery (which, as Milton would have remembered, is *ombra* in Italian, or "shade".) Through the obscurity (or non-differentiation) of *as* ("as the wakeful bird"), the poet both joins and severs when he constructs an image: he joins unlikes to affirm that they are like (poets and nightingales, for example), and yet, even as he joins them, he severs them, for the very effort involved in joining them evinces their difference. Or, at least, this is the hope of the poet. The *as* may be so obscure that the likenesses or the differences disappear and confusion results. The poet dwells always on the brink of confusion, there with Satan on the edge of chaos. Satan's lust, of course, is "'others to make such / As I'" (*PL* 9.127). Milton emphasizes this malice as early as Book 2:

> for whence,
> But from *the Author of all ill* could spring
> So deep a *malice, to confound the race*
> *Of mankind in one root, and Earth with Hell*
> *To mingle and involve?*   [*PL* 2.380–84; emphasis added]

It is hardly coincidental, much less insignificant, that the description of Satan's end as "confound[ing]" (confusing—see also *PL* 6.291; and 10.391–92) should also be the first of many occasions in the poem on which he is called "Author." Satan is the perverse author—the anti-author, if you will—from whom Milton must labor to differentiate himself. And he must so labor because authority itself always runs the risk of confusion: authority names (any) A *as* (some) B, and if by naming A as B, authority should irrecoverably alter A, then authority, unlike God, will have "'destruction with creation . . . mixed'" (*PL* 8.236).[10] Thus if Satan's lust is "'others to make such / As I,'" Milton's desire must be to make others *not* such as he. But this means, in effect, that he must make himself not such as others. He, Philomela, must not (let himself) become Procne—recall Philomela's "'Omnia turbasti . . .'." He must hold himself apart, distinct; he must be severe (severed) in order to be sufficiently singular (not confused), to join with another in that duality which creates unity. And

he must be so, that the terms of his images might be so. Milton is no
drunken boat (though malt do its utmost).

Yet he might be. Hence the terms of his first nightingale simile:
they insist on darkness, obscurity, mystery, so as to name, and thus
ideally master, the threat of Philomela's fate. If the nightingale sings
with that spontaneity that the poet craves—"Then feed on thoughts,
that voluntary move / Harmonious numbers"—she also sings in the
dark, our of and through confusion. Milton, too, sings in the dark, but
he must be ever vigilant against confusion. And this vigilance, finally,
is to see, to see even in the dark. Not to be blind, not to be like the
Thracians (with the exception of the *Thracians* Orpheus and
Thamyris)[11] or the people of Pandion, or Tereus, but to see, to see
inwardly. Milton continues the invocation to Book 3, and we are
prepared now to see why he continues it, with a discourse on his
blindness:

> Thus with the year
> Seasons return, but not to me returns
> Day, or the sweet approach of even or morn,
> Or sight of vernal bloom, or summer's rose,
> Or flocks, or herbs, or human face divine;
> But cloud in stead, and ever-during dark
> Surrounds me, from the cheerful ways of men
> Cut off, and for the book of knowledge fair
> Presented with a universal blank
> Of nature's works to me expunged and razed,
> And wisdom at one entrance quite shut out.   [*PL* 3.40–50]

All around Milton, as all around the nightingale, [outside him] is
confusion; everywhere else, the works of nature and the cheerful
ways of men, but for Milton only "cloud" and "dark." And yet this
condition does "*cut* [him] *off*" (*PL* 3.47)—sacrifice him (*témnō*)—sever
him, singularize him, liberate him from confusion, so much so that it
empowers him to hope and to pray:

> So much the rather thou celestial Light
> Shine inward, and the mind through all her powers
> Irradiate, there plant eyes, all mist from thence
> Purge and disperse, that I may see and tell
> Of things invisible to mortal sight.   [*PL* 3.51–55]

In exchange for the confusion of the "universal blank," Milton hopes
to have, and in the event believes he does have, no confusion within,

"all mist from thence / Purge[d] and disperse[d]." For the physical blindness, freedom—freedom from the blindness of the sighted, which haunts the story of the nightingale, freedom to see and sing in the dark.

If Milton's use of Ovid's text here is stunning, it is no less so in the other two allusions to the nightingale. Crucial is the involvement of silence, the other element in Ovid's strategy. The third allusion, we know, establishes the antithesis to Milton as nightingale; this masculine bird, of Satan's invention for Eve's benefit, is *not* the bird that Milton conceives himself to be. Moreover, this bird is also antithetical to the nightingale in the second allusion: it is to "*his* love-laboured song" [that] "silence yields," whereas "silence was pleased" by "*her* amorous descant." The difference here measures the distance between confusion and harmony, or order.

But neither is it as simple as that. Begin with the barely latent personification in "silence yields," "silence was pleased," and "silence accompanied." For if we remember the personal response, the pleasure, of silence in the second allusion when we read the third, we begin to suspect that "silence yields" in the third because *she* has been forced by *him*, the *male* nightingale. A hint, if only a hint, emerges of that original rape; and the hint serves to suggest that now silence is the victim—and to suggest perhaps more, that then, too, silence was the victim. For the rape of Philomela was, ultimately, a perverted sacrifice of the signifier, or the tongue. If the signifier is the mark of difference, that which differences,[12] then the tongue is one of the instigators of that mark. And to sever the tongue is therefore to eliminate difference. In particular, it is to eliminate the difference between speech and silence, and that is to eliminate both speech *and* silence, for where there is no speech, there can be no silence, and where there is no silence, there can be no speech. In the absence of speech and silence, there is only noise and muteness.

Hence the rape of Philomela is, finally, a wounding of silence. In effect, Tereus reduces silence to muteness in Philomela. Silence is a human prerogative, a choice—beasts only growl or roar, they are mute—and to fall silent—to exercise the choice—is also to communicate. But her tongue torn out, Philomela has no choice (no *different* alternative), and instead of silence, she has only muteness. And, as Ovid says, "os mutum . . . caret indice." Lacking an "index," Philomela resorts to a "text" (the tapestry) which really is no text, which becomes a "carmen" which really is no song, which is read and "silet"—where *silet* marks the final abuse of silence, for Procne is mute (stricken dumb, as we would say), and speech is no real alternative for her (*Meta.* 6.582–83). Now at last we can revise my earlier, premature conclusion and give it precision: the perverted sacrifice of Philomela produces pseudo-silence, which produces pseudo-texts, which produce pseudo-silence. And this is a model of textual production which Milton abhors, as did Ovid before him. In this model, silence is *not* pleased.

To please silence, to render it no longer the victim, a different model of textual production and a different product are needed, a model and a product not contaminated by violence. Silence will accompany and be pleased with, will not be forced to yield to, the text of love, whose model is true, not perverted, sacrifice. This text and its model (Satan's perversion of which in the third allusion Milton signals by the parody of the Song of Songs)[13] are an "amorous descant," not a "love-laboured song," which pleases silence and thus *produces* silence, real silence. Moreover, this descant which pleases silence contains the "a" which marks the difference (and différance) between Adam and Eve's love and the love-song they hear, on the one hand, and the "descent" into laboured love and violated silence produced by Satan, on the other. This one letter, and the word it distinguishes, in a sense, make all the difference: Milton's poem would be a desc*a*nt, and as such able to receive the descent of Urania (*PL* 7.1), rather than only a desc*e*nt, such as Satan's "foul descent" (*PL* 9.163) into the confusion of angel and "bestial slime" (*PL* 9.165). His poem would be both descant and descent, *a* and *e* and therefore *a* not *e*, *e* not *a*, or the absence of confusion.

6

Incest, Chastity, Productivity

Our search for an understanding of true sacrifice by its contrary is not yet complete. For there is a confusion even worse than that begotten by the rape of Philomela. It is perhaps—for Milton, I believe it *is*—the ultimate confusion, the terror-inspiring confusion of incest.

Sin, we know, is the pretext of the sign in *Paradise Lost*. As the confusion of the Fall is the pretext for poetry (musing and punning and so on), so sin, the embodiment of that confusion—the daughter by parthenogenesis of her father, begotten incestuously by him with death—is the pretext for signs, of which poetry is made. But if sin embodies confusion, if sin *is* the confusion of good and evil, the first victim of that confusion is, necessarily, apartness—for the good, to be good, is apart from its Creator to be a part of its Creator. But in sin, apartness becomes the simulacrum of itself; it is confused with a (per)version of itself. In sin, apartness is confused, because it looks like itself, or the apartness which would be creative. Sin, for example, is the daughter of Satan and therefore, apparently, apart from him. Tereus, another example, is the husband of Procne and therefore, apparently, apart from Philomela. But in fact, in sin, apartness is not itself—it is, rather, perverted connectedness. Sin couples with her father and gets death; Tereus rapes Philomela and is thus "geminus coniunx."[1] The apartness of sin, then, is the simulacrum of apartness.

Hence the incontrovertible decorum of the narcissism imagery which names the "relationship" between Satan and Sin (*PL* 2.761–65): narcissism is the simulacrum of selfhood and identity. Hence also the stunning maneuver of coupling *Sin* and *sign* in the same line: take but the *g* away, and the sign becomes sin; that is to say, take but the *g* away and confusion results. Signs, which depend on apartness, lie forever precariously on the margin of their pretext, or the simulacrum of apartness. He who works in signs, Milton well knew, is only the letter from sin.

And the gravest sin he risks committing is the sin of incest, Satan's sin with his daughter Sin. "In incest it is the signifier that makes love with its signifieds,"[2] the poem with its meanings, the poet with his imagery. And the product of incest, as Milton clearly saw, is the anti-product death. Incest produces the ultimate confusion, or indistinctness—the randomized particles of the once-shaped, now decayed individual (recall the "'vast unhide-bound corpse'" [*PL* 10.601]). Incest is the ultimacy of narcissism: in incest, the image in the water (or glass) is made flesh, and Narcissus's desire is realized, or better, reified—the self becomes just enough not-self that it can couple with itself. But immediately this is said, it also becomes evident that incest is the parody of production, for in incest, the self would produce itself without the alienation of *re*production. In incest, the self would differentiate itself without submitting to the pain of difference (the principal pain of every marriage)—the one lover so little different from the other as to be the same (see chapter 12 below, on *Samson Agonistes*). In incest, the self would become other without the (b)other.

Incest, then, is the model of inward-turning, autotelic reflexivity which can produce nothing (no thing) but its own producing, for a thing would be a difference, whereas incest can see no difference.[3] Hence, for example, the problematic figure of Melancholy, the daughter of Saturn by his daughter Vesta—"in Saturn's reign,/Such *mixture* [or, confusion] was not held a stain" ("Il Penseroso," lines 25–26; emphasis added). As the whole tradition recognizes, Melancholy is near kin to Death, the (non-) product of incest, because in fact, it is the death of the self to the outer world (where the truth of the trope "death of the self" is more real than naive realism can suspect.)[4] Thus Milton, the Puritan poet, also therefore necessarily a poet of work—who, moreover, did not consider work a punishment for sin (see *PL* 4.618–19)—finds in this one trope a poetic, theological, and technological figure of the ultimate degradation of creation, for, in the tradition from which Milton emerges, creation is differentiation, the infinitely bountiful production of the good by the good (see chapter 1).

The attraction of the trope must have been great in other ways too, for in the greatest Latin fable of incest, Ovid's account of Myrrha, Milton would have found several significant elements of his own design, and chiefly the emphasis on confusion.[5]

Ovid's fable of Myrrha (*Meta.* 10.298–502) cannot be understood apart from its immediate context in the poem. It is preceded by his account of Pygmalion (*Meta.* 10.243–97) and followed by that of Venus and Adonis (*Meta.* 10. 503–739), Adonis being the product of Myrrha's incestuous love for her father. It is therefore enclosed in an elaborate and profound discourse on imagery and the production of imagery, and forms, moreover, part of a 500-line text incessantly *re*produced by European poets—for example, Alain of Lille, Jean de Meun, Dante, Chaucer, Boccaccio, Petrarch, Shakespeare,[6] and, perhaps most important for our purposes, Spenser, in Book 3 of the *Faerie Queene*, on which more in a moment. In this text, Ovid concentrates on Myrrha's excruciatingly painful awareness of the evil she is contemplating and eventually performs; and, more specifically, he has her rehearse, in distaste and self-loathing, the predictable results:

'Et quot *confundas et iura et nomina*, sentis!
tune eris et matris paelex et adultera patris?
tune soror nati genetrixque vocabere fratris?'

[*Meta.* 10.346–48; emphasis added]

['Think how many ties, how many names you are confusing! Will you be the rival of your mother, the mistress of your father? Will you be called the sister of your son, the mother of your brother?']

To increase sympathy for the illusionless girl, Ovid has her bitterly remark that

'Humana malignas
cura dedit leges, et quod natura remittit,
invida iura negant.'

[*Meta.* 10.329–31]

['Human civilization has made spiteful laws, and what nature allows, the jealous laws forbid.']

Thus he also introduces the crucial theme of nature (*phýsis*) versus convention (*thésis*). Next, when Myrrha and Cinyras actually consummate the act, Ovid writes, with chilling brilliance, that

Forsitan aetatis quoque nomine 'filia' dixit,
Dixit et illa 'pater,' *sceleri ne nomina desint.'*
                                                    [*Meta.* 10.467–68; emphasis added]

[It chanced, by a name appropriate to her age, he called her
'daughter,' and she called him 'father,' that names might not be
lacking to their guilt—literally, lest the names should be lacking to
their crime.]

Of course the names must not be "lacking to the crime," for in a
sense the names *are* the crime—were it not for the names "daughter"
and "father," this carnal intercourse would be no crime, only "quod
natura remittit." It is the names—which are difference—that intro-
duce the difference which declares Myrrha and Cinyras to be too
similar to copulate. Were there no names, Myrrha and Cinyras
would be sufficiently different to copulate without crime (or with
much less crime certainly). But put this way, the problem appears in
all its stark complexity, for if Myrrha and Cinyras were *that* different, she would not want him with anything like the same passionate
intensity (although want him she still might). It is the similarity,
product of their names, which more than anything else fuels Myrrha's relentless desire.[7] Without the names, there would be no
crime; but without the names also there would have been no (or
much less) lust in the first place. The names are the crime.

But they are the crime only in the sense of the instrumental
cause, not the efficient cause. The efficient causes are Myrrha and
Cinyras: they are the guilty ones. The names may be the crime, but
they are not guilty. The instrument is never guilty—unless it, too, is
conscious.[8] Ovid himself assumes the guilt of incest, in the special
way a poet can commit incest in language, in order to emphasize
how names or predications can be crimes and to show, at the same
time and in the same way, how both the crime and the guilt can be
avoided. Immediately following the conclusion of Myrrha's story, as
he opens his account of her son Adonis, Ovid stresses the surpassing
beauty of the boy:

. . . . modo formosissimus infans,
Iam iuuenis, iam uir, *iam se formosior ipso est.*
                                                    [*Meta.* 10.522–23; emphasis added]

[Now a youth, now a man, now himself more beautiful than he is—
to give a very literal translation.]

I suppose the initial, obvious reaction to such language would be to tame it by saying something like, O just another bit of Ovid's sophisticated rhetoric. But such a judgment—virtually a dismissal— is actually an evasion. What does it *mean*, what *can* it mean, to say that "he is more beautiful than he himself is"? To be sure, we feel something like, Well, he must be very beautiful indeed. But we supply this feeling in the absence of any retrievable meaning. Of course, "se formosior ipso est" is grammatically possible, just as the copulation between Myrrha and Cinyras is naturally possible, but neither the Latin nor the copulation is conventionally possible: convention—in the one case of meaning, in the other of morality—is offended and flaunted. All is not meaningful that grammar or nature permits. And the Latin phrase "se formosior ipso est" is just as incestuous in its way as the copulation of Myrha and Cinyras, for it posits a difference which is specious—morphologically, this difference consists of the adjectival comparative term *-ior* plus the dative of the reflexive pronoun *ipso*, in order to escape with indulging a similarity of self-coincidence only possible in grammar. And Ovid commits this crime, this incest, of language, in which nothing is produced but the producing itself, in which grammar (if you will) only grammars,[9] so as to remind himself and us of how and how easily men can "confundere et iura et nomina."

I think it is obvious now in what way I will suggest that Milton found Ovid's text of Myrrha attractive. But there is more to the matter than this, for Milton did not only read Ovid, he also read all the versions of Ovid which subsequent great poets deposited, and in particular those of Shakespeare and Spenser. In *Venus and Adonis*, for example, Shakespeare emphasizes the issue of productivity so significant to our understanding of Satan in *Paradise Lost* and crucial, I will eventually argue, to understanding the central thesis of *Paradise Regained*, or God's producing of the man Jesus (*PR* 1.150–55; see also chapter 11 below). Early in the poem, for example, and most pointedly, Shakespeare writes:

'Is thine own heart to thine own face affected?
Can thy right hand seize love upon thy left?
Then woo thyself, be of thyself rejected—
Steal thine own freedom, and complain on theft.
    Narcissus so himself himself forsook,
    And died to kiss his shadow in the brook.

'Torches are made to light, jewels to wear,
Dainties to taste, fresh beauty for the use,
Herbs for their smell, and sappy plants to bear:
Things growing to themselves are growth's abuse.
  Seeds spring from seeds, and beauty breedeth beauty—
  Thou wast begot—to get it is thy duty.

'Upon the earth's increase why shouldst thou feed,
Unless the earth with thy increase be fed?
By law of nature thou art bound to breed,
That thine may live when thou thyself art dead.
  And so in spite of death thou dost survive
  In that thy likeness still is left alive.'   [V & A, lines 157–74]

It is unimaginable that Milton overlooked or forgot these lines. Most attractive in them obviously is the way in which they derive the issue of productivity from the formulation of Adonis's narcissism. The narcissist *does* "grow to himself" and thus "abuse growth," and the incestuous, who realize and incarnate their narcissism, reifying it in another's flesh, even when they do produce a child, produce one who, in Shakespeare's version anyway, resists all further production, preferring rather sports of death (hunting), the pursuit of destruction, to life and the getting of life (Adonis never does couple with Venus in Shakespeare's poem). Much else in *Venus and Adonis* doubtless appealed to Milton, but I think Shakespeare's articulation of what I would like to call the *avaritia sui* of the narcissist (see chapter 1 and 3 above) must have attracted him particularly strongly. If the root of all evil is greed (1 Tim. 6:10), then Milton, Shakespeare concurring, might well have concluded that those rooted in evil the deepest are narcissists—like Satan.

If the explorations of narcissism and incest in *Venus and Adonis* attracted Milton to Shakespeare, the Ovidian configurations of these issues in *The Faerie Queene*, Book 3, must have provoked and challenged him the most. There is no question here, of course, of my undertaking anything like an analysis of this whole book, one of the most famous and most difficult of the poem.[10] My concerns are much narrower, and my remarks therefore hardly comprehensive or complete. I will proceed from the obvious to the only slightly less so, pausing at times to emphasize crucial connections.

Most obvious in terms of Milton's interest are Spenser's overt contrasts of Britomart with Narcissus, for the purpose, I take it, of distinguishing her from him—although, since to contrast is also to

compare, traces of Narcissus do finally linger about her still, as I
suppose they must about someone whose chief task in life is to deposit her image in the world (*FQ* 3.iv.11). The most important of
these contrasts takes place in canto ii, in which Myrrha is also ad-
duced so that Britomart may be distinguished from her too (*FQ*
3.ii.40–41). Britomart herself, having looked into her father's mirror
(Merlin's "globe," called "mirror" at *FQ* 3.ii.38) directly acknowledges her likeness to Narcissus:

> But wicked fortune mine, though mind be good,
>   Can have no end, nor hope of my desire,
> But feed on shadowes, whiles I die for food,
> And like a shadow wexe, whiles with entire
> Affection, I doe languish and expire.
>   I fonder, then *Cephisus* foolish child,
>   Who having vewed in a fountaine shere
> His face, was with the love therof beguild—
> I fonder love a shade, the bodie farre exild.   [*FQ* 3.ii.44]

Immediately, her nurse, Glauce, patterned obviously on Myrrha's
nurse (*Meta*. 10.382) for the sake of the difference between them,
objects to Britomart's despairing self-analysis:

> 'Nought like (quoth she) for that same wretched boy
>   Was of himselfe the idle Paramoure,
> Both love and lover, without hope of joy,
> For which he faded to a watry flowre.
> But better fortune thine, and better howre,
>   Which lov'st the shadow of a warlike knight,
>   No shadow, but a bodie hath in powre:
> That bodie, wheresoever that it light,
> May learned be by cyphers, or by Magicke might.'   [*FQ* 3.ii.45]

Though almost certainly not to *her* way of thinking, Glauce's objection manages to leave some room for doubt about Britomart, since to
love a shadow, no matter how *shadow* may be qualified, is to resemble Narcissus; and perhaps Spenser realized that this lingering resemblance is necessary, for, as he has the old woman say when she
learns to her relief that Britomart's love is not incestuous:

> Of much more uncouth thing I was affrayd,
> Of filthy lust, contrarie unto kind:
> But this affection nothing straunge I find,
> For who with reason can you aye reprove,

To love the semblant pleasing most your mind,
And yield your heart, whence ye cannot remove?
No guilt in you, but in the tyranny of love.

Not so th' *Arabian Myrrhe* did set her mind.

[*FQ* 3.ii.40.3–41.1; emphasis added]

About any amorous desire, there is this much of Narcissus anyway,
and necessarily, that to love at all, the lover must form "the semblant
pleasing most [his] mind." If that semblant be *only* his own projection, then he is damned, but some semblant there must be, at the
beginning, for love to happen at all.

Clearly Spenser intends us to understand that Britomart's semblant is more than her projection: it is rather, and much more, productive "love [which] does alwayes bring forth bounteous deeds,/
And in each gentle hart desire of honour breeds" (*FQ* 3.i.49.8–9).
Thus already in canto i, Spenser emphasizes the productivity of love
as opposed to narcissism. With her love Artegall, Britomart will produce "from the sacred mould / Of her immortall wombe" (*FQ*
3.iv.1.8–9) a long line of great kings; and as if to emphasize con-
clusively how fertile, how productive, Britomart is and will be,
Spenser is bold to liken her, when she hears her first description of
Artegall (by Redcrosse Knight), to a mother who has just given
birth:

The royall Mayd woxe inly wondrous glad,
  To heare her Love so highly magnifide,
And ioyd that ever she affixed had,
  Her hart on knight so goodly glorifide,
  How ever finely she it faind to hide:
The loving mother, that nine monethes did beare,
  In the deare closet of her painefull side,
  Her tender babe, it seeing safe appeare,
Doth not so much reioyce, as she reioyced theare.   [*FQ* 3.ii.11]

Similes are dangerous, as Spenser well knew. After all, it is he who
wrote, I am sure to Milton's delight as well as to A. B. Giamatti's:[11]

So tickle be the termes of mortall state,
  And full of subtile sophismes, which do play
  With double senses, and with false debate,
T'approve the unknowen purpose of eternall fate.   [*FQ* 3.iv.28.6–9]

Only in Hell or in Heaven is the single, or unisemous, sense possible; here among mortals the "double sense" is needful, if also usually painful. And the double sense—I would prefer, for distinction's sake, to say the "dual sense"—of remarking that Britomart rejoices *more* than a just-delivered mother when she hears Artegall highly praised is to suggest that she somehow is also giving birth to Artegall, who will be her lover. The suggestion of incest, in short, is inescapable.

And intended, I think.[12] If Britomart is to be the true opposite of Narcissus and Myrrha, she must also, as opposites do, resemble them. Hence Spenser is shrewd enough and bold enough to suggest, so as to comprehend and justify, Britomart's motherhood vis-à-vis Artegall; for, of course, throughout the fin'amors tradition, the Lady is the mother of her lover's virtues—the Lady *does*, in that second of the "double" or dual senses, give birth to her lover.[13] Hence Spenser can suggest Britomart's amorous maternity and yet also purify it of incest, insisting thus on its true, authentic copia (see especially *FQ* 3.iii.3). Moreover, in doing so he can play delightfully with Ovid's text by using the Tree of Jesse tradition (Isaiah 11:1) to suggest that Britomart is a tree, the tree, and if you will, the main root, from which will spring the British monarchy (*FQ* 3.ii.17, 3.iii.18, and especially 3.iii.22), thus to suggest also that she is again the anti-Myrrha, since Myrrha, of course, gave birth to Adonis from her trunk, *after* she had metamorphosed into a tree (*Meta.* 10.503–14). Furthermore, with this suggestion, Spenser can also intimate that the root of the British monarchy is different from the root of all evil. It was, after all, Elizabeth who told her subjects, in the "Golden Speech" before Parliament in 1601:

> Of myself, I must say this: I never was any greedy, scraping grasper, nor a strict, fast-holding prince, nor yet a waster; my heart was never set upon any worldly goods, but only for my subjects' good. What you do bestow on me, I will not hoard up, but receive it to bestow on you again: yea, my own properties I account yours, to be expended for your good, and your eyes shall see the bestowing of it for your welfare. . . . And though you have had, and may have, many princes more mighty and wise, sitting in this state, yet you never had, or shall have, any that will be more careful and loving.[14]

A queen of copia if ever there was one.

If Spenser insists on Britomart's copia by systematically distinguishing her from—but also likening her to—Narcissus and Myrrha, he also demonstrates her copia by an emblem of its opposite, or Malbecco, of whom we are told:

> For all his dayes he drownes in privitie,
> Yet has full large to live, and spend at libertie.
>
> But all his mind is set on mucky pelfe.
> To hoord up heapes of evill gotten masse,
> For which he others wrongs, and wreckes himselfe.
>
> [*FQ* 3.ix.3.8–4.3]

Malbecco, an emblem of *avaritia* and *avaritia sui*, both, is married, we know, like Chaucer's Merchant January,[15] to a woman far too young for him, Hellenore, whose promiscuity and infidelity prompt Spenser to a crucial apology at the opening of canto iv:

> But never let th'ensample of the bad
>   Offend the good: *for good by paragone*
>   *Of evill, may more notably be rad,*
>   *As white seemes fairer, macht with blacke attone*
>   Ne all are shamed by the fault of one:
>   For lo in heaven, whereas all goodnesse is,
>   Emongst the Angels, a whole legione
>   Of wicked Sprights did fall from happy blis
> What wonder then, if one of women all did mis?
>
> [*FQ* 3.ix.2; emphasis added]

Of course, we have here yet another instance of the tradition of "By his contrary is everything declared." But we have more than that actually. What Milton would have read here is not only a position on the inevitable "blend" (*FQ* 3.ix.7) of good and evil, but also the emergence of this awareness from a book, the "Legend of Chastity," intimately concerned with doubles and duality and doubling and the sorting of doubles. Artegall, for example, is, of course, "Arthur's equall" or dual, though hardly his copy; Belphoebe's grandmother is Amphisa, or "double Nature."[16] Therefore, Milton must have also found in this legend a spur for his own commitment to the chastising of confusion, its purification into copia, the copia of chastity.

Thus the problematic of incest leads to the question of chastity. This question, especially as it concerns productivity, we can most fruit-

fully address in Milton's early, most Spenserian poem, the masque
Comus.

One of the minor, but still significant, cruces in the masque occurs
when the younger brother expresses his fear " 'Lest some ill-greeting
touch attempt the person / Of our *unowned* sister' " (*C* 405–06; emphasis added). Carey observes in his note to line 406 on the word
unowned that "no other occurrence of the word in the sense 'lost' is
recorded: usually it meant 'not possessed as property.' "[17] And indeed
it means that here, too, in addition. Milton's whole strategy in the
masque, in fact, can be precipitated from the meaning of this word.
We may comprehend it most clearly if we make use of the French
word *propre* and its multiple meanings, translating "unowned" into
impropre.[18] As long as the Lady is "lost," she is also no one's property;
as long as she is (at least potentially) "unclean," she is again, also no
one's property—no individual owner's property—because she is (or
would be) promiscuous and therefore the property of anyone who
would have her—in other words, *un*chaste. If the Lady is unclean,
she is improper—in all senses which the word will bear.

Conversely, if she is some *one's own* (*propre*), his property, she is
also clean, or chaste—which, of course, is the condition which obtains in marriage. Hence Milton's language in *Paradise Lost*, Book 4:

> Hail wedded love, mysterious law, true source
> Of human offspring, *sole propriety*
> *In Paradise of all things common else.*   [*PL* 4.750–52; emphasis added]

Marriage, or more properly, chastity in marriage, is the origin of
"propriety"—both proper-ness and property.[19] Everything else in
the pre-lapsarian world is common, obviously, because of the earth's
death-less abundance (*PL* 4.624–32, for example). The consistency of
Milton's argument from *Comus* to *Paradise Lost* is only less impressive
than the purity of his vision: were there no death, property in human
life would be sole, alone; just as there would have been only one sign
of our obedience left, there would have been also only one propriety
in our lives; and just as that one sign would have enabled all the others
to let the sunshine in, so the sole propriety would have left everything
else as common, as free, as the sunshine.

From this purchase on Milton's argument, we can briefly collect
the significance of the economic imagery elsewhere in *Comus*, and
demonstrate its relevance to Milton's idea of chastity. Most of this

imagery derives from Comus himself, who, of course, wants the Lady
to spend herself on him and for him, for if she buys his line, then he
owns her in the parody of ownership, peculiarly his, which makes the
proper common (promiscuous). Hence, for example, in a famous
passage, he accuses the Lady—his "purchase" according to her elder
brother (*C* 606)—of "hoarding":

> 'List Lady be not coy, and be not cozened
> With that same vaunted name virginity,
> Beauty is Nature's coin, must not be hoarded,
> But must be current, and the good thereof
> Consists in mutual and partaken bliss,
> Unsavoury in the enjoyment of itself
> If you let slip the time, like a neglected rose
> It withers on the stalk with languished head.'   [*C* 736–43]

The temptation to *Quellenforschung* here is great, but happily it can be
resisted by invoking the tradition which Comus (so to speak) most
wants to suppress so as to succeed in his seduction, namely, "Moneta
Dei sumus."[20] The tradition that man is God's coin is so ancient and
various that I can hardly detail it here. Suffice it that Milton himself
directly alludes to it and its pretext in the voice of the Attendant
Spirit:

> 'And here to every thirsty wanderer,
> By sly enticement [Comus] gives his baneful cup,
> With many murmurs mixed, whose pleasing poison
> The visage quite transforms of him that drinks,
> And the inglorious likeness of a beast
> Fixes instead, unmoulding *reason's mintage*
> *Charactered in the face*.'   [*C* 523–29; emphasis added]

In the Christian tradition, man is God's coin because "reason's mintage / [Is] charactered in the face." God created man in his image and
likeness (Gen. 2:6), and the image and likeness reside in man's mind,
especially in his reason.[21] Hence the "mintage" of reason "charactered in the face" is the proof that God owns this coin—he issued it if
you will. After the Fall, however, the likeness to God was destroyed
by sin, and all that remained were traces of the image in man's reason,
which thus has only the power of something fragmented.[22] Hence, it
is just as Milton writes: "The inglorious likeness of a beast / Fixes
instead" on the face of any fallen human who is not vigilant in the

exercise of reason, the preservation of "reason's mintage." (Incidentally, so much also accounts for Milton's observation, when Adam and Eve awaken after their fallen copulation, that they are "in face / confounded" [*PL* 9.1063–64]—it is in man's face that the effects of his fall, his confusion, are first and most nakedly seen). This much said, we can pause to remark the emphasis early in the masque on the "human countenance": Comus offers " 'to every weary traveller,

> His orient liquor in a crystal glass,
> To quench the drought of Phoebus, which as they taste
> (For most do taste through fond intemperate thirst)
> Soon as the potion works, *their human countenance,*
> *The express resemblance of the gods*, is changed
> Into some brutish form of wolf, or bear,
> Or ounce, or tiger, hog, or bearded goat,
> All other parts remaining as they were,
> And they, so perfect is their misery,
> Not once perceive their *foul disfigurement*,
> But boast themselves more comely than before
> And all their friends, and native home forget
> To roll with pleasure in a sensual sty.'   [*C* 65–77; emphasis added]

Here Milton is laying the groundwork not only for the masque's emphasis on temperance, and expecially chastity, but also precisely for its economic tropes figuring the image of God in man.

Comus, we can now observe, wants above all to deface, or disfigure, "reason's mintage," in order himself to hoard God's coin. Hence his argument that Nature mints beauty. We can find a very similar argument in quite reputable authorities; Alain of Lille, for example, has *Natura* say " '[God] appointed me as a sort of deputy, a coiner for stamping the orders of things'."[23] But Alain premises what Comus suppresses, namely that Nature is God's "vicaria." As his vicaria, she mints what God issues; God's authority is prior, and *his* image, not beauty or any other, is the truest and most real. This, of course, Comus cannot endure. Hence his repeated, fallacious recourse to Nature as primary. Earlier, for example, he had argued with the Lady:

> 'Why should you be so cruel to yourself,
> And to those dainty limbs which nature lent
> For gentle usage, and soft delicacy?

> But you invert the covenants of her trust,
> And harshly deal like an ill borrower
> With that which you received on other terms,
> Scorning the unexempt condition
> By which all mortal frailty must subsist,
> Refreshment after toil, ease after pain,
> That have been tired all day without repast,
> And timely rest have wanted, but fair virgin
> This will restore all soon.'   [*C* 678–88]

The argument is venerable and partly true ("'that hath been thy craft, / By mixing somewhat true to vent more lies'" [*PR* 1.432–33]): we have what we have in this world only on loan, and we are not to bury our talents.[24] But we know that this version of the argument is ultimately a perversion of it as soon as we hear the cadences of Spenser's Despaire: "'Refreshment after toil, ease after pain'" (line 685). Milton quotes just enough of Despaire's speech to Redcrosse Knight (*FQ* 1.ix.40.7–9), evokes just enough of its hypnotic rhythm, to signal the murderous singleness that Comus intends. Comus seeks to im-pair the Lady (from God), to undual her, and to double her, confuse her, with beasts and the bestial: what Comus owns (*propre*) is always unclean (*impropre*). But she detects, and says so, precisely his "'base *forgery*'" (*C* 697), and refuses to commit virtual suicide. Her virtue is proof against such baneful confusion, even though she walks "' in the *blind mazes* of this *tangled* wood'" (*C*, 180; emphasis added), where "'*Chaos* . . . reigns . . . / In *double* night of darkness, and of shades'" (*C*, 333–34; emphasis added). She has prayed, "'Eye me blest Providence, and *square my trial* / To my *proportioned* strength.'" (*C* 328–29; emphasis added), and her prayer is answered: her reason (which is *ratio*), with Providence's help, has balanced and proportioned her strength against the one who tries her, and she resists, pure.

     She remains her *own*, her own property, because she remains first and foremost *God's* own:

>   'but when lust
> By unchaste looks, loose gestures, and foul talk,
> But most by lewd and lavish act of sin,
> Lets in defilement to the inward parts,
> The soul grows clotted by contagion,
> *Embodies, and imbrutes*, till she quite lose
> The *divine property* of her first being.'   [*C* 462–68; emphasis added]

The "divine property of her first being" reads dually: the soul *owns* divine property, but the soul also *is* divine property, and as long as it is divine property, so long does it own divine property, never being reduced to the poverty of confusing ("embod[ying]" and "imbrut-[ing])" itself with, becoming common with, anything else in creation. And the soul is divine property—this is Milton's ultimate point—as long as it is chaste (where chastity, as *Paradise Lost* teaches, is also possible in marriage).[25] Chastity has this power to preserve divine property, and thus to generate property, because it converts (the opposite of perverts) the human into the divine:

> 'So dear to heaven is saintly chastity,
> That when a soul is found sincerely so,
> A thousand liveried angels lackey her,
> Driving far off each thing of sin and guilt,
> And in clear dream, and solemn vision
> Tell her of things that no gross ear can hear,
> Till oft converse with heavenly habitants
> Begin to cast a beam on the outward shape,
> The unpolluted temple of the mind,
> And turns it by degrees to the soul's essence,
> Till all be made immortal.'   [*C* 452–62; emphasis added]

Chastity is, as it were, a divine converter, generating energy to transform the world, as it transforms the image of God in man back into likeness with God. But chastity is also more than this, and other.

If we read the lines just quoted, remembering as we do so Milton's description of his relationship with his muse (*PL* 7.1–39), we can grasp, I believe, why he prized chastity so highly. Especially the lines 456–57—"'And in clear dream, and solemn vision / Tell her of things that no gross ear can hear'"—alert us to the reason behind Milton's choice of chastity. Chastity is not only a converter, it is also a conductor, singularizing the self to a filament which can incandesce with the divine. Chastity thus renders the self immortal, which is to say death-less or change-less, and the self in this way resembles the deathless bounty of pre-lapsarian Nature: the self, like Nature, differentiates, which is to day, produces—in Milton's case, song.

If the chaste self produces, and the chaste Milton produces song, then we can readily understand why he would figure the Lady in *Comus* as a nightingale, *his* bird, the bird of the bard: he and she alike are ardents of chastity. The nightingale, victim of force, is the figure of chastity in this post-lapsarian world, for chastity is always assailed (cf. *C* 587–91), always in the position of (about to be) a victim. And this because the fallen world, heavy with mortality, always tends to confusion, to the random, to the opposite of chastity and chastity's difference. Hence the Lady is a " 'poor hapless nightingale' " (*C* 565; cf. 233–35), whose song is such

> 'that even Silence
> Was took ere she was ware, and wished she might
> Deny her nature, and be never more
> Still to be so delighted.'   [*C* 556–59]

Wherever in Milton the nightingale is, there silence is too. In *Paradise Lost*, when the nightingale sings and silence is pleased, the bird and her song accompany Adam and Eve to their slumber in a world at peace; but when *he* (that is, Satan) sings and silence yields, Eve remembers Satan's seduction, with the strife and chaos of his relentless hatred. In *Comus*, Milton writes " 'Silence / Was took,' " and the phrase " 'Was took' " admits of an impressive, an impressively honest (and I suspect intended) duality: Silence was not only "charmed,"[26] but also seized, appropriated—note that she " 'wished she might / *Deny her nature*' " (emphasis added)—and this second sense admits that chastity, even chastity, in *this* world is not innocent or ignorant of violence. Even the nightingale is at times a bird of prey: if chastity produces property, sometimes it does so by displacement (line 559), by the violence of appropriation. In this world, productivity and violence can never be separated ultimately.

7

Sacrifice: The Meaning of Meaning

A Tooth upon Our Peace
The Peace cannot deface—
Then Wherefore be the Tooth?
To vitalize the Grace—

The Heaven hath a Hell—
Itself to signalize—
And every sign before the Place
Is Gilt with Sacrifice—
—EMILY DICKINSON, #459

True sacrifice we are ready at last to distinguish from perverted sacrifice. In true sacrifice, I resign myself up for another; in perverted sacrifice, I resign another up to myself. True sacrifice, therefore, promotes the significance of another; it re-signs the victim as proper to, belonging to, the other—it expands and enhances the property of the other with the victim, making a new sign of victim and other alike.[1] Perverted sacrifice, on the contrary, re-signs the other as proper to myself—it reduces the property of the other to my own, my self, where my self, by definition, is not new, but the same as it always was, for I would not have sacrificed the other to myself if I had not wanted at all costs to preserve and promote myself. Perverted sacrifice is devil's work, "'others to make such / As I'."

Sacrifice, we know, is also the structure of signification. In signification, the mind, on the one hand, and reality, on the other, are sacrificed to words, which cut them up and cut them off so as to share (portion) them among others. Language itself is fallen. And words can dual for the mind and reality only by partitioning them. Such is the substitution (replacement) which the mind and the real must suffer after the Fall. We are the victims of words, and the sacrifice demanded by words is, by definition, perverted, since words always seek their own (their proper and property). If we are to be redeemed from this predicament, substitution (replacement) itself must first be

[101]

redeemed. This is the work of the Word, the Logos, the Son of God, who sacrifices himself for man. In the Incarnation and the Crucifixion, the polarity of substitution (replacement) is reversed: the Word gives up its own, its proper and property (see 1. Cor. 13:5). The Whole replaces, substitutes for, the part; the part does not replace the Whole. In the Incarnation, God (the Whole) becomes man (the part); the Word (the cutter—Philo's *lógos tomeús*) becomes flesh (cut, separated, dispersed); the Victimizer becomes the victim, the Word unites rather than severs, and metaphor, by a primal Aufhebung, transumes metonymy, and sacrifice becomes the meaning of meaning.

Metonymy is the work of contiguity. It is the "change of name" (met-onomázo) from the name proper to the referent to the name of something contiguous with the referent.[2] It is the figure of association of parts. Metaphor is the work of similarity. It is the "bearing beyond" (meta-phéro) the name, although within the name, of the multiple meanings related to the name.[3] It is the figure of assimilation of parts.[4] If there were a metaphor that was also a metonymy, assimilation would fuse with association, whole-ness with part-ness, and there would exist a part which is the whole and a whole which is a part. Such, in fact, is Christ, the Word of God: he is a part of God that for man is the whole of God:

> Beyond compare the Son of God was seen
> Most glorious, *in him all his Father shone*
> Substantially expressed.   [*PL* 3.138–40; emphasis added][5]

He is the metonymic metaphor.[6] As the metonymic metaphor, Christ is an image (as all words are) that is *not* (as all words are) part (and partializing) but all, the whole, of his referent. To love Christ, Milton would argue, is not to love a part in place of God but to love God (although Christ is not numerically or substantially God).[7]

We may the better grasp these distinctions by considering briefly contemporary Protestant and Puritan theories of sacramentality. These theories rely almost exclusively on metonymy, indeed to the point of warning against metaphor.[8] Their approval of metonymy and suspicion of metaphor provide a key to our concerns at this point.

Calvin states the basic principle very clearly:

> For a kind of perpetual rule in regard to all sacraments is that the sign receives the name of the thing signified.[9]

Further, Wallace, summarizing Calvin's position, writes:

> In the sacraments we have such a close connection between the symbol and the spiritual gift which it represents that we can 'easily pass from the one to the other' in our speech and refer to the bread as being indeed the body of Christ.[10]

William Perkins, Milton's countryman, will posit similar arguments:

> [The] sacramental relation is the cause of so many figurative speeches and *metonymies* which are used: as the sign is used for the thing signified, the name of the thing signified is given to the sign, the effect of the thing signified is given to the sign, as circumcision is a covenant, that which properly belongeth to the sign is attributed to the thing signified.[11]

If metonymy is assigned this privilege by these writers, it is because they are Protestants, who want above all to distinguish themselves from Roman confusions. Wallace writes:

> Calvin is concerned to maintain a middle course between Papists who confound the reality and the sign, and profane men who separate the signs from the realities. 'The efficacy and use of the sacraments will be properly understood by him who shall connect the sign and the thing signified, in such a manner as not to make the sign unmeaning and inefficacious, and who nevertheless shall not, *for the sake of adorning the sign*, take away from the Holy Spirit what belongs to him.'[12]

This dualism—for that is what it is—is repugnant to Milton, monist that he is. And so, in his monism, he brilliantly unites metaphor with metonymy, understanding as he does so, that metonymy (contiguity) inhibits confusion in metaphor—if Christ is *part of* God, he cannot *be* God—even as metaphor (assimilation) completes the associativeness of metonymy—if Christ is the similitude of God ("Begotten Son, divine similitude" [*PL* 3.384]), he expresses the whole of God.

These heady abstractions need chastening, of course, by the finitude of examples. When Eve recommends suicide to Adam as their best alternative, she reasons that they will thus "'destruction with destruction . . . destroy'" (*PL* 10.1006). Immediately, the Satanic reiteration warns us to beware of these words. Eve would have her and Adam signify the destruction of destruction, but, in the infinite regress that characterizes unredeemed signification,[13] they

would only replace destruction with destruction—the sign would
signify only a sign (more of itself, the identical, as in Satan's " 'spite
with spite shall be repaid' " [*PL* 9.178])—and thus they would be the
victims of fallen language.

When, on the other hand, Jesus agrees to be in man's place, a
" 'man among men on earth' " (*PL* 3.283), God addresses him thus:

> "*Thou therefore whom thou only canst redeem,*
>   Their nature also to they nature join;
>   And be thyself man among men on earth,
>   Made flesh . . . '   [*PL* 3.281–84; emphasis added]

"Thou whom thou only canst redeem" is not Satanic reiteration,
though necessarily it resembles it, because Christ is a true du*a*l, God
and man. He, the Son, is whole without self-coincidence—without
the "cutting" that separates him from himself to unite him with himself—because he is the Word of God, and thus he can replace himself
(Son of Man) with himself (Son of God) without reiteration or mere
copying: if he, as Son of God, redeems himself, he also, as Son of
Man, redeems man. The infinite regress of signification is halted by
the metonymy (the part) that is also metaphor (the whole). Because
Christ is the part that is the whole (able to become the part), those who
believe on him will not " 'hard be hardened, blind be blinded more' "
(*PL* 3.200); he will " 'pay / The rigid satisfaction, death for death' "
(*PL* 3.211–12), and in paying it, cancel all mere reiterative substitution—hard . . . hardened, blind . . . blinded, death . . . death (and
also the "habitual habitant" in the garden, Sin [*PL* 10.588]). In his
love, the faithful are no longer the victims of words—of definitions,
categorizations, labels, and their infinite regress—for, in his love,
they have each become like him the Word.

Sacrifice, then, is that event in which the resignation of the victim
(beast, human being, individual self) re-signs the victim and those for
whom the victim "substitutes," to a meaning (a whole) completely
different from and other than the meaning expected for the victim.
(Communication, the next degree of mutuality below sacrifice, is that
event in which free exchange of wills within the whole preserves in
harmony and sympathy meanings already achieved and agreed to, in
order that these may grow or change, to the satisfaction of the com-

municants, in the course of time.) The merit of these definitions is that they clearly demonstrate that sacrifice is the structure of signification (of the making of meaning) and the victim a medium, a means.

From this position, we can turn now to Milton's explanation of the necessity of Christ's sacrifice:

> To whom thus Michael: "Doubt not but that sin
> Will reign among them, as of thee begot;
> And therefore was law given them to evince
> Their natural pravity, by stirring up
> Sin against law to fight; that when they see
> *Law can discover sin*, but not remove,
> Save by those *shadowy expiations* weak,
> The blood of bulls and goats, they may conclude
> Some blood more precious must be paid for man,
> Just for unjust, that in such righteousness
> To them by faith imputed, they may find
> Justification towards God, and peace
> Of conscience, which the law by ceremonies
> Cannot appease, nor man the moral part
> Perform, and not performing cannot live.
> So law appears inperfect, and but giv'n
> With purpose to *resign* them in full time
> Up to a better cov'nant, disciplined
> From shadowy types to truth, from flesh to spirit,
> From imposition of strict laws, to free
> Acceptance of large grace, from servile fear
> To filial, works of law to works of faith."
>
> [*PL* 12.285–306; emphasis added]

The sacrifice of the law, "shadowy expiations weak," cannot remove the sin which the law "discover[s]"; and so, the Law and its sacrifices, "inperfet," are "but giv'n / With purpose to resign" men "to a better cov'nant." But if weak and imperfect, these sacrifices still do "resign" because such is the work of sacrifice, to resign/re-sign. Milton, of course, from his Christian perspective narrows the resignation/resignation of these weak and imperfect sacrifices to the one different sign, Christ, whose sacrifice he understood to be full, final, and perfect (*CD* 1.15,16); but his word *resign* derives nonetheless from his understanding that sacrifice is the structure of signification.

Milton's strategy in explaining the necessity of Christ's sacrifice will also help to explain why and how his poem and he are sacrifices; hence this passage bears further consideration. Milton has attributed to the law the work ("resign") of one of its functions (sacrifice) so as to expose more powerfully and more glaringly the principal shortcoming of the law—its literalness, or its limited capacity to signify. In this matter, we need, for the moment, to hear in *resign* more the sense "resignation" than "re-sign." Because the law is inadequate, it "resigns" men—that is, gives them up—"to a better cov'nant"; it renounces, so to speak, any claim on them. To be sure, as sacrifice, the law also re-signs men, but only so far—no farther, in fact, than it resigns them. The re-signing of the law goes no farther than its resigning, because the law is incapable of metaphor. The law is strictly literal: "Thou shalt not" leaves no room for multiplicity of reference, no dwelling place for the improper sense. The law has no tolerance for the improper (moral as well as rhetorical, or course). The law is written on tables of stone, not tables of flesh (2 Cor. 3:7), whereas the metaphor, the trope, the improper figure "tables of flesh" insists, by contraries, on the limitedness and rigidity of the Law. The law cannot inscribe tables of flesh, as St. Paul to his sorrow learned: "For I delight in the law of God, in my inmost self; but I see in my members another law, at war with the law of my mind and making me captive to the law of sin in my members" (Rom. 7:22–23). The merely human cannot endure the inscription of the Law. Sacrificed to the law, to the letter of the law, the merely human can only be a victim of its impartial wholeness—the Law takes the part of no man. Christ, on the contrary, takes the part of every man. He, the Mediator, inscribes the law in tables of flesh: or, again, as St. Paul learned, "not I but Christ in me" (cf. Gal. 2:20) obeys the law. Only Christ, the fulfillment of the law, can crown the literal with the spiritual sense (cf. Rom. 8:2–4). Only he can transcribe the law from tables of stone to inscribe it in the hearts of men, tables of flesh; and this because he is the Word *made flesh*, the metonymic metaphor—the ultimate improper, a scandal to the Greek and a stumbling block to the Jew (1 Cor. 1:23).

Metaphor or trope, figurative discourse generally, is improper in a number of senses. Here the French words *propre* and *impropre* will help us again. A trope is improper—that is unowned and unclean—because it is polysemous or multiple in sense (*not* ambiguous—that is a different, special case, to be discussed in a moment). If we are careful with the words, we can say that a trope is promiscuous, precisely in that it belongs to no one individual, or we can say that it is indiscrete, in that it extends itself to everyone. The trope of *fruit* in *Paradise Lost* is thus promiscuous, indiscrete, polysemous, improper, because it can and does generate new meanings constantly as it forms new wholes of meaning with succeeding generations of readers. No one owns—makes his own or propre—such tropes: they are improper or impropre because at any time a new reader can du*al* with the trope, creating a new coinherence of individual elements, which produces a new and exciting and desirable meaning, which other readers of the poem then adopt as theirs too. In this way, then, it is possible to say that the trope or figure is improper: it ex*propr*iates the proper sense of a word, of *fruit*, say—which everyone who speaks English owns by convention—and renders that proper improper or unowned (and therefore without its own) by any *one* individual so that *any* one may form a new whole with it to produce new meaning (which is now its own).

The figure, being improper, is thus also unclean, promiscuous, indiscrete in its multiplicity; and just so, both the Hellenic and the Judaeo-Christian worlds have always suffered a horror of figurative or tropic discourse, because, like the endless fertility of woman, it always exceeds the individual and the individual's own proper definiteness. Or, as Yeats puts it in one of his "Songs":

> Odour of blood when Christ was slain
> Made all Platonic tolerance vain
> And vain all Doric discipline.[14]

Christ the Word is indeed the ultimate improper (God *and* man is a scandalous notion), and when he was slain, he was emptied, thus to become the fullest signifier in history, as subsequent events were to prove, for the Word, in his endless polysemy, generated the whole of Western culture as we know it. Platonic tolerance and Doric discipline were transformed in his fertility; consider only the fourfold method of Biblical exegesis (to which Dante applied the word "polysemous")[15] and you will see my point. The Word produced and multiplied, was unclean, in fact, indiscretely disseminating in the process the Hebrew God to the Gentile nations. Little wonder the Law has no tolerance for the improper—metaphor is its end—and therefore equally little wonder that the great prophets were such masters of metaphor—when they predicted and proclaimed the end of the Law, Messiah.

And their utterances, like the utterances of the prophet Milton, were not ambiguous, because ambiguity is pseudo-figuration, pseudo-trope. Ambiguity is not true, productive polysemy because, as we can see in Satan's "ambiguous words" (*PL* 6.568), ownership, the proper and the property of words, is not expropriated in ambiguity. On the contrary, the speaker sides with words, hides behind the property they still own. In an ambiguous utterance, such as Satan's "'propound'" (*PL* 6.567), the word or phrase owns a surplus of meaning, and some individual hoards part of that surplus, even as that word or phrase at the same time admits of a different proper and property, even as it admits of another ownership. Indeed, the cruel pain of all ambiguity in our personal lives is precisely this, that, when we confront an ambiguity, we do not know who owns the proper meaning of this situation or what is the propriety in this predicament; we cannot sort out and define who owns what, because ownership, the proper, is double, or duplicitous, and claims to the proper are in conflict. Satan owns one meaning of *propound* (which thus, of course, also owns him), and the other meaning, quite proper in itself, is, as far as he is concerned, only a decoy to entice Michael and the heavenly hosts to submit to the meaning he owns.

To expand on this argument. Satan *appears* to sacrifice himself to the meaning "propound"—he appears to own it (cf. the locution "I own that it is so") and it, him—but in reality, behind this pseudo-sacrifice, this cruci-fiction, he owns and owns to the meaning "pound." Thus, he makes a distinction—even a fallen archangel can still reason—but he makes it only to obscure it: this, we know, is duplicity. Compared to Satan (and the comparison is useful at this point), Adam in the moment of his fall is not duplicitous, since, *pun*theist that he is, he is only wantoning in the various senses (or meanings). The Devil, on the contrary, is using one sense as a decoy for the other, sounding the word at war with itself. Or, we can say, he reduces the word to cannibalizing itself: *pound* consumes *propound*, leaving only its letter(s) behind. Milton himself justifies this argument when he writes of the fall of Adam and Eve that

> At that tasted fruit,
> The sun, as from Thyestean banquet, turned
> His course intended.   [*PL* 10.687–89]

It was Thyestes who ate his sons when his brother Atreus fed them to him, and by means of this simile, Milton is strongly suggesting that the original sin was cannibalism of sorts. Adam and Eve, in fact, are cannibals, eating their own species, or the sign: they and the apple alike are signs of God's will. And when they eat the apple, they consume their own kind in a perversion (also pre-version?) of that eating by which the faithful consume the sign, too, the Word—but to communion, not confusion. The cannibalism of the faithful upon the body of Christ is cannibalism with a difference: it repeats that original cannibalism in the Garden—only this time with the sign consenting of its own free and loving will to be consumed. This time, that is, the sign is a sacrifice *for* them, not *to* them. But Satan, on the contrary, sacrifices *propound* to *pound*, which consumes all of *propound*'s substance but the letter(s). And the letter, as Satan knows, killeth (2 Cor. 3:6).

Satan, as usual, deliberately confuses the situation with a double meaning because, also as usual, he seeks sovereignty in and over the situation. Satan in his avarice always seeks to appropriate meaning to himself. But this is because he is ultimately meaningless—ruinously single, divided, alone, afraid, and unable to die. For death is precisely the difference between ambiguity, or pseudo-figuration, and polysemy, or truly multiple, productive tropes. In ambiguity, the proper and properties do not die: they still own and someone still owns them, which is why the predicament is felt as ambiguous, as a *di*lemma. In metaphor, however, the proper, the own, does die, so as to be expropriated into the new property of a new meaning or meanings (whereupon, of course, it lives again, reborn, resurrected). And if Christ is the consummate metaphor, the Word made flesh, it is because he is the Word made flesh which also, oppositely from Satan, dies. Christ was willing (if afraid) to die, to empty himself (Phil. 2:5–8), to sacrifice himself, and therefore he is the eternally full signifier. He is not his own, he is another's, and, as another's, he is, and is full. Satan, on the contrary, never rests from his avarice, trying instead to fill himself forever with ownership of the creation, and therefore he is eternally empty, full of sound and fury.

We may approach this issue of property from a different but equally advantageous perspective, one afforded by Milton's greatest precursor, Shakespeare, in "The Phoenix and the Turtle." To be sure, if the ideas in this extraordinary lyric are often obscure, the syntax is on occasion seemingly unintelligible. Thus, it is a very difficult text, even in Shakespeare's canon, and it is made doubly difficult for us because Milton, I will argue, took exception to some of its positions and hypotheses. Still, we will profit from a reading of it, even as Milton did.

Probably Milton was most attracted to, and thus also most disturbed by, the last line of stanza 7:

> So they lov'd as love in twain
> Had the essence but in one
> Two distincts, division none:
> Number there in love was slain.

It is easily seen, I am sure, in light of the argument that has intervened, how pertinent this stanza is to Milton's thought on number and numbers: if love is real and true, then love in two persons does have its essence in one—$1 + 1 = 1$—and in such love, there are two distinct persons without division. However, Milton would agree that "number there in love was slain" *only* if it were agreed beforehand that such slaying, like the death of the phoenix, is followed by rebirth. For Milton, number is not slain, but realized or fulfilled in the duality of partnership.

Hence it is also that Milton would define his own position on property (see also chapter 11 below) in opposition to Shakespeare's stanzas 9 and 10:

> So between them love did shine,
> That the turtle saw his right
> Flaming in the phoenix' sight;
> Either was the other's mine.

> Property was thus appalled,
> That the self was not the same;
> Single nature's double name
> Neither two nor one was called.

For Milton, I am suggesting, it would be truer to say that property obtains, if at all, precisely in that "the self [is] not the same" as itself: he or she is proper / propre who is owned, the property of an other; the self is itself because it is an other's ("not the same")—"either was the other's mine." Metaphor, inversely, is improper because it always exceeds personal or private ownership. Hence, moreover, Milton would transume the last two lines quoted above into another meaning: the single nature of lovers does have a double—Milton, I think, would say "dual"—name (their "proper" names) which "neither two nor one [is] called," because the duality of love is precisely "neither two nor one"; it is rather one plus one equals one, the proper names summed.

From this transumption, which I impute to Milton, the next two stanzas (11 and 12), notoriously difficult though they seem, are actually quite simple:

> Reason, in itself confounded,
> Saw division grow together,
> To themselves yet either neither,
> Simple were so well compounded:

> That it cried, 'How true a twain
> Seemeth this concordant one!
> Love hath reason, Reason none,
> If what parts can so remain.'

If reason is "confounded" (confused) at this sight, it is because, it is very much fallen reason, Milton would argue. Division in love does obtain: to be a part of, one must be apart from. And yet it also grows together, be reason never so dismayed. Moreover, just so, to themselves neither love is either (possessed exclusively by himself or herself) because each is the other's. Each sacrifices to the other for the other out of his/her free will. The dual, then, is precisely a well-compounded simple—$1 + 1 = 1$. Fallen reason seeing such a mystery retains at least enough ratio, Milton would argue, to see that Love has reason, or ratio, which exceeds it; and in this ratio what parts—two lovers who are apart to be each a part of the other ("a true twain")—remains a "concordant one," beyond (mere) reason's reason.

In "The Phoenix and the Turtle," I would argue, Milton found his own position on number and property and the proper, but in a version he could not quite accept. He could not accept it, not only because Shakespeare assumed that "number there in love was slain," but also because, in the "Threnos," (stanza 3), he claims that the phoenix and the turtle leave

> no posterity,
> 'Twas not their infirmity,
> It was married chastity.

For Milton, just the contrary, married chastity, "sole propriety / In Paradise of all things common else"(*PL* 4.751–52) is fertile, "true source / Of human offspring" (*PL* 4.750–51), because it is the very type of the dual that generates appropriation and expropriation.

Metaphor, similarly generative, is thus a marriage, too, the "consorting" of meanings: Metaphor and love go together—poets are lovers, as we all know—because coupling is the way in which they share. Better to say, however, that in the fallen world, metaphor is the constant oscillation between marriage and divorce. Metaphor is the divorce of a word from its proper sense so as to wed or at least couple it with another sense. In the fallen world, metaphor is impossible without indiscretion or promiscuity (without *common* names), and the consequent divorcing of meaning from words. And any marriage that cannot be dissolved, at least in theory, is meaningless, a totalitarian (con)fusion of an otherwise free signifier and signified. There is no absolute adequation of sign to signified in a fallen world. But, though divorce is necessary, in discourse as well as in intercourse, marriage and married chastity are the truest and the best duality—they make the community possible. Shakespeare opens "The Phoenix and the Turtle" as follows (emphasis added):

> Let the bird of loudest lay,
> On the sole Arabian tree,
> Herald sad and trumpet be,
> To whose sound *chaste* wings obey.

And, just so, it must have seemed to Milton that he had been invited to rewrite this extraordinary, often unintelligible, lyric.

Be that as it may, a consideration of property and the proper confirms that death is structural in metaphor. (Divorce, we might observe, would be the metaphor of death's structure in metaphor.) And if the Law is deadly to human life, it is so precisely because of its inability to die—it can kill, as can its letter (2 Cor. 3:6), but it cannot die. Or, put it this way, the Law is deadly because it is not incarnate, it is not fleshed, it has no body—the Law is im(not)partial. Christ had to die because the Law could not; the Law was too deadly to die (the Law is always dead already), and thus, from the human perspective, the Law was "inperfet," incomplete, in its very perfection, its very completion. So perfect as to be inhuman, the most the Law could do, Milton tells us, was to kill "Bulls and Goats"; and neither the victim in this sacrifice nor those for whom the victim substituted could be resigned by it to the new significance of a new life—at most, they could be released by it from the debts and bonds of an old life (cf. Heb. 10:1). In Christ, however, the Law could and did die, to be reborn, resigned, to the new significance of Love, the Love that decreed the Law in the first place. Christ fulfills the Law because he loves the Law (is the Love of Law and the Law of Love), loves it so completely that he obeys it completely, even to the ultimate difference of dying for it. And obeying it completely, unto the death, makes it thereafter possible for the human to love the Law completely by loving him completely—one can love a man (God) far more readily and deeply than one can love laws inscribed in stone.[16] In Christ, the Law suddenly ceases to be literal, becomes capable of metaphor; or, as Milton might have put it, in Christ (the ultimate sacrifice), the Law is made spiritual.

8

Authority: The Duel between
the Adversary and the Son

If we now know the meaning of meaning, sacrifice, this knowledge
will lead us to the vision of authority in Milton's poetics, his understanding of the genealogy (family tree) of meaningfulness. This vision
involves at least three fundamental notions: the verse or the trope and
its perversion in the Adversary, a philosophy of the meaning of equality, and a doctrine of proof. Strictly speaking, these notions are inseparable; and so, in a sense, I am faced with the same problem which
confronted Milton when he revised the ten-book *Paradise Lost* into a
twelve-book poem. I could write one very long concluding chapter or
three shorter concluding chapters, one on authority, one on equality,
and one on proof. In choosing the latter strategy, I have artificially
separated—and the point of this aside is to acknowledge that the
separating is artificial—the three closely related notions that inform
Milton's vision of authority. However, this artificiality is the price I
must pay for a sufficient measure of clarity on an issue otherwise very
tangled indeed—and I would not willingly be guilty of introducing
confusion just where Milton is most rigorous in excluding it. Hence I
will proceed with the next three chapters, openly acknowledging that
in many ways they are really one chapter, which might have been
entitled "Originality: Dualing with the Father."

First, then, the perversion of the verse in the Adversary. We must, in
fact, never forget to hear *vers* in *adversary:* the Adversary "turns"
(ultimately "plows"), he also "tropes," and thus, finally, in some

sense, he is a maker of verses.¹ The Adversary "turns" one thing into another, I would like to suggest: " 'Nor hope to be myself less miserable / By what I seek, but *others to make such / As I* " (*PL* 9.126–28; emphasis added). And he himself suffers what he does to others. If he confuses others with himself, he is himself permanently confused. Hence, when he first addresses Beelzebub after the Fall, he must begin: " '*If* thou beest he' " (*PL* 1.84). Similarly, when he tries to persuade himself that

> 'The mind is its own place, and in itself
> Can make a heaven of hell, a hell of heaven,'
>
> [*PL* 1.254–55; emphasis added]

he must ask himself: " 'What matters where, *if* I be still the same'?" (*PL* 1.256; emphasis added). Satan's "if" is not Milton's "of" (*PL* 1.1—though, to be sure, only 83 lines and two graphs separate them): the genitive is appalled by the doubleness of doubt, the *o* of generation by the *i* of rebellion. Moreover, in addition to the irony in "if," Milton also insists that Satan

> with his horrid crew
> Lay vanquished, rolling in the fiery gulf
> *Confounded* though immortal.   [*PL* 1.51–53; emphasis added]

In short, Satan has become (confused) what he did (confuse), his substance forever reduced to this one catastrophic act—he who "turned against" now turned into "Turned Against." And, to add to his punishment, this corollary: whatever "turned against" he attempts to turn into himself, or evil, God turns into good (see *PL* 1.217–18; 2.622–23; 7.615–16; and especially 12.471—" 'and evil turn to good' "), so that all Satan's acts are incomplete tropes of God's authorithy which his Word will complete beyond Satan's comprehension, to Satan's confusion.

Satan forever is (confused) what he does (confuses). Conversely, he can only do what he is. He always and only reduces *as* to (the simulacrum of) *is:* he confuses *as* and *is.* If Adam is created to be *as,* or *like,* God (Gen. 2:6), then Satan's end is to seduce Adam and Eve into believing (confusedly) that they can *be* God, or at least gods (cf. *PL* 9.547, 732). When the serpent uses the *as* which descends from Genesis (3:5)—" 'ye shall be as gods / Knowing both good and evil' " (*PL* 9.708–709; and again at 9.710)—this *as* already is the simulacrum of *is*, since it is part of the whole Satanic illusion. The most Adam and Eve can be, properly, is *as* God (ever more like him),[2] but Satan means by *as*, in the illusion which he is spawning, what Eve all too surely takes him to mean—*is*—for, as Milton says: "nor was godhead from her thought" (*PL* 9.790). The Adversary, in the serpent, promises to turn Eve into a goddess (and rhetorically, he does), but only in order to turn her into such as he, a rebel against God.

The effect of the simulacrum of *is* we can grasp even more completely by turning to the early part of Book 9, during the argument between Adam and Eve as to whether she will part from him for the day—and remember, an argument is necessarily an adversarial exchange, though not necessarily a hostile one. At one point in the argument, Milton remarks:

> To whom [sc. Adam] the virgin majesty of Eve,
> *As* one who loves, and some unkindness meets,
> With sweet austere composure thus replied.
>
> [*PL* 9.270–72; emphasis added]

The Adversary, we see, is indeed already in the garden, contaminating it with the simulacrum of *is* (with doubt and its ambiguity, too; see *PL* 9.279–81). Eve is the only one in the garden "who loves, and some unkindness meets"; there is no one else (pardon my syntax) whom she can be *as*. Thus, Milton's narrative voice—(which, of course, is postlapsarian)—indicates the contagion of the Adversary: the simile, imported from post-lapsarian experience, says, in effect, Eve is *as* herself, where *as* can only be the simulacrum of *is*. Moreover, in saying as much, the simile betrays its illusoriness: where, in a simile proper, two produce one, here, one generates the illusion of two (Eve *as* Eve). From this betrayal, we may infer the structural (if not psychological) narcissism of the adversarial simile. For another example, "'if death / Consort with thee, death is *to me as* life'" (*PL* 9.953–54; emphasis added), says Adam to Eve just before he eats of the apple, where "to me" is the sign of the narcissism in the "as." And when Milton writes, near the end of *Samson Agonistes* that "'Samson hath quit himself / Like Samson'" (*SA* 1709–10), he asks us, in effect, to decide, first and foremost, whether this is an adversarial simile or not, and if not, why not (see chapter 12 below).

But this is to have gotten ahead of ourselves. Next to be considered among the notions of the verse and the Adversary is the matter of contraries. This matter cannot be seriously considered apart from Milton's prose writings, especially the crucial argument in *Areopagitica* quoted in chapter 1 above, that, "assuredly we bring not innocence into the world, we bring impurity much rather; that which purifies us is triall, and triall is by what is contrary" (YE 2:515). In light of this argument, we can suggest that the Adversary's—which is also to say, the Contrary's—punishment is the most exquisite in that he is forever involved in the *process* of purification—"'the hateful siege / Of *contraries*'" (*PL* 9.121–22; emphasis added)—without ever becoming, or being able to become, pure. The Adversary is forever "on trial":

> 'To do aught good never will be our task,
> But ever to do ill our sole delight,
> As being the contrary to his high will
> Whom we resist.'   [*PL* 1.159–62]

There is no end to his trial because there is no end to his contradiction. "'For only in destroying I find ease / To my relentless thoughts'" (*PL* 9.129–30), or, even more telling, "'Save what is in destroying, other joy / To me is lost'" (*PL* 9.478–79). The Adversary is forever bound to Whom he opposes, forever subject to his Judge, forever chained to what he would destroy; and all this because "they" *are* "he," his projections from within him—"'Myself am hell'" (*PL* 4.75), or, as Abdiel puts it, "'Thyself not free, but to thyself enthralled'" (*PL* 6.181; cf. *PL* 4.79–102). Like Oedipus, the ultimate figure of confusion in the classical world, Satan, the Adversary, has never separated from the Father (nor, therefore, from him*self*): to kill the father, as to oppose the Father, is to bind oneself to the father (and to the "self" thus bound). Hence to adapt Lacan's etymological play (note 54 of chapter 1 above), Satan cannot "procède à sa parturition" because he has never completed "sa partition": he has never submitted to the other. Rather, like Oedipus, he remains—or, even more accurately, re-sists—forever in the father's place: Oedipus in Jocasta's genitalia, Satan in the cosmos of God. And anything he "begets" there will be, like Oedipus's children, confusion: they are brothers *and* sons, sisters *and* daughters; his offspring are Sin and Death—his daughter, wife, son, and brother (see *PL* 9.11–13 and Rom. 5:12). Satan, like Oedipus, is always redundant, Satan literally so, since he "boils" (*PL* 4.16) and "rolls" (*PL* 9.631) just like a wave ("unda").[3]

The Adversary is redundant and unfree because he refuses to admit the mystery of derivativeness: to be original, you must be a copy—you must copy originally some precursor whose priority and authority you admit, in order to differentiate and distinguish yourself from him—you must dual him rather than duel him, though duel him too you will. But admit this priority—once be his son—and you then create him: it is your copy of him which proclaims him the original.[4] Or, to put this now in Milton's words:

> in their looks divine
> The image of their glorious maker shone,
> Truth, wisdom, sanctitude severe and pure,
> Severe but in true filial freedom placed;
> Whence true authority in men.   [*PL* 4.291–95]

It is frighteningly easy to under-read these lines, to underestimate their boldness. "Filial freedom"—or "bound liberty," we might say, hearing the son's *duty* as well as the son in "filial"—is probably the most volatile, as it is certainly the most far-reaching, oxymoron in the poem. Almost more stunning, however, at least upon reflection, is the "but" of line 294. The "sanctitude" of Adam and Eve is "severe"—that is, severed, cut off, apart, and separate from their Maker—*but*—that is to say, though severe—is still "in true filial freedom placed." Adam and Eve are separate from their Maker (severed) and thus more nearly complete than Satan—though, of course, neither he nor they are born, but made—and yet, even so, they place their sanctitude in "filial freedom," from "*whence true authority in men*"—by being offspring, separate, who bind themselves still in sonship, they are free to exercise true authority. Adam and Eve are the image of their Maker; they are *not* adverse to him. On the contrary, such is their authority (through derivativeness) that, at least as far as appearances are concerned, *they* author *him*—"in their looks divine" / The image of their glorious maker shone" (see also *PL* 3.44; and 4.364, where even Satan sees the "divine resemblance" in them).

I hope that I have not weakened the force of these lines. They are, if I read them aright, a proclamation of poetic authority. I have argued that Milton's model of textual production is the structure of signification itself, or sacrifice, like the sacrifice of Christ. But the sacrifice of Christ is supremely an exercise of "filial freedom . . . whence [his] true authority." Hence I conclude that Milton's model of textual production, ultimately his poetics, is a poetics of "filial freedom"; and it is this poetics which engenders and empowers the authority of his originality and the originality of his authority. His sonship is creative apartness which begets the Father in begetting the image of the Father. Milton's originality is to beget his origin.[5]

We are now in a position to see and recognize for what it is one of the most startling features of *Paradise Lost*. Every figure of note in the poem is, at some point or other, said to be an author, except Christ. Milton's theology of the Son, I will argue, precludes the Son's direct access to the Father's authority: he can only participate in that authority (see *CD* 1.5, YE 6:227, 233, 266, for this position). And this participation—this dualing, if I may, of the Father by the Son—is the origin of Milton's vision of authority.

Next to be considered, obviously, if this position is to be convincingly argued, is the unequivocal status of God as *supreme* Author "'Who [is] alone / From all eternity, for none [He] know[s] / Second to [Him] or like, equal much less'" (*PL* 8.405–07). Several passages affirm that he is the one, unequalled Author of creation—"thee author of all being," sing the angels in Book 3 (line 374), for example (see also *PL* 5.188)—but without doubt the most important of these is the one in which God identifies himself to Adam at Adam's creation. Adam tells Raphael:

> 'Rejoicing, but with awe
> In adoration at his feet I fell
> Submiss: he reared me, and "Whom thou sought'st I am,"
> Said mildly, "*author* of all this thou seest
> Above, or round about thee or beneath."'
>
> [*PL* 8.314–18; emphasis added]

Most important here is the allusion to Exodus 3:14 and the tetragrammaton: the Author of all things is also I AM. I speculate that a good deal of the motivation for Milton's anti-Trinitarianism is just this name of God: I AM brooks no plurality (see further *CD* 1.5, YE 6:214, 234 and note).[6] Be that as it may, in this passage, the authority of God and his singularity are closely coupled, and this prepares for the crucial discourse on unity some hundred lines later, to which I will return in a moment.

Before we can discuss unity, however, we must discuss equality, for Milton's definition of equality is much stricter than that ordinarily ascribed to the word, and this stricter definition is indispensable to his vision of authority. Equality for Milton implies difference, and this implication informs all his thinking on the Father and the Son, on originality and authority.

After naming the beasts, Adam cries out to God, " 'how may I / Adore thee, *author* of this universe' " (*PL* 8.359–60; emphasis added). He then goes on to complain of his solitude (*PL* 8.363–66), whereupon God asks him " 'What call'st thou solitude' " (*PL* 8.369)? Adam answers:

> 'Hast thou not made me here thy substitute,
> And these inferior far beneath me set?
> Among unequals what society
> Can sort, what harmony or true delight?
> Which must be mutual, in proportion due
> Given and received.'   [*PL* 8.381–86]

In his rejoinder, God first observes that Adam "wil[l] taste / No pleasure, though in pleasure, solitary' " (*PL* 8.401–02):

> 'What think'st thou then of me, and this my state,
> Seem I to thee sufficiently possessed
> Of happiness or not? Who am alone
> From all eternity, for none I know
> Second to me or like, equal much less.   [*PL* 8.403–07]

Then follows the crucial explanation. Adam reasons:

> 'Thou in thyself art perfect, and in thee
> Is no deficience found; not so is man
>
> .   .   .   .
> . . . man by number is to manifest
> His single imperfection, and beget
> Like of his like, his image multiplied,
> In unity defective, which requires
> Collateral love, and dearest amity.'   [*PL* 8.415–16; 422–26]

Whereas God, " 'already infinite,' " (*PL* 8.420) is " 'through all numbers absolute, though one' " (*PL* 8.421), Adam is " 'in unity defective' " and must therefore be two in order to be one; moreover, in " 'his single imperfection' " (and let us note well, it is called an "imperfection"), he must " 'beget / Like of his like' "—something which God never does. God *creates* his like—"in His image and likeness created

He them"—but he does not beget "like of his like." No likeness of him intervened when he begot his Son. In fact, God "'alone / From all eternity'" knows "'none . . . / Second to [him] or like, equal much less'" (*PL* 8.406–07). Not even the Son, Christ, is *like* God—"the Word is not of the same essence as God" (*CD* 1.5, YE 6:239)—for the Son is begotten, not made (in the words of the Nicene Creed), and being begotten, issues directly from the Father, later than the Father. God's Son is not "like of His like," because there is no likeness prior to him which he can be like—He is God's *only* begotten Son. Hence he is not *like* God, he is *of* God—and therefore later than and less than God ("'none / Second or like, equal much less'"). *Of* God, the only begotten, Christ, resembles God ("Begotten Son, divine similitude" [*PL* 3.383–84]), but is not like him, because God does not beget his like—he begets (once and only once) "of his own substance" (*CD* 1.5, YE 6:209).[7] He makes or creates his likeness according to his image.[8] Hence he can say, and Milton can have him say, that he "'knows none / Second to [Him] or like, equal much less,'" precisely because he is "absolute": he is prior, he is one, and one can have no second or like or equal; only two can have a second or like or equal. Hence, Christ can be "enthroned in highest bliss / Equal to God, and equally enjoying / God-like fruition" (*PL* 3.306–08) because he and God are two, with God always first and absolute. In other words, Christ can be equal to God, God willing, but God is never equal to Christ—as one is never equal to two. God knows "'none second to [Him] or like, equal much less'" because as one, he is singular, "alone" (*PL* 8.405; see also chapter 11 below).

God's authority is without similar, without like, without equal. God is one. Christ, the Son, therefore, cannot be "author," because he can in no way accede to the inviolate unity of the Father's authority.

In fact, the closest He can come is, God willing, *simile:*

> 'but all ye gods,
> Adore him, who to compass all this dies,
> Adore the Son, and honour him *as* me.'
>
> [*PL* 3.341–43; emphasis added]

The beauty of Milton's accuracy here is considerable, though subtle and austere. This *as* is hardly the simulacrum of *is*. Christ is so dissimilar to God, so unlike him, so unequal to him, that God can permit him to enter into simile with him, commanding the angels to " 'honour him as me' "; and we understand God to mean in this command Christ's difference from him (see chapter 11 below), because he, God, *also* addresses the angels as gods—" 'all ye gods' " (see also *CD* 1.5, YE 6:233)—which title they may enjoy only if they shun Satan's error of (at)tempting to *be* God. The angels may be "gods," and Christ supremely may be "God," in every way except *being* God: numerically, they are never God (One)—as it were, the quotation marks must never be deleted. In short—and this is the crux of the matter—unlike Satan, God makes no one such as he (that is, identical with himself), but will let any of his sons who truly loves him be *as* God: "But as many as received him, he gave them power to be made the sons of God, to them that believe in his name" (John 1:12). As Satan confesses, too late, " 'heaven's free love [*is*] dealt equally to all' " (*PL* 4.68). Because Christ himself honors God first, and above all other creatures, he may in turn be honored *as* God. All his authority, in other words, derives from this original homage; all his authority is derivative, what God has delegated to him (cf. especially *PR* 1.289 and *CD* 1.5, YE 6:266). Or, to put the matter precisely, Christ, the Son, is the Word, the uttered; God, the Father, is the Author, who utters: "Creation . . . is always qualified as being through Christ; not by him, but by the Father. . . . It is understood that the Father is the first or major cause in everything" (*CD* 1.5, YE 6:267–68). Hence, for example, when God creates man "in His image and likeness," he lets the Son be his image (*CD* 1.5, YE 6:233), and then through him creates his likeness in man. But he does not make man, nor does he make anything else, *such as* he.

Milton never predicates "Author" of Christ because the "authored"—the "expressed," say—cannot be the "author."[9] Two passages, in particular, confirm this argument. In the first, note how the syntax insists on the derivation from the Father:

> He said, and on his Son with rays direct
> Shone full, he all his Father *full expressed*
> Ineffably into his face *received*,
> And thus the filial Godhead answering spake.
>
> [*PL* 6.719–22; emphasis added]

Here, "full expressed" must be a participial adjective qualifying "Father" which is the direct object of "received" ("the Son himself reports that he received from the Father . . . also whatever else he has"

[*CD* 1.5, YE 6:259]), and thus the Son cannot himself have uttered or expressed or authored. So much is even clearer in the second passage:

> So spake the almighty, and to what he spake
> His Word, the filial Godhead, gave effect.   [*PL* 7.174–75]

The Son is the effect, the spoken, not the cause, the Speaker (see, further, *PL* 10.65–67).

From these two passages we may turn, briefly, to a moment in which Alastair Fowler finds a suggestion that "*the filial power* is at least jointly in apposition to *Author and end*," and propose a different (actually more customary) reading.[10] Here is the passage, with Fowler's emendation:

> when at the holy mount
> Of heaven's high-seated top, the imperial throne
> Of Godhead, fixed for ever firm and sure,
> The filial power arrived, and sat him down
> With his great Father (for he also went
> Invisible, yet stayed [:] such privilege
> Hath omnipresence) and the work ordained,
> Author and end of all things.   [*PL* 7.584–91]

The emendation, the colon combined with the opening of the parenthesis, is a valiant effort to read the presumed apposition between Father and Son; "he" in the emendation must refer to the Son. But the by now standard punctuation, which suggests the Father's independence of the Son (especially in the adverb "also")—

> Father, for he also went
> Invisible, yet stayed (such privilege
> Hath omnipresence)—

is closer to correct, we can suggest now, with "he" referring to the Father, because on the other occasions when the Son has "expressed" the Father, Milton has been careful to separate him from and subordinate him to the Father, has been at pains to show him as derivative from the Father. At the same time, we can note also in light of the present argument, that on all these occasions (*PL* 6.722; 7.175; 7.587) Milton also stresses sonship—the word *filial* figures prominently when the Son "expresses" the Father. And we are equipped to understand this now, because we now know that "filial freedom" is the source of "true authority," in men and the Son of Man alike.

Christ the Son is not an author, because he is the Word of God.

But he participates in "true authority" by His obedience in "filial freedom": as long as he distinguishes himself from Satan and confesses his derivativeness and secondariness, he has authority in heaven and earth. And just as men in "true authority" author God (as far as appearances are concerned), so, although to a much greater degree, does Christ, in "true authority" author God. And so it is that Milton can write, without contradiction—(although it is hardly a piety of mine to spare Milton from his contradictions)—what is certainly the most stunning case of the Son authoring the Father, or his revision of the Father, in the opening of Book 3: " 'That be from thee far,/That far be from thee, Father' " (*PL* 3.153–54). And note well that Milton concludes this revision of the Father—in what we now know is the only way he could have concluded it—by reference to the Son's "filial obedience":

> His words here ended, but his meek aspect
> Silent yet spake, and breathed immortal love
> To mortal men, above which only shone
> *Filial obedience: as a sacrifice*
> *Glad to be offered*, he attends the will
> Of his great Father.   [*PL* 3.266–71; emphasis added]

Precisely because of his "filial obedience," the Son is free to author the Father—indeed, so much is what the Father authored him to do. And it is obviously of no little importance, especially to the present argument, that, after "filial obedience," Milton continues with "as a sacrifice / Glad to be offered, he attends the will / Of his great Father," for, as I contend, sacrifice, which obviously must here be construed as virtually in apposition to "filial obedience" (lineation and enjambement demand it) is the model of textual production—that is to say, authority—which Milton posits and obeys. Do not ask whence true authority flows—it flows (through "filial obedience," "filial freedom") from sacrifice.

Moreover, the sacrifice in this case grants an authority in which silence can speak without confusion: "his meek aspect / Silent yet spake." Unlike the perverted sacrifice of Philomela, the sacrifice of the Son does not wound silence. Quite the contrary, it liberates silence and liberates it because the Son is the opposite of silence, the Word. The Son is so obedient, unto death (Phil. 2:5–8), that he submits so as to empower his opposite. Indeed, this is his very first action in creation:

'*Silence*, ye troubled waves, and thou deep, peace,'
Said then the Omnific Word, 'your discord end.'

[*PL* 7.216–17; emphasis added]

The Word's first word is the opposite of the word: he does not make others such as he. So much is the humility of creation.

Finally, we may conclude this part of the argument concerning authority by considering for a moment the last occurrence in the poem of *filial*. We have looked at the passage before:

'So law appears imperfect, and but given
With purpose to resign them in full time
Up to a better covenant, disciplined
From shadowy types to truth, from flesh to spirit,
From imposition of strict laws, to free
Acceptance of large grace, *from servile fear*
To filial, works of law to works of faith.'

[*PL* 12.300–06; emphasis added]

From "servile fear to filial" fear (for "fear" is definitely implied) is one with the re(-)signation from flesh to spirit, law to faith, letter to spirit. Milton implies—he could hardly do less—that in filial fear, men put off the oldness of the letter and put on the newness of the spirit (Eph. 4:22). But this is to imply, further, a rule of hermeneutics: it is in filial fear that men read according to the Spirit. But this is also to say that, in reading according to the Spirit, they read with the authority ("filial" authority) that authors its original. And is this not Protestantism?

Every believer is entitled to interpret the scriptures; and by that I mean interpret them for himself. He has the spirit, who guides truth, and he has the mind of Christ. . . The pre-eminent and supreme authority . . . is the authority of the Spirit, which is internal, and the individual possession of each man. [*CD* 1.30, YE 6:583, 587]

9

Equality: Dual, not Duel

To continue the argument on authority in *Paradise Lost*, we must consider the problem of equality with regard to other figures of the poem, too. We can best do that, however, if we first digress to the sestet of Sonnet 7, a reading of which will prepare us to see the issue more clearly.

This sonnet, which begins, "How soon hath time", is rightly considered both crucial in Milton's career and difficult to get a purchase on.[1] My concern with the sestet is very limited and specialized, but my remarks will, I think, be of use to understanding the poem as a whole, and this because the poem must be read, I believe, from and through *Paradise Lost*, which is its most appropriate gloss. The two nodes of connection are the emphasis on *even* and the play between *as* and *is:*

> Yet be it less or more, or soon or slow,
>> It shall be still in strictest measure even
>> To that same lot, however mean or high,
> Toward which time leads me, and the will of heaven,
>> All is, if I have grace to use it so,
>> As ever in my great task-master's eye.
>>> [Carey ed., pp. 148–49, lines 9–14]

Eventually, I will argue that *eye* in the last line must also be heard as its homophone, *I*, if the sestet is to yield up its full relation with *Paradise Lost*. But for now consider the phrase "even / To" (I eliminate the comma since, crucially, "the Trinity MS draft . . . is, with the exception of a comma after 'me' [12], entirely unpunctuated."[2] The phrase means "level with"[3], but also, I think we can agree, "equal to"; and therefore, Milton does *not*, as Eve, self-deluded, did, dream of becoming "more equal" (*PL* 9.823). His authority will, so to speak, seek its level—a minimum pre-condition for filial obedience and freedom—be that level "however mean or high."

High, of course, is the word of Satan[4] which Milton attempts to purify and reclaim (*PL* 1.24: "the highth of this great argument") "with no middle flight" (*PL* 1.14)—hence the risk he runs of himself becoming Satanic.[5] And yet here, as before (see chapter 5 above), Milton transcends his dilemma by assuming it. He welcomes the risk so as to discipline himself to coming "even to" or "equal to" his height (the height of his "lot")—hence the accuracy of the phrase "in strictest measure," which is a clue to the nascent poetics of the sestet. *Paradise Lost is* written in strictest measure (and without rhyme, to up the degree of difficulty) because strictest measure, the opposite of Satanic discord and contrariety, is the obedience, the self-disciplining and -chastening, which makes way for "filial freedom." But—and this is Milton's trump—by writing in strictest measure to become even to the height of his lot, he will "equal the most High," because, "in filial freedom / Whence true authority in men," he will, as far as appearances are concerned, image, or "author," God.

Milton will (and does) "justify the ways of God to men." His "reason" will (and does) "equal" God, though in a way totally beyond what Satan the rebel comprehends in those words when he utters them (*PL* 1.248–49). Milton comes even to, or level with, God and his ways because his humility exalts him to their height. In the poem's words:

'Because thou hast, though throned in *highest* bliss
Equal to God, and equally enjoying
Godlike fruition, quitted all to save
A world from utter loss, and hast been found
By merit more than birthright Son of God,
Found worthiest to be so by being good,
Far more than great or *high;* because in thee
Love hath abounded more than glory abounds,
Therefore *thy humiliation shall exalt*
With thee thy manhood also to this throne,
Here shalt thou sit incarnate, here shalt reign
Both God and man, Son both of God and man.'
                         [*PL* 3.305–16; emphasis added]

If any object to my implying that Milton is the son of God, I reply that I do no more than follow St. John, who teaches that "as many as received him, he gave them power to be made the sons of God, to them that believe in his name" (John 1:12). Though Milton is a son of God by adoption only (Gal. 4:5–6), whereas Christ is Son "by merit" (*PL* 3.309)—a status impossible for mortals (cf. Eph. 1:5; Titus 3:5–6)—his sonship ("filial obedience") may still be such that he can equal the Most High, if, imitating Christ, he empties himself first. "[T]hat which purifies us is triall, and triall is by what is contrary" (*Areopagitica*, YE 2:515); just so, if he would be full, Milton must empty himself, following the Apostle's injunction:

> For let this mind be in you, which was also in Christ Jesus, who being in the form of God, thought it not robbery to be equal with God; but emptied himself, taking the form of a servant, being made in the likeness of men, and in habit found as a man. He humbled himself, becoming obedient unto death, even to the death of the Cross. [Phil. 2:5–8]

But emptied of self, what kind of vessel will Milton be? A vessel of wrath, to destruction (Rom. 9:22)? A vessel of clay, housing treasure (2 Cor. 4:7)? The conclusion to the sestet of Sonnet 7 suggests an answer. After his confident prediction of steadfastness in and to his lot, Milton writes:

> All is if I have grace to use it so
> As ever in my great taskmaster's eye.

These lines suggest equality with the Most High, but they do so without any hint of any contamination from the Adversary. In them a real and profound opposition marks the jointure where "I" *is as* the Other. "I" is the vessel of the Other when *as* is not the simulacrum of *is*. When *as* is truly *as*, pseudo-identity vanishes and equality emerges, "for equality cannot exist except between two or more essences" (*CD* 1.5, YE 6:275). *As* is the boundary between essences. *As* is the medium of the vessel, preserving its distinctness from the contents.

Let *as* be the medium, and confusion, such as in puns, is arrested. Because of *as* in line 14 of the sestet, we do not think what we otherwise hear, namely, "All is if eye have grace to use it / As ever in my great task-master's I." *If* we heard this pun, then Milton would *be* his great taskmaster, and his *eye* would see only what his *I* sees—this, of course, is precisely the damnation of Satan, who sees Eden, for example, and cries out, " 'O Hell' " (*PL* 4.358). But because *as* mediates between—that is to say, interrupts—*I* and *eye*, insisting on their difference (unlike the simulacrum of *is* in Eve *as* Eve—see chapter 8 above), we hear and understand that Milton desires to be emptied and then filled with the vision of the Other. If he has grace to use everything in creation as it is in his great task-master's eye, then he will be using it as it is Other: he will be so using it as to let it be what it is, not so as to make it such as he is. He will use it as if using it not.[6] And in this event, his *I* will contain that *eye* without confusion ("two or more essences"), for *I* will see as the *eye* of the Other, and seeing as the *eye* of the Other, *I* will be able to say, all is—*I* will know the creation, as it is.

The logic of the sestet, then, is this. If Milton comes "even / To" his lot, that humility exalts him to equality with the Most High, where equality means, not identity (except "by adoption"), but difference of essence; equal in this way, he can see *as* the Most High, his great task-master, sees, and thus finally he can claim to "justify the ways of God to men."

Milton does not see *what* God sees—no mortal can do that—rather he sees *as* God sees. He sees as a part of God, creatively apart from God. Satan, however, is contrarily apart from God and sees only as his own *I* (*eye*) sees. Hence, he is precisely not what Eve catastrophically mistakes him to be, an " 'author unsuspect' " (*PL* 9.771); he is very much, rather, a suspect author who produces texts which are only "such as he"—Sin and Death, for example. Sin three times refers to Satan as "author" (*PL* 2.864; 10.236, 356), and on the first two of these occasion, she refers to him as explicitly her (and Death's) author. And as we know, she and Death are literally "such as he," for they are of the same essence as he, begotten by him of himself. We may conclude, therefore, that narcissism (with incest)—the form of Satan's authoring of Sin and Death—is also Milton's trope for suspect authority.

This conclusion helps us to pursue further the vexed issue of equality. Narcissism, we know, is the illusion of two where, in reality, there is only one. Equality, however, obtains only where there

are "two or more essences" (or so Milton understood the matter). Real
equality, then, is the impossibility of narcissim and incest, even as it is
also the impossibility of identity. Equality demands apartness, difference. Therefore, wherever in *Paradise Lost* we encounter equality
without demonstrable difference, we know we are confronting
pseudo-equality, which is perhaps also narcissism or incest. And if
Satan is the "Author of all ill" (*PL* 2.381), the "Author of evil" (*PL*
6.262), this is *not* because he sought equality with God, but because,
under *the guise* of seeking equality with God (see *PL* 5.763), he actually
sought the identity of God (*PL* 6.89 and 4.50–51), thus seeking, in
effect, to confuse creation, ruining two essences by collapsing the one
into the other—God into himself, Satan. The author of all ill, then, is
precisely the author of confusion; and, as we remember, Milton in-
sisted on as much from the beginning:

> for whence,
> But from the Author of all ill could spring
> So deep a malice, to confound the race
> Of mankind in one root, and earth with hell
> To mingle and involve.   [*PL* 2.380–84]

To this important passage we may now add several at the end of Book
2 which emphasize confusion, both the confusion of Chaos and Night
and the confusion soon to follow upon Satan's flight through Chaos.
For example, Satan, Sin, and Death see, when the "infernal doors"
(*PL* 2.881) first open:

> where eldest night
> And chaos, ancestors of nature, hold
> Eternal anarchy, amidst the noise
> Of endless wars, and *by confusion stand*.
>   [*PL* 2.894–97; emphasis added]

Or, again, after Satan addresses Chaos,

> him thus the anarch old
> With faltering speech, and visage *incomposed*
> Answered.
> .   .   .   .
>   'go and speed;
> *Havoc* and spoil and *ruin* are my gain.'
>   [*PL* 2.988–90, 1008–09; emphasis added]

These and other passages in Book 2 (*PL* 2.910–14, 951–54, 996) all insist, either directly or indirectly, that where Satan is, there confusion is too: Satan's authority can never found, only *con*found—he is the great unoriginal (cf. *PL* 1.84).

Here is the same argument from a different perspective and a different moment of the text. After Abdiel's valiant effort to persuade the rebels to repent, Satan, "more haughty," sneers:

> 'That we were formed then say'st thou? And the work
> Of secondary hands, by task transferred
> From Father to his Son? Strange point and new!
> Doctrine which we would know whence learned: who saw
> When this creation was? Remember'st thou
> Thy making, while the maker gave thee being?
> We know no time when we were not as now;
> Know none before us, self-begot, self-raised
> By our quickening power, when fatal course
> Had circled his full orb, the birth mature
> Of this our native heaven, ethereal sons.
> Our puissance is our own, our own right hand
> Shall teach us highest deeds, *by proof to try*
> *Who is our equal.*'   [*PL* 5.852–66; emphasis added]

The whole speech reeks of narcissism, we quickly perceive: the "self" that "begets itself" is precisely an illusion of two—the boy by the pool. But even more important is the obvious irony of " 'by proof to try / Who is our equal'," for the meaning of this statement and the sense of the words are rhetorically contrary to each other: the meaning or intention can only be that no one is our equal, and the sense of the words is betrayed by this meaning. Irony, which is the momentary confusion of sense and meaning, followed by the contradiction of sense by meaning, proves the Adversary's desire for confusion, which is to say, identity—his desire to be God. And from this vantage, finally, we can observe that all Satan's authority is and ever will be confusion— " 'Evil be thou my good' " (*PL* 4.110) constituting, it seems to me, only the most stunning of numerous instances.

This confusion is realized and acted out in the seduction of Eve, and the subsequent, similar lapse of Adam. And there is abundant evidence that Milton understands this dire event as an occasion of confusion. The most pertinent evidence for the present argument is Eve's misconceived desire for equality:

> 'Shall I to him make known
> As yet my change, and give him to partake
> Full happiness with me, or rather not,
> But keep the odds of knowledge in my power
> Without copartner? So to add what wants
> In female sex, the more to draw his love,
> And render me more equal, and perhaps,
> A thing not undesirable, sometime
> Superior; for inferior who is free?'   [*PL* 9.817–25]

Eve's desire to be "more equal" sounds at first like an understandable, though not excusable, because fallen, human impulse; however, when in the next breath, she desires more—to be " 'sometime / Superior, for inferior who is free?' "—we hear the ominous notes of pride, rebellion, and self-delusion; moreover, we understand that the desire to be "more equal" is only a feint (of self-delusion) on the way to the desire for superiority (and power). That desire, in turn, bespeaks further, hidden desires, not only for the ruin of creation by the destruction of order and degree, but also for—this, utterly Satanic—Adam's place: Eve would be in the man's place.

Milton insists on this error of hers in Christ's chastisement of Adam prior to his judgment of him:

> To whom the sovereign presence thus replied.
> 'Was she thy God, that her thou didst obey
> Before his voice, or was she made thy guide,
> Superior, or but equal, that to her
> Thou didst resign thy manhood, and the place
> Wherein God set thee above her made of thee,
> And for thee, whose perfection far excelled
> Hers in all real dignity: adorned
> She was indeed, and lovely to attract
> Thy love, not thy subjection, and her gifts
> Were such as under government well seemed,
> Unseemly to bear rule, which was thy part
> And person, hadst thou known thyself aright.'   [*PL* 10.144–56]

The answers to the questions which open this speech are, of course, no but yes: no, she was not Adam's God, but yes, he let himself act as if she were. Hence he resigned to her his manhood and " 'the place/ Wherein God had set [him] above her'." Adam gave Eve, Christ is hardly deceived, what she wanted, the man's place. More, he re-

signed (line 148) his place to her. This resignation is the perversion of
the resignation we have previously noticed in the poem. Whereas
unfallen (and eventually also repentant) man resigns the world by
re-signing it to its ultimate authority, thus never confusing any sign
with an end in itself, Adam fallen (and unrepentant) re-signs his
manhood and place to a sign (Eve) confused now with an authority—
or, say, he re-signs a sign as an authority (confusing an instrument
with an agent), thus arrogating to himself an authority he does not
have. Note finally that, in order to do this, Adam must act in contradiction of what he knows to be the real and the true—he must act as if
Eve were due his place, and hence, profoundly, the imagery of the
stage which Milton chooses for Christ's description of Adam's error:
" 'to bear rule, which was thy part / And person'." Adam resigned
and re-signed his " 'part / And person' " to Eve—as if either of them
really had more than a *character's* authority in God's play, as if Eve had
any script to make Adam such as she, or Adam any directions to let
her make herself such as he.

And yet such is Eve's desire: to be in the man's place, to enjoy his
privilege, exercise his power, possess his (greater) completeness.
Eve's desire, at its root, is to compensate her lack, "adjust" her deficiency, with " 'the *odds* of knowledge' "—a phrase which, for its reper-
cussions, can hardly be equaled, even in the rest of Milton.

Just how misconceived and confused Eve's desires are we can
measure from the conclusion to her subsequent seduction of Adam:

'Thou therefore also taste, that equal lot
May join us, equal joy, as equal love;
Lest thou not tasting, different degree
Disjoin us.'   [*PL* 9.881–84]

We hear almost instantly the terrible confusion with which Eve is
afflicted: *if* she were to become equal to Adam—what she desires so
much now that she is fallen—then " 'different degree / [Would] disjoin' " them, for equals are of "two . . . essences." Eve literally does
not know what she is saying: she asks for the opposite of what she
really wants, for if she really wants to be *con*joined to Adam, then she
must be unequal to him. When she complains:

'If this be our condition, thus to dwell
In narrow circuit straitened by a foe,
Subtle or violent, we not *endued*

> *Single* with *like* defense, wherever met,
> How are we happy, still in fear of harm?'
>
> [*PL* 9.322–26; emphasis added]

she does not understand that if they were single, they would *not* be *en-du*-ed: they would not be two ("du-") so as to be one; to be two so as to be one, they must not be "endued / single," which is a contradiction in terms—they must be endued dual (cf. *PL* 9.339). They are not finally separate; rather, they are parts, she of him and he and she of the whole human, and the parts cannot be single.[7]

With this formulation, we have approached the critical mass of Milton's thought on equality (and so also on authority, human and divine). Because Eve is so much *a part* of Adam (his rib), she is not truly se*par*ate from Adam—rather, with dire consequences, she is radically dependent on, conjoined to, his "'higher intellectual'" (*PL* 9.483)—and therefore she carries a propensity (like a congenital defect?) for making up the odds, for desiring to be equal, for seeking separation (*PL* 9.1153 especially). Built into Eve is the potential to desire to be more because she is less. Built into Eve is lack: "though both / Not equal, as their sex not equal seemed" (*PL* 4.295–96). Eve lacks what Adam has.[8] If man (Adam) is "'in unity defective'," woman (Eve) is even more so. And her greater defect, if we stop to think about it, is owing to her confusion with Adam: she is a part of him, not sufficiently apart from him, still closely connected to him, still "'collateral'" (that is, "with-sided"; cf. *PL* 8.426). Both Adam and Eve have growing to do—so much Raphael makes clear (*PL* 5.493–503)— but Eve has further to go because she begins one step behind Adam, or one degree "inferior" to him (numerically, not substantially).

At this juncture and in this way, we are at last prepared to address one of the most perplexing passages in *Paradise Lost*, also one of the most notorious—Eve's awakening as (a feminine) Narcissus (*PL* 4.449–91).[9] Immediately after she first awakens, Eve hears a "'murmuring sound / Of waters [that] issued from a cave and spread / Into a liquid plain, then stood unmoved / Pure as the expanse of heaven'" (*PL* 4.453–56). "'With unexperienced thought'" (*PL* 4.457), she approaches this "'smooth lake, that . . . seemed another sky'" (*PL* 4.459) to her, and there she sees her image:

> 'I started back
> It started back, but pleased I soon returned,

Pleased it returned as soon with answering looks
Of sympathy and love.'   [*PL* 4.462–65]

She would have lingered there " 'till now, and pined with vain desire,

Had not a voice thus warned me, 'What thou seest
What there thou seest, fair creature, is thyself,
With thee it came and goes, but follow me
And I will bring thee where no shadow stays
Thy coming, and thy soft embraces, he
Whose image thou art, him thou shalt enjoy
Inseparably thine.'   [*PL* 4.466–73]

Eve followed this mysterious speaker who brought her to Adam,

'fair indeed and tall,
Under a platane, yet methought less fair,
Less winning soft, less amiably mild,
Than that smooth wat'ry image.'   [*PL* 4.477–80]

She immediately fled from Adam but heard him call:

'Return, fair Eve,
Whom fli'st thou? Whom thou fli'st, of him thou art,
His flesh, his bone; to give thee being I lent
Out of my side to thee, nearest my heart,
Substantial life, to have thee by my side
Henceforth an individual solace dear;
Part of my soul I seek thee, and thee claim
My other half.'   [*PL* 4.481–88]

She returned to him then, has remained with him since.

It is a strangely moving scene, both haunted and haunting. Let us begin at the end with the clues there. Adam claims Eve as his other half, part of his soul, and an individual (that is, inseparable) solace. Clearly, the stress is on their connectedness, thus on the potential for confusion between them—as if Eve could almost lapse back into Adam. If we work backward through the scene from this emphasis, we see that Eve's nature is to be attracted or repulsed (*PL* 4.478–80)— connected, we might say, or disconnected. From this we can conclude that she is always defined, and to be defined, in terms of Adam; and hence we may further conclude, perhaps most importantly, that she is a reflector and, in one sense anyway, reflective—" 'he / *Whose image thou art*' "." In Eve, Adam sees his image (reflected; see also *PL* 5.95). Working backward further from this point, we infer the reason for the allusion to Narcissus, he who reflects himself. It is Eve's very essence to reflect, to image forth, to be a mirror—for all this was she made[10]—and therefore, quite appropriately, even logically, the first thing she does upon awakening is reflect. She fulfills her function. That is all, initially—she simply fulfills her function.

We have always known, of course, that it is not Eve's *fault* that she for a brief moment resembles Narcissus; we have always known that she is innocent, created so. And we have often been embarrassed by Milton's apparent prejudicing of the case against her, implying, it seems, that even when she is innocent she is somehow guilty. But now we can see that it is the function, not Eve, which is guilty, or at least potentially guilty. It is reflection, it is imaging, it is imitation, or, as I prefer to say, iconicity, which is guilty. Recall Adam's confession:

> 'But man by number is to manifest
> His single *imperfection*, and beget
> Like of his like, his *image multiplied*,
> *In unity defective*, which requires
> Collateral love, and dearest amity.'   [*PL* 8.422–26; emphasis added]

Multiplying his image, begetting like of his like, is man's imperfection and defect—Milton insists on it. Imaging is an imperfection and an image of imperfection. It is not yet an evil—one element is yet lacking for that—but it is an imperfection and a defect.[11] And if Eve upon awakening is a feminine Narcissus, that is, we now clearly see, ultimately because of man's and woman's, but especially woman's, " 'single imperfection'."

Or say it this way. Before the Fall, Eve is the supplement that is also a complement. She is not just the supplement to Adam because he himself is not perfect or complete: "The supplement adds itself, it is a surplus, a plenitude *enriching another plenitude*, the *fullest measure* of presence. It cumulates and accumulates presence."[12] The supplement is a supplement because it 'enrich[es] another plenitude." But Adam is not another plenitude; rather, he complains of his "single imperfection." Moreover, the supplement "supplements. It adds only to replace. . . [It] is *exterior*, outside of the positivity to which it is super-added, alien to that which, in order to be replaced by it, must be other than it. Unlike the *complement*, dictionaries tell us, the supplement is an *exterior* addition."[13] But Eve is from *within* Adam (his rib) and is therefore, strictly speaking, in fact his "complement"—she is the supplement that is also a complement. Yet, she is also Adam's sign— " 'manlike' " (*PL* 8.471). She is the sign, before the Fall, which signifies Adam without making Adam a victim of her significance. Rather, she completes as well as "suppletes" (if I may).

But after the Fall, she only suppletes. She suppletes (and supplants) Adam, sacrificing him to her significance. Now by her sin *outside* Adam, she finishes Adam (and finishes him off) by adding herself to him so as to add him to her— " 'so to add what wants / In female sex. . . / And render me more equal' " (*PL* 9.821–23). She suppletes, or supplements, Adam, making him the margin and herself the center. Similarly, Adam subsequently supplements, and suppletes, Eve. In his fallen misery and self-commiseration, he will complain of Eve as having been " 'supernumerary / To my just number found' " (*PL* 10.887–88), arguing as if he *had* been a plenitude originally and Eve only a dangerous supplement. Supplementation, we can say, is also the fall of language—language not full.

The one element lacking for imaging to become evil is the conscious will to make someone else one's image— " 'others to make such / As I' "—the will to supplement without complement and, precisely therefore, without compli*m*ent either. Such a will is the will of thought that has experienced the creation and chosen itself, thus experienced (" 'with unexperienced thought' " can lie no evil), before all others and to the exclusion of all others. Such a will can only confuse creation with itself. Add such a will, the Satanic will to duplicate and reduplicate oneself in others, and evil, or deliberate confusion and hence ruin of created entities, must follow inevitably. Even when Eve " 'with unexperienced thought' " looks " 'into the clear / Smooth lake',," where she sees (that is, makes) her image, the lake seems to her " 'another sky' " (*PL* 4.458–59)—in other words, lake and sky are confused, are confused even when the reflector is innocent. Let the reflector be guilty, with thought experienced in evil, and confusion ruinous in its consequences will follow. When, for example, Eve seduces Adam, she urges, " 'On my *experience* freely taste' " (*PL* 9.988; emphasis added), and we instantly perceive, if we had not realized it before, that she is, Satanically, making another such as she, making Adam in her own image, confusing Adam with herself in the same sin, confusing him with her experience. "On Eve's experience," where, so to speak, he does not belong, Adam may "freely" confuse himself with Eve to his ruin—his "'effeminate slackness'" (*PL* 11.634) *adam*brating lack in his (and his children's) being.

Experience is the individual's private, personal version of the world, which can only be a perversion of the Other if it is imposed the "other to make such as I."[14] Milton stresses the exclusivity and distortedness of private experience in Eve's first speech after eating the apple. She immediately praises the virtues of the fruit and then exclaims:

> 'Experience, next to thee I owe,
> Best guide; not following thee, I had remained
> In ignorance, thou open'st wisdom's way,
> And giv'st access, though secret she retire.'   [*PL* 9.807–10]

But immediately following this effusion of praise, she wonders, *sotto voce*, in a furtive aside: "'And I perhaps am secret'" (*PL* 9.811). So always with private experience: it borders forever on the secret and inclines the mind to secrecy, even through a non-sequitur (mere association) such as Eve's here. Private experience is necessarily limited, discrete, partial. Thought privately experienced is necessarily deprived; consider, for example, how Eve's thought, as she decides to eat the fruit, is at least in part Satan's thought, her own deprived of its rightful place and function, and confused, moreover, with his. We should hasten here to distinguish thought privately experienced from thought experienced in solitude: thought experienced in solitude may be the most richly informed and communicative thought possible—it is open (not secret) thought.[15] Thought privately experienced, however, has severed itself from the Other, and if it goes on, reflecting (imaging), "'others to make such / As I'," it proves itself damned in confusion. Such thought proves that it has chosen itself before all others. Such thought also, therefore, proves that all its images are false and damned.

Adam resigned his part and person to Eve, confusing himself and his image with her. Before proceeding any further with the argument, it will be helpful to secure our understanding of Adam's fault here, lest the analysis of Eve's fault mistakenly appear to have been biased and unjust. Adam's fault is graver than Eve's, because he knew better; he acted on what clearly can only have been private experience—in the teeth (if you will) of the evidence. He knew full well that Eve was *not* "'beyond / Compare'" (*PL* 9.227–28)—only Christ is "beyond compare" (*PL* 3.138). She was rather to be "paired with," first God and then himself. And had he done both, especially the latter, he would not have fallen, as Raphael explains quite clearly:

> 'weigh with her thyself;
> Then value: oft times nothing profits more
> Than self esteem, grounded on just and right
> Well managed; of that skill the more thou know'st,
> The more she will acknowledge thee her head,
> And to realities yield all her shows.'   [*PL* 8.570–75]

Had Adam paired himself with Eve, dualing the two of them properly, he would have valued himself aright; however,

> So little knows
> Any, but God alone, to value right
> The good before him, but perverts best things
> To worst abuse, or to their meanest use.   [*PL* 4.201–04]

Adam was, in fact, a poor judge of the good before him; his reason did not proportion (ratio/*ratio*) his and Eve's values properly. Indeed, he could not get enough distance on the situation for such a judgment: he was unable to se*par*ate himself enough from Eve (*PL* 9.915–16, 957–59) to make a proper com*par*ison; and so, confused with her, he fell. The model for his behavior, as distinct from the Scriptural authority (1 Tim. 2:14), Milton found in Ovid's Medea (*Meta.* 7.1–452), a character (and a story—that of the Golden Fleece) who strongly supports his understanding of the Fall of Man.

For some time, readers of Milton have recognized Medea in Adam at the crucial moment when he tells Raphael, "'yet still free / [I] approve the best, and follow what I approve'" (*PL* 8.610–11); it is difficult at this moment, if not impossible, not to hear Medea saying "'video meliora proboque, / Deteriora sequor'" ("'I see the better and approve it, but I follow the worse'".)[16] In light of the emphasis on "proof" in *Paradise Lost*, Medea's "probo" in Ovid can only strengthen the probability of alluson; moreover, the whole clause sounds so like St. Paul—"for I do not the good which I will; but the evil which I hate, that I do" (Rom. 7:15)—that Milton must here have been challenged by the provocative similarity between pagan and Christian sentiments. His response to the challenge is to use Medea's self-consciousness, not only in this instance, but also later, to expose and weigh Adam's conscious, willed act against necessity. If Adam "scrupled not to eat / Against his better knowledge, not deceived, / But fondly overcome with female charm" (*PL* 9.997–99), it was largely the same (though to my knowledge no one has noticed this before) with Medea's decision to obey Jason and serve him: " 'Quid faciam, video; nec me ignorantia veri / Decipiet, sed amor' " ("'I see what I am about to do, nor shall ignorance of the truth be my undoing [literally, nor shall ignorance of the truth deceive me], but love itself' " [*Meta.* 7.92–93]). In the moment of his fall, Adam, like Medea, chooses to act against his certain knowledge ("nec . . . ignorantia") of the error he is commiting. In his case, however, he does not directly acknowledge his conscious decision; rather, it is Milton who does that. This difference, as we might expect, is significant.

In Ovid, Medea endures a long psychomachia, or internal debate, over whether she should love and follow Jason (*Meta.* 7.11–73). By the conclusion of this debate, she has decided in the negative. But then, by chance, she sees Jason again right away, and her love suddenly aroused once more, she capitulates to it, uttering the crucial phrase already quoted. The two passionate monologues, interrupted by this fateful encounter with Jason, generate considerable sympathy for Medea, which Ovid almost certainly intended (see especially *Meta.* 7.85). And it is just this sympathy which Milton wishes to exclude from his text. He wants to insist—and this is probably the first motive in fact for the allusion—that, just as Medea cannot divorce herself from Jason, although she knows that she should (*Meta.* 7.11–18 especially), neither can Adam divorce himself from Eve, although he knows that he should.[17] But Milton does not want us to sympathize with or pity Adam, for Adam *did* know better—his "higher intellectual" was not deceived—and therefore, he quotes Medea of Adam's behavior. The "distance and distaste" (*PL* 9.9) thus achieved—especially by substituting for Medea's matter-of-fact " 'sed amor' " the tinnily alliterative "but fondly overcome with female charm"—insist on the extent of Adam's guilt, as well as on the helplessness of man who cannot do what he knows full well is best for him.

And he *is* so helpless just because he assumes he is *not*. This Ovid's text also makes clear. If Medea chooses Jason against her better knowledge, she does so in part because she believes that

> '*Maximus intra me deus est.* Non magna relinquam,
> Magna sequar'
>
> > [*Meta.* 7.55–56; emphasis added]

['and the greatest god is within me! I shall not be leaving great things, but going to great things']

and that

> 'quo coniuge felix
> Et dis cara ferar et *vertice sidera tangam.*'
>
> > [*Meta.* 7.60–61; emphasis added]

['with him as my husband I shall be called the beloved of heaven, and with my head shall touch the stars.']

Both these presumptions must have seemed apt descriptions to Milton of Adam's and Eve's inner states (their pride) on the occasions of their falls. Moreover, when we add to these connections Ovid's evocation of Virgil's Dido (see *Aeneid* 4.172) in Medea's mocking question to herself,

> 'Coniugiumne putas speciosaque nomina culpae
> Imponis, Medea, tuae?'
>
> > (*Meta.* 7.69–70

['But do you deem it marriage, Medea, and do you give fair-seeming names to your fault?']

we can hardly resist assuming that Milton remembered this condemnation of rationalization, especially in the passage in his own text in which Adam manages to convince himself that

> 'what thou art is mine;
> Our state cannot be severed, we are one,
> One flesh; to lose thee were to lose myself.'   [*PL* 9.957–59]

What Adam will not admit to himself, Medea (and Dido) amply supply.[18] And such opportunities as these it is not like Milton to miss.

And even less likely is he to have missed the other opportunity afforded by the story surrounding Medea, the resemblance between Jason and Eve; for as Eve plucked the apple, so Jason seized the

Golden Fleece, and in each case, the action was a theft of mediation, of an intercessor, which resulted in betrayal and death.

Just how the apple on the Tree of the Knowledge of Good and Evil is a mediator I have already described and discussed at length (see chapter 2 above). The Golden Fleece is also a mediator, although, obviously, not in the same way. To be precise (and as brief as possible), in the various versions of the myth which Milton would have known, there is frequent emphasis on voluntary sacrifice, either by Phrixus or by the ram who carries him away to safety before he is offered up. For example, Hyginus writes:

> Quod cum Athamas se facturum abnuisset, Phrixus ultro ac libens pollicetur se unum civitatem aerumna liberaturum. itaque cum ad aram cum infulis esset adductus.
>
> [Phrixus voluntarily and readily promised that he alone would free the state from its distress. Accordingly he was led to the altar, wearing the fillets (of sacrifice.)][19]

Or, again, Apollonius Rhodius remarks that "Phrixus / . . . [was] the sacrifice prepared by his father'."[20] Moreover, Apollonius also notes that "the ram, at its own prompting, he then sacrificed to Zeus."[21] These emphases suggested to Milton, I think, that the Golden Fleece is a sign of the work of sacrifice, which mediates or interrupts, for the sake of its beneficiaries, the evil or suffering which it absorbs into itself. Metonymically, then, he could have associated the Fleece and the apple. The appeal of this association must have been great, since Jason had to abrogate all innocence for the Fleece, seduce Medea, deceive Aetes, and practice violence—all in order to *steal* what is itself the gift, as several ancient sources note, of Hermes, who is himself god of thieves and merchants, as well as the psychopomp who mediates between the worlds and gives his name to the science of interpretation (hermeneutics).[22] The Fleece probably appealed to Milton, then, as the kind of liminal object which, like the apple, represented, and therefore prevented, a host of evils, including the accursed science of interpretation (which would not have been necessary had it not been for the Fall).

And so it is that Milton can consider Eve another Jason. Like Jason, she steals a sacred object in order to augment her power; like Jason after the theft, she betrays her spouse, although she manages to convince herself that she is behaving in his best interests (whereas

Jason simply abandons Medea because she is a witch—the very characteristic which made it possible for her to help him steal the Fleece in the first place); like Jason's, her betrayal leads to death (Medea kills her brother as well as her children by Jason); and, finally, like Jason, she changes the whole world—the *Argo* was the first long ship ever made, and after its successful voyage (which would have been impossible without Medea), civilization was never so innocent again.[23]

One more point remains to be emphasized. If Milton was attracted to Medea because she and Adam resembled each other, and to Jason because he and Eve resembled each other, he was also attracted to them both, as well as their story, because they reverse the sex roles in the account of the Fall of Man. If Adam was "fondly overcome with female charm," this is because something in him was female; and Medea, a female Adam, is able to represent this precisely because she also possessed a "higher intellectual." If Eve aspired to godhead and its power and dominion, it is because something in her was masculine; and this Jason, a male Eve, is able to represent precisely because he also manifests consummate fickleness. In short, in Medea and Jason, Milton found a model of human corruptibility and culpability less sex-determined than that in Genesis, and this model attracted him, I believe, as a way of enriching the human characterizations of Adam and Eve.

10

Proof: Fruit of the Dual

For the fruitfulness of a gift is the only gratitude for the
gift.

—MEISTER ECKHART

To prove oneself apostate by choosing oneself, one's private experience, before all else is not, we have just learned, a particularly male or
female error. Indeed, we should remember what we perhaps too often
forget, that the first apostate was male—Satan. And as he says in yet
another outburst of confused authority, not unlike " 'Evil be thou my
good' ": " 'Yet all his good *proved* ill in me, / And wrought but malice' " (*PL* 4.48–49; emphasis added). But this outburst, if not so stunning as the former, is of at least as much importance. It isolates the
crucial role of proof in the larger question of authority in the poem,
and in doing so, leads us toward the conclusion of the present argument.

Proof is inconceivable apart from experience and experiment,
which themselves are inconceivable apart from authority. If someone
experiences something or experiments with something, he is by definition an authority with regard to that item: he can give proof in
witness of his experience or to demonstrate his experiment. Proof we
may define as the result or the issue or—most daring perhaps, but
also most truthful—the *fruit* of an action, which affirms or denies
some predicate of the action or the agent. When "good prove[s] ill" in
Satan, the fruit of "ill" affirms confusion to be the case with him (" 'By
their fruits ye shall know them' " [Matt. 7:16]).

Or again, a different example. When Satan begins his seduction of
Eve, she

Yet more amazed unwary thus replied.
  'Serpent, thy overpraising leaves in doubt
The virtue of that fruit, in thee first proved.'   [*PL* 9.614–16]

The (apparent) speech and reason of the serpent (*PL* 9.553–59) affirms the special virtue of the fruit, proves such virtue to be the case. But that is hardly all we can or should say in this particular instance. The line "The virtue of that fruit, in thee first proved" makes the point even more vividly. If we read the line for the moment as if "proved" were intransitive (which, of course, it can be), then it says "The virtue of that fruit in thee first proved"—that is, *become* proof. The line can also say that the fruit first becomes proof, first assumes the nature of proof, in the serpent/Satan.[1] Which, of course, is the truth, since fruit in the sense of "consequence" and fruit in the sense of "ovary" are possible only after the Fall, when God created the world for repair[s]. In the fall of Satan, fruit proves proof, and therefore, by the logic of the felix culpa (by the Logos of the One) in the creation, proof proves fruit—the proof of man's obedience proves, becomes, a piece of fruit interdicted to his taste. In the prohibition on the Tree, God in a sense asks man not to reiterate Satan's crime: he asks him not to prove (that is, taste, that is, experience) so that he might indeed fruit. The only thing that man, his " 'creature late so loved, [his] youngest son' " (*PL* 3.151), has to prove to God is fruitful; the only thing he has to prove is *im-prove*ment (obedient) in fruition.[2]

As much can also be inferred from God's explanation of man's freedom:

'Not free, what *proof* could they have given sincere
Of true allegiance, constant faith or love,
Where only what they needs must do, appeared,
Not what they would?'   [*PL* 3.103–06; emphasis added]

God implies that some proof or fruit, unspecified, will affirm "true allegiance, constant faith [and] love" of Adam and Eve. Free, they will prove fruitful.

At the same time, however, he also implies that some proof or fruit may deny these attributes of them. Proof, by definition, can go either way. Proof, in other words, is also proof of option—it necessitates choice between alternatives or options. If " 'all his good proved ill' " in Satan, it is because Satan chose " 'Evil be thou my good'." Or, a different but equally useful example, when Eve seduces Adam into sinning with her, she praises his love for her, saying that " 'good proof [of it] this day / Affords' " (*PL* 9.967–68). Then she continues:

'[thou] declaring thee resolved,
Rather than death or aught than death more dread

> Shall separate us, linked in love so dear,
> To undergo with me one guilt, one crime,
> If any be, of tasting this fair fruit,
> Whose virtue, for of good still good proceeds,
> Direct, or by occasion hath presented
> This happy *trial* of thy love, which else
> So eminently never had been known.'
>
> [*PL* 9.968–76; emphasis added]

The fruit occasions a trial of love (see also the beginning of the speech, " 'O glorious trial' " [*PL* 9.961])—that is, a *choice* of loves—and Adam proves his love for Eve by choosing her rather than God.

But such choice, at least initially, is still an act of reason—" 'reason also is choice' " (*PL* 3.108)—and it is, therefore, an exercise of freedom or " 'true liberty which always with right reason dwells' " (*PL* 12.83–84). Choice may, in the event, as in the event of Adam's falling in with Eve, cancel true liberty and obliterate right reason, but it begins as proof of both. Proof, therefore, is proof of freedom (" 'Not free, what proof . . .' "). Or, to put this most significantly now, proof is a *sign* of freedom. But if proof is a sign of freedom, it is also a sign of signs or signatures. Hence, finally, the logic of God's sentence:

> 'if I foreknew,
> Foreknowledge had no influence on their fault,
> Which had no less *proved* certain unforeknown.
> So without least impulse or shadow of fate,
> Or aught by me immutably foreseen,
> They trespass, *authors* to themselves in all
> Both what they judge and what they choose; for so
> I formed them *free*, and *free* they must remain,
> Till they enthrall themselves.'   [*PL* 3.117–25; emphasis added]

Freedom is the minimal pre-condition for authority, and proof is a sign of that freedom, which is "filial freedom" (*PL* 4.294), "whence true authority in men." To be able to prove is to be an author, free, free because created free. Conversely, to deny creatureliness, as Satan does, is to deny freedom, which is thus to become a suspect author, no longer able to prove. But what is it to be no longer able to prove?— if not to be no longer able to choose?—if not forever to inscribe the *same* sign?—if not forever to be arrested in one stage of growth, incapable of any new *fruit?*

'But say I could repent and could obtain
By act of grace my former state; how soon
Would highth recall high thoughts, how soon unsay
What feigned submission swore.'   [*PL* 4.93–96]

Evil is to reenact the same choice forever, to "author" the same "sign" forever (which is no authority at all), to remain in the same "fruition" forever.[3]

Conversely, good is to choose, repeatedly, what reason approves: " 'yet still *free* / [I] *approve* the best, and follow what I *approve*' " (*PL* 8.610–11; emphasis added). We have already learned (in chapter 2 above) that because, before the Fall, evil was mediated and was not a medium, it " 'into the mind of god or man / May come and go, so *unapproved*, and leave / No spot or blame behind' " (*PL* 5.117–19; emphasis added). Because before the Fall, good is the medium of evil, evil may enter the mind as a mediated datum which the mind can disapprove even as it approves the good. The mind can choose the good rather than the evil. But this is to say that the mind (ap)proves the *signs* of the good (for the good is everywhere a sign of the Maker). But what is it to (ap)prove the signs of the good if not to make, or author, a new text with those signs? Proof of the choice of the good is a new story; to prove the signs of the good is to weave them into new texts. Proof that one has reaped fruit of the good is the ongoing creation itself. And the ongoing creation is proof of the fruit of the good. Hence, for example, when Adam led Eve " 'to the nuptial bower' " (*PL* 8.510),

'she what was honour knew,
And with obsequious majesty approved
[His] pleaded reason.'   [*PL* 8.508–10]

And her ap*prov*al, of course, is to issue there, within the bower in creation, the fruit of her womb, their offspring, who are to continue the story of creation.

" 'God made thee perfect, not immutable' " (*PL* 5.524), Raphael tells Adam. Adam and Eve were made, then, to *change*—more precisely, to *grow:*

'And from these corporal nutriments perhaps
Your bodies may at last turn all to spirit,

Im*proved* by tract of time, and winged ascend
Ethereal, as we, or may at *choice*
Here or in heavenly paradises dwell.'

[*PL* 5.496–500; emphasis added]

Change, the change of growth or fruition, is wholly good, leading to
the proofs of "im*prove*ment" which themselves enfranchise further
choices. Not to change, forever to remain the same, is proof of damnation. But there are two species of change: that which makes new, or
change-to-fruition, and "mortal change" (*PL* 10.273), which brings
death into the world. It is the office of Christ the Mediator to transform the latter into the former after man has fallen—" 'Death, thou
shalt die' " (1 Cor. 15:55; Hosea 13:14; and see also *PL* 3.252–53).[4]
More on such conversion in a moment. For now, note only that before
the Fall, the good of change was its significance for the fruition and
growth of creation.

Obedience guarded and preserved this good, this significance, for
obedience—more precisely, honoring "the only sign of obedience
left"—preserved all the other signs of good, which were also proofs
and fruits of good, so that they could grow into the ever variegated
text of creation. Obedience, in other words, preserved the constancy
of change toward the good. Even in heaven. Witness Abdiel:

'. . . .for this [says God to him] was all thy care
To stand approved in sight of God, though worlds
Judged thee perverse.'   [*PL* 6.35–37]

God's approval of Abdiel proves that Abdiel (ap)proved God—signified God who otherwise was absent from Satan's camp—but Abdiel (ap)proves God only by obeying him, obeying him rather than
Satan, where such obedience is precisely " 'for the *testimony* of truth' "
(*PL* 3.33; emphasis added), for the text of creation.

Such obedience, the obedience of those " 'who approve not to
transgress / By [Satan's] example' " (*PL* 4.880–81), is the right of way
to the good. But without such obedience, the constancy of change
toward the good dissolves, the right of way is lost, and change turns to
"mortal[ity]." Hence the accuracy of Adam's warning to Eve:

'Seek not temptation then, which to avoid
Were better, and most likely if from me

> Thou *sever* not: trial will come unsought.
> Wouldst thou ap*prove* thy constancy, ap*prove*
> First thy obedience.'   [*PL* 9.364–68; emphasis added]

Eve must change and grow; she must prove her fruition—she cannot
remain almost confused with Adam. All this Adam knows. Indeed, in
a sense, he acted on this very knowledge, though to his sorrow:

> 'Too facile then thou didst not much gainsay,
> Nay didst permit, *approve*, and fair dismiss.'
>   [*PL* 9.1158–59; emphasis added]

Adam knew that Eve must " 'from [him] / . . . sever'," in order to be
creatively apart from him and thus truly a part of him. He knew that
he must (ap)prove her independence if she were to prove her freedom
and the authority which would flow from it. But to approve the
constancy of her necessary change, she must—he was right, and we
know why he was right—(ap)prove her obedience first. Her obedience is the sign of the good of her authority.

Her authority, however, was not constant. When, after the Fall,
Adam concludes, lamentingly,

> 'Let none henceforth seek needless cause to ap*prove*
> The faith they owe; when earnestly they seek
> Such *proof*, conclude, they then begin to fall.'
>   [*PL* 9.1140–42; emphasis added]

he is again right, though this time regrettably too late. The quest for
such proof is itself the termination of proof. The quest for such proof
is already proof that faith is gone; and by the very nature of creation,
that proof is the terminal proof, for after faith and obedience, it is no
longer possible to prove, to author, to reap fruition—faith is the
minimal pre-requisite for signification. They who seek such proof
must necessarily already believe themselves (mistakenly) capable of
proving their faith beyond the simple obedience demanded of them—
they "seek needless cause," as Adam implies—and this pride (excess)
is proof of the vitiation of their reason (which also is choice, which also
is proof). It is also, this terminal proof, proof that they have ceased to
grow.

Such a conclusion is predictable also from Adam's uxorious rap-
tures in the presence of Raphael:

'but here
Far otherwise, transported I behold,
Transported touch; here passion first I felt

. . . .

Or nature failed in me, and left some part
Not *proof* enough such object to sustain,
Or . . .

. . . .

                    when I approach
Her loveliness, so absolute she seems
And in herself complete . . . '

                    [*PL* 8. 528–30, 534–35, 546–48; emphasis added]

The speech is much lengthier than this, of course, but enough has
been quoted to make the point. Confronted with Eve's loveliness,
Adam thinks her "absolute" and "complete"—that is, grown,
finished, beyond fruit. And he thinks so because "some part" of him
is "not proof enough such object to sustain." Adam's confusion here is
precisely his inability to hear the truth of what he is saying: any *part* of
Nature in him is by definition not proof enough because the part
alone cannot fruit, cannot produce fruit. Indeed, as Raphael will say
to Adam in reproof: " 'Accuse not Nature, she hath done her *part*' "
(*PL* 8.561; emphasis added). Nature has not "failed"—she has done
her part, all she can do. She has left him, Adam, part (his "single
imperfection") and therefore precisely not proof enough by himself to
sustain such an object *if* that object is "absolute" and "complete." If
Eve is absolute and complete, then she might as well be God—which,
of course, is exactly what she does become for Adam in the moment of
the Fall, only for him later to complain that she was not " 'mature,
proof against all assaults' " (*PL* 10.882). In short, if Eve is God, then of
course Adam cannot sustain an object such as she.

Hence his thinking must be clarified. Evil has come into his mind
and has almost been ap*proved*. And when his thinking is clarified (by
Raphael), he is told to distinguish, to " 'weigh with her [him]self,
/ Then value' " (*PL* 8.570–71). Which would be to recognize that he
and Eve are both parts—neither is absolute or complete—and that
they must both continue to grow, to be proof enough, fruit enough, to
sustain the absolute and complete toward which they tend and aspire.

Regrettably, Raphael's lesson is forgotten, unheeded, and Adam and Eve terminate their growth, lose their faith, eat the fruit (proof), which thus does not let them prove (fruit) their obedience. Happily, however, the termination of their growth is not permanent:

> Thus they in lowliest plight repentant stood
> Praying, for from the mercy-seat above
> Prevenient grace descending had removed
> The stony from their hearts, and made new flesh
> Regenerate grow instead.   [*PL* 11.1–5]

"The stony," of course, is a fitting image for the static, the fixed, the ungrowing, the (de)ceased. But in its stead, happily, "new flesh" is growing. And growing with this new flesh are certain fruits:

> 'See Father, what first *fruits* on earth are sprung
> From thy *implanted* grace in man, these sighs
> And prayers, which in this golden censer, mixed
> With incense, I thy priest before thee bring,
> *Fruits* of more pleasing *savour* from thy *seed*
> *Sown* with contrition in his heart, than those
> Which his own hand manuring all the trees
> Of Paradise could have produced, ere fallen
> From innocence.'   [*PL* 11.22–30; emphasis added]

Note, in passing, that we could substitute "proofs" for "fruits" in this speech (although I hasten to admit that "fruits" is the more pleasing choice by far). Be that as it may, clearly something new is growing in Paradise. And at its sublimest, what is growing there is a *new story*. Although Adam and Eve have aborted proof or fruit by their choice of evil, thus releasing signs of evil into all the world, reducing the world to reenactment of the *same* story, the history of evil, Christ crosses this abortion with his sacrifice, which leaves behind one *un*ambiguous sign of the good in the world, in proof of which is the new story of the Redemption or, more generally, of the felix culpa.

Christ de-termines the story of men and women after the Fall. He both cancels the premature termination of their growth and gives shape and direction to their subsequent history. Without him, "mor-

tal change," or death, would be absolute. With him, mortal change is
transformed into conversion, change-to-fruition. To be sure, death
the unthinkable fact, remains; but Christ the Word can—and for the
faithful, does—transform it, convert it, in their conversion to him,
through metaphor into fruition (thus the unthinkable becomes imaginable and sayable). In effect, then, the Word changes the death
which Adam and Eve have incurred into their birth into a new world,
a new story.

Hence the birth imagery subtly introduced into the poem at certain crucial moments: Adam and Eve are finally expelled from paradise as the fetus is expelled from the womb. The imagery first con-
fronts us in the obvious evocation of the pudendum in the first
mention of Paradise:

> delicious Paradise,
> Now nearer, crowns with her enclosure green,
> As with a rural mound the champaign head
> Of a steep wilderness, whose hairy sides
> [Are] With thicket overgrown, grotesque and wild.   [PL 4.132–36]

The imagery continues and is perhaps most moving at the moment(s)
of the Fall:

> So saying, her rash hand in evil hour
> Forth reaching to the fruit, she plucked, she ate:
> Earth felt the wound, and nature from her seat
> Sighing through all her works gave signs of woe,
> That all was lost.   [PL 9.780–84]

> he scrupled not to eat
> Against his better knowledge, not deceived,
> But fondly overcome with female charm.
> *Earth trembled from her entrails, as again*
> *In pangs, and nature gave a second groan.*
>   [PL 9.997–1001; emphasis added]

In the present perspective, the word *again* in the second passage is
most important, for it helps to suggest that in both moments of the
Fall, Milton would have the reader perceive, however dimly and
distantly, the onset of labor pains—Adam and Eve being born, o felix
culpa![5]

Milton needed only these few hints to plant the seed in our minds.

Adam and Eve do not die finally because they are born; nature and the earth expel them from the "womb" (so to speak) of Paradise, "down the cliff . . . / To the subjected plain" (*PL* 12.639–40). And if Nature *sighs* when she gives "*signs* of woe" in her labor, still the confusion wrought by the Fall is blocked, if barely: *sigh*[*s*] does not become *signs*, by the grace of one graph, and therefore sighs *can* be signs (similarly at *PL* 10.1090–91 and 1102–03). In conclusion, if Milton chooses the imagery of birth to suggest the overcoming of confusion (sin), it is ultimately, I believe, because birth makes all the difference in the world: with birth, $1 + 1 = 3$.

11

Christz:
Son of God, Lord of Difference

This chapter on the brief epic *Paradise Regained* most properly begins with a statement of what it is *not*. It is not a complete analysis of the poem; it is not a character study; it is not a source study nor a genre study; especially, it is not an explanation of this obscure and difficult poem in the sense of "planing" or "flattening out" its excrescences, oddities, and contradictions. What follows is a piety of a different sort. I am concerned only with the ways in which *Paradise Regained* completes the argument begun in *Paradise Lost* regarding the sign and its repair. This concern and the chapter, therefore, intentionally exclude all other matters, but such exclusion should not be misconstrued as implying that other matters are unimportant, only that they are irrelevant to the present, admittedly narrow concern.

The argument Milton begins in *Paradise Lost* culminates in *Paradise Regained*. At the end of Book 4, as sure of his poem as of his doctrine, Milton has the angelic choir address the Son in the following manner:

> 'True image of the Father whether throned
> In the bosom of bliss, and light of light
> Conceiving, or remote from heaven, enshrined
> In fleshly tabernacle, and human form.'   [*PR* 4.596–99]

Jesus the Son is the true image of the father. Milton means his readers to understand by this triumphant affirmation that the "trial" (*PR* 3.195; 4.206) of Christ by Satan has "by proof" demonstrated Jesus to be "the *undoubted* Son of God" (*PR* 1.11; emphasis added). Here we may assume *proof* to mean what it means in *Paradise Lost* (see chapter 10 above): the "spirit" (*PR* 1.8) brings Christ from the desert, "by proof undoubted Son of God," by authoring the story of the "duel" (*PR* 1.174) between him and Satan; and this authority, of the spirit, to submit this proof, is derivative entirely, from Heaven and the Father (*PR* 1.289). Moreover, this same spirit "inspires" (*PR* 1.11) Milton's "prompted song *else mute*" (*PR* 1.12; emphasis added) because, without the spirit that proves, the spirit of proof—and therefore of reason, choice, and liberty—would also be absent, and the song could only be the pseudo-song ("mute") of Philomela (see chapter 5 above).

But the song is not mute, any more than the spirit is. Rather it is Satan who is now "mute" (*PR* 1.459), for

> 'God hath now sent his living oracle
> Into the world, to teach his final will,
> And sends his spirit of truth henceforth to dwell
> In pious hearts, an inward oracle
> To all truth requisite for men to know.'   [*PR* 1.460–64]

And the inward oracle of Milton notes the teachings of God's living oracle in order to insist that he is the "*undoubted* Son of God." The word is big with Milton's vision. Only in Hell and Heaven, though oppositely, can any sign—and the Son is a sign, *the* sign, the Word—be undoubted. Christ is the *undoubted* Son, He who cannot be doubled or duplicated or counterfeited Son of God, because, oppositely from the damned and their signs, he has always and already chosen differentiation; he has chosen forever to be different; he has chosen *not* to be God, and, therefore, by this merit (*PR* 1.166), of perfectly honoring the independent deity of the Father, he can be called the Father's Son. Christ is the only creature perfectly himself, the only creature who not only "dares be" but always *is* "singularly good" (*PR* 3.57), and therefore, he can never desire to usurp the Father's place, for who, of men or of angels, in full and eternal possession of himself, would ever want to be someone else?

Because Christ never wants to be someone else, he never wants either, unlike Satan, " 'others to make such / As I' " (*PL* 9.127–28). Why would Christ want to make someone else such as he? Such a desire would argue at least a deficiency, if not also a perversion, of self-love. Rather, Christ wants every man and woman to be only, or—more daringly, but also more truthfully—singularly such as he or she is. Christ wants (but does not lack) the difference of every creature he made in obedience to the Father's authority. Therefore, strictly speaking, every creature would be such as he insofar as every creature would be singular and different; but he himself would never *make* another creature such as he, for this would be to subvert the creature's liberty. The creature is free to *imitate* the Son (*Of Education*, YE 2:366–67; see also chapter 1 above), but, by this imitation, he or she would become only such as he—*as* in this case could never be the simulacrum of is. In other words, so uniquely and singularly different would each creature become that he or she could be son or daughter of God (though by adoption only, since Adam fell), because neither he nor she could ever want to *be* God.

Christ, the Word, is the opposite of confusion. He is, rather, difference incarnate. He is so different from every other creature, especially humans, that he can enter into relationship with a creature—he can du*al* (with) a creature—and become the significance of that creature's life without compromising either himself or the creature. He can become the creature's sign; he can become the creature's Word—confusion will never threaten.

And this, of course, is in fact what he did. He became man, God incarnate, which should have been the ultimate confusion, but which was and is, on the contrary, the beginning of wholeness. Christ became man, in St. Paul's words, by emptying himself (Phil. 2:5–8; see chapter 3 above). Christ was so wholly, in fact eternally, in possession of himself that he could empty himself without fear of loss—logically, he could never finally *become* empty, because he always willed to *be* empty, thereby remaining always full of the *will* to empty himself for others, which of course is his *love* for others. Christ became man in order to show man the significance of who he, man, is. Jesus Christ is the only creature who ever became fully and perfectly a man—"'this perfect man'" (*PR* 1.166). Jesus Christ is the only man who ever lived. All the rest of us always have been, are, and will be less than men (though we may choose or refuse to be human as we like). And that Jesus Christ is the only man who ever lived is the *proof* that he is the Messiah, the Son of God.

Hence Milton's emphasis, from the very opening of the poem, on Jesus the man:

> I who erewhile the happy garden sung,
> By one man's disobedience lost, now sing,
> Recovered Paradise to all mankind,
> By one man's firm obedience fully tried
> Through all temptation, and the tempter foiled
> In all his wiles, defeated and repulsed,
> And Eden raised in the waste wilderness.　　　　[*PR* 1.1–7]

There is no ambiguity, no confusion, no doubleness (though, to be sure, duality remains): man recovers Paradise. And indeed only so could Paradise be recovered, for if any covering other than man could re-cover Paradise, we, mere humans that we are, could never see it, and therefore would never strive to regain it. We can be the more certain that this is the intended emphasis because of Milton's syntax: by writing "recovered Paradise," which makes "recovered" a participial adjective qualifying "Paradise," Milton insists as much on the attribute "re-covered" as on the action of "recovering." Hence the point, namely that Paradise is not only recovered, it is also re-covered, by man; and therefore mankind can regain it.

Moreover, man re(-)covers Paradise "by . . . firm obedience fully tried / Through all temptation." It is his obedience, flowing from his absolute difference, which makes Jesus the Son of God, and, therefore, it is also his obedience which makes him the perfect man. Since to obey is first and foremost to have faith in whom one obeys, it is Jesus's faith which is also fully tried, and since the ontological (but unnatural) opposite of faith is doubt, and since, moreover, trial, which purifies us, is by what is contrary (see chapter 1 above), clearly the chief agency of Jesus's trial must be doubt or doubleness, and the agent, just as clearly, the embodiment of doubleness, or Satan.[1]

Doubt and related words occur thirteen times in *Paradise Regained*, and the importance of doubt to the poem's meaning has long been recognized as part of the difficult question of when and how Christ knows himself to be Son of God.[2] Jesus himself marks the issue most clearly in his condemnation of oracles. Late in Book 1, after Satan has boasted of the "'advice'" which he gives men "'by presages and signs, / And answers, oracles, portents, and dreams'" (*PR* 1.394–95), Jesus declares:

> 'Deservedly thou griev'st, composed of lies
> From the beginning, and in lies wilt end
>
> .　.　.　.　.　.　.　.　.　.　.　.　.　.　.

The other service was thy chosen task,
To be a liar in four hundred mouths;
For lying is thy sustenance, thy food.
Yet thou pretends'st to truth; all oracles
By thee are given, and what confessed more true
Among the nations? that hath been thy craft,
By *mixing* somewhat true to vent more lies.
But what have been thy answers, what but dark
Ambiguous and with *double sense* deluding.'
                    [*PR* 1.407–08, 427–35; emphasis added]

These passages constitute the clearest and most direct position, apart
from *Areopagitica*, which Milton took on the problem of doubleness,
and it is important, I believe, that he inflects this position, which
alludes to John 8:44 (where Jesus says that Satan " 'is a liar, and the
father thereof' "), with the imagery of food and sustenance, for if
Satan, composed of lies, feeds on lies, which are composed of words,
the redeemed Christian feeds on the Word, or Christ himself, who is
the opposite of lies and who never " 'with double sense delude[s]'.''
Milton thus once again (see chapter 7 above) opposes communion to
confusion—Satan " '*mix*[es] somewhat true to vent more lies' "—even
as he also prepares the brilliant irony of Satan later reporting to his
cohorts that he has " 'found him [Christ], viewed him, *tasted* him' ''
(*PR* 2.131; emphasis added). Testing Christ, Satan has tasted him,
and this food is definitely not to his liking. Duplicity can never assimi-
late unity.

Every doubt or doubleness in the poem to do with Christ is systematically dissolved, its illusion (result of confusion) penetrated.
Satan himself first acknowledges the principle of the matter:

'And he himself among them was baptized,
Not thence to be more pure, but to receive
The testimony of heaven, that who he is
Thenceforth the nations may not *doubt*.'
                    [*PR* 1.76–79; emphasis added]

It is, of course, fitting that he should do so, since being compelled to
perform the contrary of his desire only serves to continue his punishment. Indeed, here in *Paradise Regained*, as also in *Paradise Lost* (as at
5.73), Milton insists on this "rule" (so to speak) of Satanic existence:

to the coast of Jordan . . . [Satan] directs
His easy steps, girded with snaky wiles,

Where he might likeliest find this new-declared,
This man of men, *attested* Son of God,
Temptation and all guile on him *to try*;
So to subvert whom he suspected raised
To end his reign on earth so long enjoyed:
But *contrary* unweeting he fulfilled
The purposed counsel pre-ordained and fixed
Of the Most High.   [*PR* 1.119–28; emphasis added]

Satan only does (confuse) what he is (confused): if he attempts X, he achieves Y; contradiction is his (anti-)essence. But Milton has done more than merely work the "rule" of Satanic existence; he has produced a Satan whose confusion is the source (instrumental cause) of the poem's action. Because Satan doubts who "this man of men" is, he duels him, trying (unsuccessfully) to double him, and thus, himself the spirit's instrument, he proves him "undoubted Son of God." Satan sees the dove descend (*PR* 1.82–84) but does not know what " 'it meant' " (*PR* 1.83); he sees that " 'man he seems / In all his lineaments, *though* in his face / The glimpses of his father's glory shine' " (*PR* 1.91–92; emphasis added). What Satan cannot do is believe, have faith in, the possibility that a man can be the Son of God. As a consequence, he tries the man, and fails: his doubt fails to double (counterfeit) Christ with any other creature—angel, beast, or human—and therefore his doubt proves Christ a man, "this man of men," and this perfect manhood, in its turn, by its singularity, proves Christ the Son of God. Finally, an all-important corollary can be drawn from this argument: Christ knows without doubt that he is Son of God the moment he knows that it is Satan himself who is trying to double him; if no less a power (though a power, to be sure, by permission only) than Satan doubts it, then it must be true. All Christ has to do from this point on (*PR* 1.346–57) is remain singular, with God's help.[3]

It will help before proceeding with any other part of the argument to defend and augment these claims. To do so, it will be necessary to engage the issue of productivity in *Paradise Regained*, and this issue will remain to the fore throughout the rest of the argument.

Not inappropriately, it is God who authorizes all the recent claims. His first address in the poem begins, as we might have expected, by emphasizing proof: " 'Gabriel this day *by proof* thou shalt behold'" (*PR* 1.130). Milton once again avails himself of the opportunity to insist that his argument has to do with proof of Christ's divine sonship (see *PR* 1.10–11). Then the speech continues with a brief account of the Annunciation which contains a crucial dual reference: "'Then toldst [Gabriel] her *doubting* how these things could be / To her a virgin'" (*PR* 1.137–38; emphasis added). The syntax permits two readings, both of which are necessary, I think. Why Mary should have doubted is, I presume, self-evident; and therefore the first reading can pass without further comment. But why Gabriel might have told her, *himself* doubting the good news, is, I am assuming, much less evident; and so this reading does need some discussion. And an adequate response is not far to seek: nothing in creation—whether angel, beast, or human—can conceive the singularity, the pure difference, of the Christ; and yet it is this singularity which enables him to be the perfect man and thus the Son of God by merit; hence the perfect manhood is also inconceivable (until it has happened); and therefore, even the angel Gabriel must doubt, if only briefly, because he cannot, although of course he tries, double, (re-produce) using anything from his experience, the Incarnation (becoming man) of the Son of God.

God continues his address to Gabriel and the other angels by announcing his exposure of Christ to Satan:

> 'He now shall know I can *produce a man*
> Of female seed, far abler to resist
> All his solicitations, and at length
> All his vast force, and drive him back to hell,
> Winning by conquest what the first man lost
> By fallacy surprised.'   [*PR* 1.150–55; emphasis added]

God (and Milton) are unambiguous: it is a *man* who will defeat Satan. Just as a man must re(-)cover Paradise, if humans are to strive for it, so a man must defeat Satan, if humans are to struggle against him. At the same time, however, this man is also the Son of God; and this, from one perspective, because God *produces* him. Milton uses the word *produce* two other times in *Paradise Regained*, and each occurrence, in its own way, makes the same point: God, and God alone, truly produces. The second occurrence is when Jesus "fervently" (*PR* 3.121) rebuts Satan's condemnation of God for God's desire to have glory. Satan concludes his harangue: "'From us his foes pronounced glory he exacts'" (*PR* 3.120). Jesus then responds:

'And reason; *since his word all things produced,*
Though chiefly not for glory as prime end,
But to show forth his goodness, *and impart*
His good communicable to every soul
Freely.' [*PR* 3.122–26; emphasis added]

Not least important about this passage is its clear implication in the Neoplatonic doctrine of creation.[4] And the verb *impart* in this context goes far toward validating my earlier claims about the importance of *part* and *pair* in *Paradise Lost* (chapter 1 above). But more important for present purposes is the evidence that Milton is obviously willing to conceive of creation as the *product* of God's Word. Creation and productivity, then, are synonymous, and this because, as I argued earlier (also in chapter 1), they are differentiation, the opposite of Satan's eternal confusion. Because of this confusion, of course, Satan himself can produce nothing but the anti-product Death (see chapter 5 above); and this incapacity for production is the burden of the third occurrence of the word *produce:*

'The kingdoms of the world to thee were given,
Permitted rather, and by thee usurped,
Other donation none thou canst *produce:*
If given, by whom but by the King of kings,
God over all supreme?
. . . .
    Wert thou so void of fear or shame,
As offer them to me the Son of God,
To me my own.' [*PR* 4.182–86, 189–91; emphasis added]

God is "over all supreme"; everything is his. Hence, Satan, confused precisely in that he considers creation his own, offers the Son of God what is already his by right of his title. "'Other donation [grant, bestowal of property] none [can he] produce'."[5] Satan can create nothing of or on his own. He forfeited the right to difference long ago. He *makes* no difference.

The issue of productivity brings us, at this last occurrence of the word *produce*, to the closely related and equally important issue of property, which we must address before returning to the concept of doubt and its role in the poem. Satan often claims property to be his (see, for example, *PR* 1.442; 2.449; 4.160–65, 185) when, as part of his punishment, it is improper for him to own any property. Property presupposes difference, and the difference of property is always sin-

gular (both one and strange, or peculiar). But difference and singularity are impossible for Satan, who confuses and is confused;
Satan lost all right to distinction when he first chose non-differentiation.

The perfect man, however, owns all property, because he
re(-)signs of his own free will all rights to distinction: by giving up,
entirely and freely, his desire (from which would flow his claims) to
be different, unique, important, famous, what have you, (and let us
acknowledge that only the Son of God could do that), he receives in
return complete self-possession—he is the slave of no desire and is
therefore Lord of all creation (2 Cor. 6:10). Or, to put it now in the
words Milton assigns to Christ:

> 'Shall I seek glory then, as vain men seek
> Oft not deserved? *I seek not mine, but his*
> *Who sent me, and thereby witness whence I am.*
>
> . . . .
>
> Yet so much bounty is in God, such grace,
> That who advance his glory, not their own,
> Them he himself to glory will advance.'
>
> [*PR* 3.105–07, 142–44; emphasis added]

We recognize here what in *Paradise Lost* is the argument of necessary
derivativeness (chapter 8 above); but in *Paradise Regained* it is further
developed to include what I will call the doctrine of appropriation by
expropriation:[6] " 'I seek not mine [expropriation], but his / Who sent
me, and thereby witness whence I am [appropriation]' "—the perfect
man is Son of God because he marks (scars, labels, soils, signs) nothing as his and therefore owns a share in all things. Say it in French,
where *propre* means "clean" as well as "own": the perfect man makes
nothing *non propre* (that is, not clean, or dirty) and therefore makes
everything *propre* (that is, his own because clean or, more important
for Milton and the study of Milton, pure). Said in either French or
English, the truth is the same: property is derivativeness.

Christ's relation to, and understanding of, property demonstrate
his origin (*PR* 3.107). They attest his sonship (*PR* 1.37, 122), where
Milton's use of *attest* also suggests the struggle or agon or duel which
Christ must undergo to prove his derivation from God. His success in
this test or trial consists in his repeatedly *dis*proving any and all
doubts regarding his sonship, including, as he clearly recognizes, his
own:

'What if he hath decreed that I shall first
Be *tried* in humble state, and things *adverse*,
By tribulations, injuries, insults,
Contempts, and scorns, and snares, and violence,
Suffering, abstaining, quietly expecting
Without *distrust or doubt*, that he may know
What I can suffer, how obey? Who best
Can suffer, best can do; best reign, who first
Well hath *obeyed*; just *trial* ere I *merit*
My exaltation without change or end.'

[*PR* 3.188–97; emphasis added]

The vocabulary of this speech informs us of a good deal, but, most important, it tells us that "distrust," or faithlessness, and "doubt" are a pair, almost synonymous; and thus it confirms my earlier claims that the trial of Christ's obedience is also the trial of his faith. And repeatedly his faith is greater than Satan's des(-)pair, his singularity purer than Satan's fragmentariness—Satan can never im-pair (him from) God, for God and Christ are truly whole.

Take, for example, the attempt, likewise a failure, through hunger and food in Book 2 (*PR* 2.302–405), an example especially attractive since Milton again raises the issue of property. After describing the banquet Satan sets before Christ, Milton has the Tempter ask:

'What *doubts* the Son of God to sit and eat?
These are not fruits forbidden, no interdict
Defends the touching of these viands pure,
Their taste no knowledge works, at least of evil,
But life preserves, destroys life's enemy,
Hunger, with sweet restorative delight.
All these are spirits of air, and woods, and springs,
Thy gentle ministers, who come to pay
Thee homage, and acknowledge thee their Lord:
What *doubt'st* thou Son of God? Sit down and eat.'

[*PR* 2.368–77; emphasis added]

The temptation here is subtle but powerful. We must unpack Satan's question if we would grasp his design. Note that he uses the title "Son of God" at both the beginning and the end of his invitation. If Jesus is Son of God, then he is alone, without any possible double—Satan knows this, at least as what he fears. If Jesus has no double anywhere, then he, the Son of God, can claim anything he wants without the fear, the doubt, that someone else might claim it as his. If the Son of God is one (both unity and singular) then he need not doubt, he need not fear a double. Inversely—and this is Satan's trap—if Jesus *does* doubt, then he proves, through his fear, the possibility of a double, and that possibility would then be the chink through which Satan could emerge triumphant—he would gladly be that double. Satan's question also asks, then, Are you truly one? Alone the Son of God? Singular? More on this in a moment.

Jesus responds in the one way, the only way, to avoid Satan's trap—"temperately":

> To whom thus Jesus temperately replied:
> 'Said'st thou not that to all things I had right?
> And who withholds my power that right to use?
> Shall I receive by gift what of my own,
> When and where likes me best, I can command?
> *I can at will, doubt not, as soon as thou,*
> Command a table in this wilderness.'
>
> [*PR* 2.378–84; emphasis added]

"This perfect man," defeats Satan, because, in his absolute and complete difference, he owns everything (*propre*) by making nothing dirty or soiled (*non propre*) with intemperate desire. And because alone perfect man could do this, and because there is only one perfect man ("by merit"), then this perfect man has no double, and therefore he is truly Son of God. That this argument is the correct one Jesus himself confirms when he says: "'I can at will, doubt not, as soon as thou,/ Command a table in this wilderness'." In other words, do *not*, Satan, think to *double* me with yourself ("'*doubt* not'"), for so little are you my double (peer, equal, and so on) that I can do whatever you can do ("'as soon as thou'"); and I prove this by choosing *not* to do what you do, thus avoiding the trap of becoming *your* double, mimicking you.

Jesus (and Milton) makes the same point earlier, when Satan first suggests providing food. Satan asks:

> 'Tell me if food were now before thee set,
> Wouldst thou not eat?'   [*PR* 2.320–21]

Jesus immediately answers: "'Thereafter as I *like* / The giver'" (*PR* 2.321–22; emphasis added). Here the verb *to like* is creatively dual, suggesting not only affection but also resemblance, and thus, here too, Jesus resists doubling Satan—he does not like this giver. In both instances (and in all others), Jesus remains singular, alone. He chooses to be himself. He chooses not to be God—he performs no miracle—and therefore he remains himself, man, and by remaining man, he utterly defeats Satan.[7]

Satan, "as mute confounded what to say" (*PR* 3.2) more than once, must ultimately concede to Christ, " 'Thou shalt be what thou art ordained, *no doubt*' " (*PR* 4.473; emphasis added) where the irony, in the seemingly harmless tag "no doubt," which is indeed mute to him, measures the full extent of his miserable confusion (and testifies additionally to the dexterity of Milton's idiom). Furthermore, he must " 'confess [that I] have found thee

> *Proof* against all temptation as a rock
> Of adamant, and as a centre, firm
> To the utmost of *mere man* both wise and good,
> Not more; for honours, riches, kingdoms, glory
> Have been before contemned, and may again.'
> [*PR* 4.532–37; emphasis added]

This much confessed—and so much confused—he continues:

> 'Therefore to know what more thou art than man,
> Worth naming Son of God by voice from heaven,
> Another method I must now begin.' [*PR* 4.538–40]

Satan's confusion, of course, is the "mere" (*PR* 4.535); he confuses humans and men, construing humans to be men, which none of them has been or yet is—men begin to be possible only after the Crucifixion and the Resurrection, after Christ's example. Satan does not comprehend, cannot comprehend, that a man is the Son of God, " 'for Son of God to [him] is yet *in doubt*' " (*PR* 4.501), and he does not know

> 'In what degree or meaning thou art called
> The Son of God, which bears *no single sense;*
> The Son of God I also am, or was,
> And if I was, I am; relation stands;
> All men are Sons of God; yet thee I thought
> In some respect far higher so declared.' [*PR* 4.516–21]

We should by now be able to see quite clearly the confusion in this pivotal moment of Satan's argument (and also in his identical claims in Book 4 [*PR* 4.196–200]). Because he is himself confused and forever "despoiled" (*PR* 3.139) of singularity, because ambiguity is part of his diet, Satan cannot penetrate the coverings of signs to the "single sense" of the "Son of God." He does not know the difference between "this perfect man" and angels, on the one hand, and "men" (that is, humans) on the other. Moreover, his claim that "'relation stands'" is an equivocation, purposely confusing the issue; the issue is not relation—of course, all men are sons of God—the issue is singularity, and Satan avoids singularity as only duplicity can. He even goes as far, for example, as to call Christ by his own name, "Adversary" (*PR* 4.527; see also *PL* 2.629), in his desperate attempt to subvert the singularity of the Son.

But all ploys fail him. He still cannot (can never) be sure (not double). Hence, his final, extreme recourse to the "highest pinnacle" (*PR* 4.549), where he tries to make Christ double by this time making him double as God:

> 'There stand, if thou wilt stand; to stand upright
> Will ask thee skill; I to thy Father's house
> Have brought thee, and highest placed, highest is best,
> Now show thy progeny; if not to stand,
> Cast thyself down; safely if Son of God.'   [*PR* 4.551–55]

If Christ falls and dies, this means that he was merely human, and Satan has won. If he stands, either alone or with the aid of angels, or if he casts himself down and angels preserve him, then Satan can claim, though only on the strength of appearances, that he really is God in disguise; and again, he, Satan, has won. Therefore, Christ does neither:

> To whom thus Jesus: Also it is written,
> Tempt not the Lord thy God, he said and stood.   [*PR* 4.560–61]

Christ, the perfect man, quotes the Law instead, and quotes the Law where it says (Deut. 6:16): "'Ye shall not tempt [i.e., make trial of, test] the Lord your God'."[8] You shall not double (make trial of, test, duel, copy, mimic) the Lord God. What amazes Satan (*PR* 4.562) is not the standing, which technically is *his* victory anyway, but the perfect faith which perfectly obeys by simply refusing to tempt the Lord God. In other words, the standing is not the differential—Satan has that eventuality covered—rather, the quotation of Scripture, which is perfect humility as well as perfect obedience and perfect faith, is the differential, the wild card, the option, which Satan could not have predicted so as to double it. As for the oft-debated ambiguity in the quotation—which, if it existed, would imply that Jesus is " 'the Lord thy God' "—the syntax precludes it.[9] Milton writes "and stood" *after* the quotation to suggest that the standing is the product of the humility, obedience, and faith. Had he been interested in suggesting, ambiguously, that Jesus is the Lord God, he could have and, I think, would have, written the lines so that the standing came first, in which case the quotation would have been a scriptural substantiation of the Deity revealed in the miraculous feat. Had Milton written the lines this way: "To whom thus Jesus, who stood, then said, / Also it is written, tempt not the Lord thy God," we would have had to feel the quotation as an illustration of the Deity revealed. But Milton was not interested in suggesting that Jesus is the Lord God, any more than he was interested in committing ambiguities. His entire point was, and is, that Jesus is the *Son* of God, a perfect man. Hence, if we have followed and understood Milton's argument up to this point, we can see clearly that, in this, as in all the other instances, Christ does not doubt (double); rather he keeps his faith, perfectly and singularly; he obeys. As for standing, that comes later—first and foremost is to love the Lord thy God with all thy heart.

The product of such love will be, and is, man, who can then love his neighbor as himself—that is, as singular and different. This, I believe, is why Milton likens Satan, falling from the pinnacle, to the Sphinx (*PR* 4.572–76): the simile cannot fail to bring to mind the answer which made the Sphinx "cast herself headlong from the Ismenian steep" (*PR* 5.575)—namely, man.[10] Satan, like the Sphinx, has been answered with "man." In his case, moreover, the answer was given by the perfect man, who is perfect because of his utter singularity, his difference. And his difference from Oedipus, who also answered "man," is precisely difference, for Oedipus is all male humans, who love their mothers and desire to kill their fathers; Oedipus is the incarnation of identity, Christ the incarnation of difference,[11] and hence, Milton's revision of the pagan myth in the very act of invoking it. Christ is the man whom Oedipus is still (and always) struggling to become. Christ is perfect, whole and complete; Oedipus is incomplete, still confused with his father and mother.

Christ, in his difference and singularity, has " 'now . . . avenged

> *Supplanted* Adam, and, by vanquishing
> Temptation, [has] regained lost Paradise.'
>
> [*PR* 4.606–08; emphasis added]

So much, of course, is just and proper, for "vengeance is mine, saith the Lord" (Deut. 32:35; Rom. 12:19), and Christ is the Word of the Lord, in this case (so to speak) uttering vengeance. In addition to being faithful to Scripture, Milton here also completes the horticultural image begun in *Paradise Lost:* Satan who *supplanted* Adam is now and forever after supplanted by Christ, in whom, since he is the perfect man, all humans may henceforth "'live transplanted'" (*PL* 3.293) *as* men and women. Finally, Milton concludes his argument about doubt and doubling with the crucial statement that Christ regains Paradise "by vanquishing temptation": temptation (trial, agon, duel) is the doubling by which some "'fair appearing good'" (*PL* 9.354) seems to give me to myself by giving me what I want, but, in fact, actually takes me from myself by fixing me in its illusion or version of what I want. Christ vanquishes temptation because he is never doubled by desire; he never doubts what he desires—he desires the Father's will ("'I and the Father are one'" [John 10:30]). Dual, therefore, and never double, he dares to be singularly good.

12

Samson:
Son of the Same,
Victim of Confusion

Near the end of *Samson Agonistes*, after Manoa has learned the manner of his son's death, he declares:

> 'Samson hath quit himself
> Like Samson, and heroicly hath finished
> A life heroic.'   [*SA* 1709–11]

In form, "'Samson hath quit himself / Like Samson'" is a fallen simile: one appears to generate two across a *like* (*as*)—note how enjambement stresses *like*—which would seem to be the simulacrum of *is*. In structure, however, this fallen simile is redeemed and redeemable, for "Samson" the name is different from Samson the man. There are two terms here, not just one—and the point is that the man finally lives up to and into his name—Samson by his death becomes a word—and therefore, this fallen but redeemed simile is the meaning, and the meaningfulness, of the play. Moreover, Samson is able to become "Samson"—that is, meaning is made—because, as Manoa also says a few lines later, Samson has done "'all this

> With God not *parted from* him, as was feared,
> But favouring and assisting to the end.'
>   [*SA* 1718–20; emphasis added]

The accuracy of the poetry is beautiful. Indeed God is not *parted from* Samson but is the *part of* Samson, paired with him, which re-pairs Samson to his name. Milton probably understood "Samson" to mean "there the second time,"[1] and in fact the play does dramatize how,

[169]

with God re-pairing him, Samson (if I may) "Samsons"—that is, arrives "there the second time" at his name or essence, from whence he fell, apart from God, into doubleness and doubt, by doubling his (and God's) secret with Dalilah. The play, in a word, enacts the meaning of Samson's name.[2]

Samson the Nazarite becomes a second time "separate to God"; Jesus of Nazareth, "by merit called" Son of God (*PR* 1.166), never falls, never parts from the Father, and therefore never has to submit to "secondariness" or doubleness. He remains always Lord of Difference. The word *Nazarite*, Carey observes, "is derived from Heb. *nazar*, 'to separate oneself', and the angel says to Samson's mother, *Judges* xiii 7: 'The child shall be a Nazarite unto God'."[3] As long as Samson remained separate to God, pairing himself with God alone, he was pure (a Puritan is also a Nazarite) and stronger than any man alive. When, however, he paired himself with Dalilah, he could not remain separate to God. He could not resist her temptation, which is unambiguously the temptation of sex;[4] and we must note here, since obviously Samson and Christ are to be compared and contrasted, that in *Paradise Regained*, Milton goes out of his way to insist, through Satan's response to Belial's suggested strategy, that Christ is impervious to sexual temptation (*PR* 2.147–234). Samson, however, is *not* a "perfect man" (*PR* 1.166), and so, as Carey quite rightly remarks, he must suffer the sexual temptation of Dalilah a second time and this time resist.[5] The first time, of course, he yielded, and thus he parted from God into doubleness—or, in the play's precision, into confusion.

After Dalilah's departure, the chorus muse long on the painful mystery of woman. First they wonder:

> 'Is it for that such outward ornament
> Was lavished on their sex, that inward gifts
> Were left for haste *unfinished*, judgement scant,
> Capacity not raised to apprehend
> Or value what is best
> In choice, but oftest to affect the wrong?
> Or was too much self-love *mixed*.'   [*SA* 1025–31; emphasis added]

And here "unfinished" and "mixed" point to confusion as the flaw in woman. Then they go on to complain:

> 'Whate'er it be, to wisest men and best
> Seeming at first all heavenly under virgin veil,
> Soft, modest, meek, demure,
> Once *joined*, the *contrary* she proves, a thorn
> Intestine, far within defensive arms
> A *cleaving* mischief, in his way to virtue
> *Adverse* and turbulent, or by her charms
> Draws him *awry* enslaved
> With dotage, and his sense *depraved*
> To folly and shameful deed which *ruin* ends.
> What pilot so expert but needs must wreck
> Embarked with such a steers-mate at the helm?'
>
>   [*SA* 1034–45; emphasis added]

Here again the vocabulary cannot fail to suggest that woman leaves man confused and in confusion. But the chorus (and Milton) are most direct at the end of their speech:

> 'Therefore God's universal law
> Gave to the man despotic power
> Over his female in due awe,
> Nor from that right to part an hour,
> Smile she or lour:
> So shall he least *confusion* draw
> On his whole life, not swayed
> By female usurpation, nor dismayed.'
>
>   [*SA* 1053–60; emphasis added]

Woman, we might as well say, with Chaucer's wit, *is* confusion: "'Mulier est hominis confusio'."[6] And though, as we shall have occasion to discuss at length later, Milton would have brooked no such "inter*mixing* comic stuff with tragic sadness and gravity" ("Of That Sort of Dramatic Poem . . . ," line 28; emphasis added), we can still learn from Chaucer's text how insistent is the tradition of misogyny in which Milton's chorus inserts itself.

 Woman, and especially Dalilah, is confusion. And Samson's lot, once he has re(-)signed to Dalilah his "'part from heaven assigned'" (*SA* 1207) is thus to be no longer distinct or separate unto God, but a victim of confusion. When the chorus first see him, he "'lies *at random, carelessly diffused*'" (*SA* 118; emphasis added). Moreover, and of course more terrible, he is blind, and he suffers thus that "universal blanc" (*PL* 3.48) which Milton knew so well; then, too, this "blanc" is

itself confusion, as Samson indirectly acknowledges when he assures
Manoa that God will " 'with confusion blank [Dagon's] worshipers' "
(*SA* 471)—to see a blank, then, is also to see confusion. Again, when
Samson meets his end (and his name) in the temple of Dagon, he is
with the Philistians " 'immixed' " (*SA* 1657), or confused, and, per-
haps most chilling, he pulls " 'down the *same* destruction on himself' "
(*SA* 1658; emphasis added). Milton goes on to inflect this crucial
observation with the terms of Greek tragedy:

> '. . . and now li'st victorious
> Among thy slain self-killed
> Not willingly, but *tangled in the fold*,
> *Of dire necessity*, whose law in death *conjoined*
> Thee with thy slaughtered foes in number more
> Than all thy life had slain before.'   [*SA* 1663–68; emphasis added]

We will see eventually that these terms are important for Milton's
purification of tragedy, but for now we need only note how the words
tangled, fold, and *conjoined* continue, if in a different rhetoric, the
emphasis on confusion.

This emphasis is supported by an ancillary emphasis on *twice,
double* or *doubt*, and similar terms or concepts. The angel who foretold
Samson's birth did so *twice* (Judges 13:3–5, 13.10–20; see also *SA* 24,
361, and 635), and Milton refers to this feature of Samson's career
several times, so as to underline how two-ness, or second-ness, figure
and indeed even pre-figure his life on earth. As for the word *doubt*, its
role in the poem is varied and complex, and it will take time to analyze
it. But this analysis, we shall see, continues along lines with which we
are by now quite familiar.

One of the first things Samson says in the play is:

> 'Yet stay, let me not rashly call in *doubt*
> Divine prediction.'   [*SA* 43–44; emphasis added]

Samson is now reluctant to doubt "divine prediction" because he
knows he has already doubled God by presuming the God-like right
in himself to divulge God's secret to Dalilah—which was at least to
doubt the swiftness of God's anger and punishment. But that punishment, not only swift, is also exact (as is Milton). He who doubt-
ed/doubled God now suffers a miserable singleness (the anti-number
to Christ's "singularity" [*PR* 3.57]), which almost becomes the murderous singleness of Spenser's Despaire—Samson's near suicide (cf.

SA 1584) Milton only just succeeds in characterizing otherwise.[7] And if Samson, as he himself maintains, "'despair[s] not of his [God's] final pardon'" (*SA* 1171), he is able to assume this stance, not only because of "'plain heroic magnitude of mind'" (*SA* 1279), but also because he is "'with *celestial* vigour armed'" (*SA* 1280; emphasis added). Were he not dualed with such vigour, he would "'scarce half. . .seem to live, dead more than half'" (*SA* 79; also 100) as he knows right from the start—his singleness the fragmentariness, the halved unwhole(some)ness, of the self sundered from God.

And yet, if halved, if nearly des-paired, Samson must at the same time suffer a cruelly ironic doubleness. The structure of human life is dual: we must be partnered. If sundered from our partner, left alone, we must again partner, or else we die. Hence, we split and fragment ourselves. Thus, for example, Samson recognizes "'Myself, my sepulchre, a moving grave'" (*SA* 102); and the chorus clearly recognize also that, as they put it to him:

'Thou art become (O worst imprisonment!)
The dungeon of thyself . . . '   [*SA* 155–56]

To have become the grave or dungeon of himself, Samson must have doubled, but precisely by halving, so as to become both incarcerated and incarcerator (cf. *PL* 6:181). Sundered from unity (which, of course, is *not* singleness) with his Maker, which alone makes unity in the self, Samson must suffer "a living death" (*SA* 100), living as the grave in which he is dead—brutal confusion.

This cruel reflexivity ("'Myself, my sepulchre'"), this doubleness by halving, which "'portend[s]'" (*SA* 590) to Samson "'*double* darkness near at hand'" (*SA* 593; emphasis added), is often the rhetorical form which his punishment takes. It is wise to proceed cautiously here, this is so important a point. Samson once

     'single *combatant*
Duelled their armies ranked in proud array,
Himself an army, [but is] now [an] unequal match
To save himself against a coward armed
At one spear's length.'   [*SA* 344–48; emphasis added]

In this diminishment he confesses that

'Nothing of all these evils hath befall'n me
But justly; I *myself* have brought them on,
Sole author I, sole cause.'   [*SA* 374–76; emphasis added]

where I assume, Milton means us to understand that Samson realizes
that "sole" is the anti-number, the contradiction, of Manoa's "single"
(*SA* 344) in the sense "singular." Moreover, Samson also clearly understands how he became himself sole author, sole cause: " 'She
sought to make me traitor to myself' " (*SA* 401). Dalilah turned Samson against himself (and thus away from God) by confusing all three
of them in Samson's mind: " 'foul effeminacy held me yoked / Her
bond-slave' " (*SA* 410–11)—where the confusion of female and male
leads to the confusion also of woman and Deity, which is Samson's
self-betrayal.[8] Samson "effeminate" has paired with Dalilah, and,
paired with her, he has parted from God, to make *her* his god. He has
thus diminished himself—that is, lost his strength and in this way
betrayed himself. And it is the very same confusion with which
Dalilah tempts him the second time.

Dalilah has come, as Samson clearly perceives, " 'to try / Her husband' " (*SA* 754–55), or, since "trial is by what is contrary," to double him; so it is that she offers him her " '*redoubled* love and care' "
(*SA* 923), " 'not *doubting*'," she says, the " 'favourable ear' " of the
Philistian lords to whom she will sue for his release (*SA* 920–21). To
persuade him to accept this offer, she must exonerate herself, and to
that end she claims, " 'Ere I to thee, *thou to thyself* was cruel' " (*SA*
784; emphasis added). Milton thus continues the insistence on reflexivity, and Samson later agrees with her:

> 'I gave, thou say'st, the example,
> I led the way; bitter reproach, but true,
> I *to myself* was false ere thou to me.'   [*SA* 822–24; emphasis added]

Having reopened the division within Samson, the doubling by halving, Dalilah plays her trump:

> 'Let weakness then with weakness come to parle
> So near related, or *the same of kind*,
> Thine forgive mine.'   [*SA* 785–87; emphasis added]

This is Milton at his most brilliant: Dalilah all but says to Samson, We
are identical. In this case, of course (and this is her intent), she would
be indeed " 'Fearless . . . of *partners* in [her] love' " (*SA* 810; emphasis
added), since not even God would have a part in Samson any longer.

This second time, however, Samson is not, he says, "'so unwary or accursed

> To bring my feet again into the snare
> Where once I have been caught.' [*SA* 930–32]

where "accursed" bodes the precise threat of doubleness. Rather, this time he turns Dalilah's temptation against her, saying:

> 'Such pardon therefore as I give to my folly,
> Take to thy wicked deed: which when thou seest
> Im*part*ial, *self-severe*, inexorable,
> Thou wilt renounce thy seeking, and much rather
> Confess it feigned.' [*SA* 826–29; emphasis added]

Of course, he knows that Dalilah will not imitate him, since, as he says, "'Thou and I long since are *twain*'" (*SA* 929; emphasis added). But still, it is a solace to turn the tables on her, for doing so reinaugurates his identity—Dalilah will *not* imitate him because he is Samson, himself again, singularly. In this moment, the reflexivity, though still punitive and painful, becomes for Samson a remedy (though hardly the final remedy) since, "self-severe," and no longer just "'self-displeased for self-offense'" (*SA* 514–15), he can sever the not-self (Dalilah) from himself so as to begin to become whole again, separate to God again, himself.

Reflexivity has become the antidote to reflexivity. Thus Milton prepares for the single most important structural point in the play, a point at once theological and dramaturgical. Samson goes on in the same speech to condemn Dalilah by turning her self-exculpation against her:

> 'But love constrained thee; call it furious rage
> To satisfy thy lust: love seeks to have love.' [*SA* 836–37]

To grasp fully exactly where we are in Milton's conception, we must now reread the opening of the preface to *Samson Agonistes:*

> Tragedy, as it was anciently composed, hath been ever held the gravest, moralest, and most profitable of all other poems: therefore said by Aristotle to be of power by raising pity and fear, or terror, to purge the mind of those and such-like passions, that is to temper and reduce them to just measure with a kind of delight, stirred up by reading or seeing those passions well imitated. Nor is nature wanting in her own effects to make good his assertion: for so in physic things of

> melancholic hue and quality are used against melancholy, sour
> against sour, salt to remove salt humours.[9]

Homeopathy, which of course, is what Milton invokes here, is ancient and venerable therapy.[10] But Milton has more in mind ultimately than just therapy. His ultimate concern is in fact the difference of the same.[11]

Love seeks to have love, reflexivity heals reflexivity, pity and terror purge pity and terror: in these cases, the same conjoins with the same, and yet confusion does not ensue, any more than it does when "'Samson hath quit himself / Like Samson'." For the same is the same because it is different. Here we are dealing, of course, with what Milton elsewhere treated under the topic of equality (chapters 8 and 9 above), "for equality cannot exist except between two or more essences," where "essences" are understood to be different entities. Two entities are equal—that is to say, they are the same—if and only if sufficient difference exists between them to effect their concord. Milton explores this mystery in *Samson Agonistes* chiefly through its failure ever to obtain. Samson and Dalilah do *not* love each other: there is, alternately either too much difference between them (Jew and Philistian, for example) or too little (they lust after each other as identical carnal objects). Samson and Dalilah prove, but only through the tragic consequences of their failure to love each other, that "love seeks to have love."

The spectacle of pity and terror purges pity and terror because I (the audience) am the same as the great tragic hero (in humanity, not stature) except for the one crucial difference, that I am not enduring his sufferings, which has the all-important consequence that I can reflect, or think, as well as feel.[12] Similar in structure is the mystery of love. Love seeks to have love because love is the will toward the other's difference within the sameness of the two.[13] In love, one person wills the being, which is the difference, of another person. Love makes my beloved a person—real, live, awake, unique, important, different—while at the same time somehow mine, the same as me, my mate. My love, then, seeks from my beloved love in return, or the affimation of my equal but opposite difference, importance, uniqueness, awakening, life, reality. Love is the difference of a being, and thus love is also the being of difference. Indeed, this is the whole point of *Paradise Regained*, that in Jesus, love, or difference, becomes incarnate: in love with Jesus, man becomes wholly himself, different.

What Samson, "son of the same,"[14] does not receive in his mortal life is the difference of the same. Dalilah covets to make him *her*, not just hers. However, her jealousy (*SA* 803–14) is as nothing compared with that of God (*SA* 1375). God will have Samson, though only after proving in Samson's flesh that he alone makes a difference. Otherwise deprived of the difference that completes (that is, makes the same), Samson lives in doubleness, though always resisting doubt, and cannot achieve his name until he has purified or separated himself again. Similarly deprived of the difference that completes by the "intermixing comic stuff with tragic sadness and gravity," modern tragedy, as Milton sees it, remains in confusion, unable to achieve its name, until he, Milton, purifies it by returning it "there the second time" to its pristine condition (defined in his introduction to the play): just as Samson in the end quits himself like Samson, so Milton's tragedy quits itself like tragedy—

> His [God's] servants he with new acquist
> Of true experience from this great event
> With peace and consolation hath dismissed,
> And calm of mind all passion spent.   [*SA* 1755–58]

As Samson becomes truly himself, so tragedy becomes truly itself (cathartic). We will encounter this analogy between Samson and tragedy again, but most important to recognize and understand is that repetition with difference is the fundamental similarity which bridges the analogy.

Repetition *without* difference, however, is what Samson must suffer while he is an exile in doubleness and confusion; as he himself clearly recognizes, he is "'. . . reserved alive to be *repeated* / The subject of their cruelty, or scorn'" (*SA* 645–46; emphasis added). Only when he has succeeded, with the aid of "'secret refreshings, that *repair* his strength'" (*SA* 665; emphasis added), in returning "there a second time" to his name, can true repetition with difference—namely, the story in the book of Judges or in Milton's play—purify his story of the Philistian insistence on "'the subject of their cruelty, or scorn'." We may pause here to note that the "persistent use of rhetorical figures involving repetition," often remarked in *Samson Agonistes*, probably finds its ground and explanation in the bearing of repetition on Samson's life and his tragic end.[15] His very name can be construed as "repetition"; while the meaning of Milton's play, as well as of Samson's life, arguably is his opportunity to repeat, so as not to make the same mistake twice—to repeat, that is, with a difference, once he is repaired with God. Samson's salvation, such as it is, lies with repetition, and, as we shall see, with being repeated (by and in fame). Until this moment of redeeming repetition, however, he is "repeated" or endlessly copied in Philistian " 'cruelty [and] scorn'," even as he repeats or copies himself, in animal drudgery " 'at the mill with slaves' " (*SA* 41). Until such time, he must ever find the hand of God, in the words of the chorus, " 'so various, / Or might I say *contrarious*' " (*SA* 668–69; emphasis added), that trial or temptation is persistent; and most persistent—far more than Dalilah's ever could be—is the trial or temptation of doubt, naked unbelief.

Samson's heroism is the conquest of doubt. And the attraction of the character Samson for the man Milton must have been greatest on just this score, for doubt, especially after his blindness, must have plagued Milton cruelly. Hence the two crucial occasions in the play, both in the voice of the chorus, when doubt is addressed and exposed as error:

> 'Yet more there be who doubt his ways not just,
> As to his own edicts, found contradicting,
> Then give the reins to wandering thought,
> Regardless of his glory's diminution;
> Till by their own perplexities involved
> They ravel more, still less resolved,
> But never find self-satisfying solution.
>   As if they would confine the interminable,
> And tie him to his own prescript,
> Who made our laws to bind us, not himself,
> And hath full right to exempt
> Whom so it pleases him.'   [*SA* 300–11]

>   'All is best, though we oft doubt,
> What the unsearchable dispose
> Of highest wisdom brings about,
> And ever best found in the close.'   [*SA* 1745–49]

These two passages frame, as it were, the central action of the play, or the temptations of Samson to doubt a *second* time. The first passage, incomparably the greater poetry and (to my mind) one of the finest passages in Milton, brings into clear focus the relationships among doubt, confusion, and reflexivity. Those who doubt the justice of God's ways "ravel" or "become entangled"[16] and "never find self-satisfying solution": and this precisely because in doubt or doubleness, the self is halved. With one half trying to convince the other half or trying to serve, haltingly, as the principle of wholeness for the other, the self can never satisfy itself but can always only be trying to satisfy itself—without an other to complete it, the self cannot find "self-satisfying solution."

In evil, there is no true other, only the illusion of an other. This is the wisdom that grounds Milton's poetry, early and late. Doubt, which can be, but is not necessarily, the beginning of evil, exposes the problem of the other in the structure of the self. Having seen how this exposition unfolds, we can deepen our understanding (and admiration) of Milton's wisdom by turning to a speech in *Comus* the special emphasis of which we are now prepared to hear:

> 'But evil on itself shall back recoil,
> And mix no more with goodness, when at last
> Gathered like scum, and settled to itself
> It shall be in eternal restless change
> Self-fed, and self-consum'd, if this fail,
> The pillared firmament is rottenness,
> And earth's base built on stubble.'   [*C* 592–98]

These are the words of a young man, not only in the masque, but also in reality—Milton was twenty-six when he wrote them—but it is a measure of that young man's courage and strength that he maintained the faith of these words all his life. As Carey notes, these lines are an important gloss on the figure of Sin in *Paradise Lost* (lines 798–800), and as we can clearly see, they also apply to the words of the chorus in *Samson Agonistes*, above all in their insistence on the cursed reflexivity of evil. Not only do the lines describe the self-raveling of evil with the word "recoil"—which will later be predicated of Satan (*PL* 4.17)—and stress the confusion caused by evil ("mix . . . with goodness"), they also state four times the *self*ishness of evil, and thus they fittingly support the insight of the chorus, that doubt can never find "self-satisfying solution."

And yet the misery and remorseless absurdity of human existence (an animal that thinks?) are such, it can and will be countered, that doubt, if not complete unbelief, is the only viable posture open to us, a posture certainly superior to blind faith. But Milton counters in turn—and again, it is the voice of the young Milton in *Comus* (line 518)—that " 'unbelief is blind'." And I have no doubt that he would have gone on to argue that the blind have this advantage over the sighted, that they can see how much faith or belief *can* see. It is the blind Samson, who must see with the eyes of faith, who says, with full understanding of what he is saying,

> 'God, when he gave me strength, to show withal
> How slight the gift was, hung it in my hair.'   [*SA* 58–59]

The issue is one of self-sufficiency. Can a man accrue to himself enough power and material possession to make himself proof against the inherent frailty of human flesh? The twentieth-century response, we know, is, yes, of course he can (if he has enough money). But Milton's response (in concert with not a few others) is, no, he cannot. For precisely in believing that he can, he proves that he cannot: the man who would be absolutely self-sufficient is so disastrously divided within himself that he has erected one-half of himself, namely his body, into a deity in whose service he will then stop at nothing. As Samson says, ironically, the second time the Philistian messenger summons him to play before the lords: " 'And for a life who will not change his purpose? / (So mutable are all the ways of men)' " (*SA* 1406–07). The merely human, for a life, for the flesh, will ditch any obligation and die content in his bed because of never having been distended or strained by the contents of man.

Samson, however, is almost a man, more than merely human; moreover, he is now a blind man, and therefore frail, whereas once he was the strongest man alive. Hence faith for him is something more than blind. Samson began life almost like Jesus, a "perfect man" (*PR* 1.166). But not quite. And it requires his disability now to teach him his original lack. Only he who is not whole understands what it takes truly to be whole. Late in the action of the play, the chorus remark of Samson:

> 'For never was from heaven *imparted*
> *Measure of strength so great to mortal seed,*
> As in thy wondrous actions hath been seen.'
>   [*SA* 1438–40; emphasis added]

God im-parted himself with Samson to partner with him his invincible strength, but he did not—and who can "confine the interminable" with the question (and term) why?—impart to him, Samson learns at last, an equal measure of wisdom:

> 'But what is strength without a double share
> Of wisdom?'   [*SA* 53–54]

> 'Immeasurable strength they might behold
> In me, of wisdom nothing more than mean;
> This with the other should, at least, have *paired*,
> These two proportioned ill drove me transverse.'
>   [*SA* 206–09; emphasis added]

Samson now knows that his "matchless . . . might" (*SA* 178) was not paired with wisdom.[17] He knows now that God did not endow him with that "double share" of wisdom which would have tripled him in relation to ordinary humans (one measure of surpassing strength plus two measures of wisdom). He, like every human, was left incomplete. Carey notes that "this aspect of M.'s Samson, his weak-mindedness, is not emphasized either in *Judges* or in the Christian tradition of Samson literature.'[18] Milton adds this feature, I believe, precisely to stress the difference between Samson and Jesus, especially since, in the whole of the Western Christian tradition, Christ the Son is assimilated to the attribute of Wisdom in the Trinity. Samson lacks what Christ is, he lacks the Son of God. But his faith makes up the difference.

We must never forget that Samson is an Old Testament hero and thus that he cannot be saved in the Christian sense of redemption. This accounts, I suspect, for the emphasis, which Milton assigns to Manoa, on death redeeming Samson. Manoa affirms before the chorus first that:

> 'His ransom, if my whole inheritance
> May compass it, shall willingly be paid
> And numbered down
>
> . . . .
> For his redemption all my patrimony,
> If need be, I am ready to forgo
> And quit: not wanting him, I shall want nothing.'
>   [*SA* 1476–78, 1482–84]

Then later, when he learns of Samson's death, he exclaims:

> 'but death who sets all free
> Hath paid his ransom now and full discharge.'   [*SA* 1572–73]

In the Christian world, of course, it is the death of Christ which pays the ransom (see Mark 10:45) for man's redemption from the second death.[19] And Milton's language is probably meant precisely to contrast the Old Testament hero with the New Testament Son of God: death ransoms Samson from Philistian bondage; Christ, by dying, ransoms man from the bondage of sin and the second death. But where there is a contrast, there is also necessarily a comparison, and there is a sense in which Samson, by dying, redeems himself (if only himself); he is not a victim of the second death—after all, Milton writes precisely that "'Samson hath *quit* himself / Like Samson'," where the economic sense of *quit* ("repaid") is hardly mute.[20] Samson *is* like the Son of God, even though he is an Old Testament hero, in that his faith is great enough to accept death as the way to life ("And to the faithful death the gate of life'" [*PL* 12.571]). And such faith he finds in himself, because, though he is painfully incomplete, he is in one respect part of and partner with God.

This respect the chorus makes most explicit:

> 'So deal not with this once thy glorious champion,
> The image of thy strength, and mighty minister.'   [*SA* 705–06]

As Jesus is the "'true image of the Father'" (*PR* 4.596), so Samson is the image of God's strength and thus the dual (not the double) of God. And because he is the dual of God in this one respect, he is paired with God, and therefore never despairs of "'his final pardon'" (*SA* 1171). Rather, as he affirms before Harapha of Gath, "'My trust is in the living God'" (*SA* 1140), and this trust, this faith, enables him to quit himself like Samson. Indeed, Harapha provides the opposition through which Samson is able to *single* himself on the way back, the second time, to unity (re-pair) with God:

> 'And now [I Harapha] am come to see of whom such noise
> Hath walked about, and each limb to survey,
> If thy appearance answer loud report.
> *Sam.* The way to know were not to see but taste.
> *Har.* Dost thou already *single* me; I thought
> Gyves and the mill had tamed thee?'
>
>   [*SA* 1088–93; emphasis added]

Of course, *single* here means first of all "separate me out for combat,"²¹—and Milton's is apparently the first recorded use of it in this sense (*OED* S1: 81–2), but he chose the verb because it also enables him to suggest that in his contest of words with Harapha, Samson regains enough of himself, the Nazarite, to single someone *with* himself—he is sufficiently single to single Harapha (think of homeopathy again). If Harapha "taste[s]" Samson, Samson believes, he will know (have "sapience" of) Samson single (one) with the living God of Israel, and in believing this, Samson comes a second time to believe in himself, which is also now to believe in God.²² Hence Harapha speaks far more than he can possibly understand when he jeers at Samson " 'thy God . . . / Hath cut [thee] off / Quite from his people' " (*SA* 1156–58), because this is exactly what God has done, made a sacrifice of Samson ("cut off"—see chapter 4 again), so that Samson can serve him unqualifiedly, and this is also exactly what God is doing through the unwitting agency of Harapha himself, who is providing the opposition through which, a second time, Samson's virtue can awaken.

In their long and perplexed muse on the nature of woman, the chorus exclaim:

'Favoured of heaven who finds
One virtuous rarely found,
That in domestic good combines:
Happy that house! his way to peace is smooth:
But *virtue which breaks through all opposition,*
And all temptation can remove,
Most shines and most is acceptable above.'

[*SA* 1046–52; emphasis added]

After the sentence "Love seeks to have love," the affirmation in lines 1050–52 constitutes probably the next most important claim of the play. The play begins with Samson on the brink of despair; he draws back, however. Then the chorus lament with him over his condition. His father finds him next, much as Adam found Eve (*PL* 10.1013–28), too ready to " 'act in [his] own affliction' " (*SA* 503) and " 'self-rigorous' " to choose " 'death as due' " (*SA* 513). Then Dalilah tempts him a second time, but he resists, and having resisted is the better able to withstand and indeed "single" Harapha; whereupon, his virtue awake, he can perceive, though dimly still, the will of God. He says to the chorus:

> 'Yet that he may dispense with me or thee
> Present in temples at idolatrous rites
> For some important cause, thou needst not *doubt.*'
>
> [*SA* 1377–79; emphasis added]

They respond: " 'How thou wilt here come off surmounts my reach' " (*SA* 1380). He rejoins:

> 'Be of good courage, I begin to feel
> Some rousing motions in me which dispose
> To something extraordinary my thoughts.
> I with this messenger will go along,
> Nothing to do, be sure, that may dishonour
> Our Law, or stain my vow of Nazarite.
> If there be aught of presage in the mind,
> This day will be remarkable in my life
> By some great act, or of my days the last.'   [*SA* 1381–89]

His life then ends (and shortly thereafter the play, too) when he " 'pull[s] down the same destruction on himself' " (*SA* 1678) as on the Philistians, having announced to them first:

> 'Now of my own accord such other trial
> I mean to show you of my strength, yet greater;
> As with amaze shall strike all who behold.'   [*SA* 1643–45]

The accuracy of the poetry here is astonishing. Samson's " 'strength' " a second time has " '*virtue* [for] her mate' " (*SA* 173; emphasis added), and this renewed virtue breaks through all opposition, removing temptation as well.

Virtue breaks through opposition by piercing the confusion and illusion which vice opposes to it. Every vice is the perversion of a virtue: it is that virtue confused with a version of it which is illusory; hence, for example, prodigality is a version of generosity which looks, superficially, like generosity (hence the confusion), but which, upon reflection, proves to be a perversion or illusion of generosity—the prodigal does not care for those on whom he lavishes his wealth, as the generous man cares for those with whom he shares; he cares only for his own ostentation. Prodigality then is only an illusion—it is real but not true—and generosity breaks through the opposition of prodigality because such opposition does not truly exist; prodigality exists, of course, for illusions are real, but the opposition does not exist, for the virtue of generosity, which is true, is the non-existence of prodigality and hence the absence of any opposition. Moreover, the virtue of generosity removes all temptation to prodigality (or avarice), for where the true obtains, all perversions of the true are exposed for the illusions which they are: where I can be generous, I will neither squander nor hoard, for generosity satisfies my appetite for truth—I feel true when I am generous.[23]

These arguments apply to Samson in the temple of Dagon. "Of [his] own accord," Samson intends to act. Milton chooses this phrase, not only to emphasize Samson's renewed self-determination against his former masters, but also to suggest that Samson is now, a second time, in accord with himself, and, if in accord with himself, also in accord with God who alone makes such self-accord possible. Milton goes on to write that Samson "mean[s]" to show his strength, and indeed, Samson is making *meaning* here, the meaning of his life, as he, the man, duals his name ("there a second time"). And he makes this meaning by "other trial . . . of [his] strength."

Suddenly there seems to be a problem with the argument. It would seem that Samson's virtue has *not* broken through all opposition if he is still on trial and in trial ("triall is by what is contrary"), if he is in fact "Agonistes"; but we must be careful with what Milton has written. If Samson is Agonistes, he is also, as Carey prudently observes, *un*opposed in the temple (*SA* 1628). Moreover, and more important, Samson says, Milton writes, that he will show "other trial" of his strength. The first trial is the performance the Philistian masters force upon him; to it Samson brings, offers, but precisely does not oppose, other or second trial which he knows perfectly well is no trial at all, for it is the strength of "the living God" with whom he is again one, which he will now show his former lords. In brief, Samson offers them more of the same, which is different: he does not oppose them, for if he opposes them, they will simply kill him, they outnumber him so; rather, he duals them, becoming like them while still remaining different, and thus makes meaning, the meaning of his life, by means of them. Samson in his virtue breaks through the opposition of the Philistians by the supreme irony of giving them, and telling them that he is giving them, exactly what they want.

The price he pays for this triumph, however fleeting of singularity and unity with God, is death and the subsequent confusion (*SA* 1657–58). He never finally escapes confusion. There is no redemption for Samson, the Old Testament hero, such as would be possible for a Christian hero.

And yet there *is* redemption, of a sort—this the burden of the notoriously problematic phoenix allusion. As we address this allusion and related passages, we must remember above all that *Samson Agonistes* is *not* a Christian play but a play, a tragedy, by a Christian.

The allusion occurs in the voice of the chorus, after they have learned of Samson's death:

> 'So *virtue* given for lost,
> Depressed, and overthrown, as seemed,
> Like that self-begotten bird
> In the Arabian woods embossed,
> That *no second knows* nor third,
> And lay erewhile a *holocaust*,
> From out her ashy womb now teemed,
> Revives, reflourishes, then vigorous most
> When most unactive deemed,
> And though her body die, *her fame survives*,
> A secular bird ages of lives.'   [*SA* 1697–1707; emphasis added]

First and most important to realize is that if Samson is like the phoenix, it is because, having "Samson'd" ("there a second time"), he too now "no second knows nor third." Samson is singular (though still not in the way that Christ is singular; see chapter 11 above). Moreover, of him too now can be predicated "self-begotten": re-paired to God ("'all this / With God not parted from him'" [*SA* 1718–19]), Samson "of [his] own accord," begot himself as "Samson"—"'Samson hath quit himself / Like Samson, and heroicly hath finished / A life heroic'" (*SA* 1709–11). Thus, like the phoenix, even to being likewise a "holocaust," Samson also enjoys the redemption proper to the phoenix: "'though her body die, her fame survives, / A secular bird ages of lives'." Milton, of course, has revised the legend: the phoenix does die, but it is eventually reborn, from the worm that forms in the ashes of its predecessor.[24] Here, however, only the fame survives the phoenix's body. And just so, only his fame survives Samson—"a *secular* [hero] ages of lives."

Samson, though "Agonistes," is neither sacred "champion" nor "saint" nor "martyr," but something entirely different.[25] His particular virtue breaks through this opposition "champion" / "saint" to a peculiarly *secular* heroism (which, I should perhaps insist, lest any misunderstanding arise, is still godly and faithful). The chorus recognize and state that Samson could be either "champion" (*deliverer* is their word [*SA* 1270]) or "saint":

'Either of these is in thy lot,
Samson, with might endued
Above the sons of men; but sight bereaved
May chance to number thee with those
Whom patience finally must crown.'   [*SA* 1292–96]

But Milton's point, I believe (and his genius) is that Samson is neither, or both, and therefore more; he is so unique a hero as to transcend the opposition "deliverer" or "saint" while, of course, still remaining a godly and a faithful man. He is even, in most respects, different from Christ—hence the oft-noted absence of explicit typological parallels between Samson and Christ in the play, where there are more often comparisons and contrasts.[26] In short, the phoenix allusion tells us that the redemption and immortality of Samson consist in the fame of a pious, but secular, hero, to last "ages of lives."

But this is not all it tells us. Dalilah had observed:

'Fame if not double-faced is double-mouthed,
And with contrary blast proclaims most deeds,
On both his wings, one black, the other white,
Bears greatest names in his wild aery flight.'   [*SA* 971–74]

The fame of the phoenix, and therefore, by all-important implication, of Samson also, I propose, is the true fame of which this beast is the illusory opposite. The fame of the phoenix is single ("knows no second nor third"), and, by implication, the fame of Samson is equally unambiguous: he quits himself, "heroicly," like an Old Testament hero, avenging himself on his enemies.

'To Israel
Honour hath [he] left, and freedom, let but them
Find courage to lay hold on this occasion,
To himself and father's house eternal fame;
And which is best and happiest yet, all this
With God not parted from him, as was feared,
But favouring and assisting to the end.'   [*SA* 1714–20]

He is, of course, not a New Testament martyr, since a martyr, after Christ, would not have killed his enemies, having been enjoined rather to love them (Matt. 5:44). Rather, Samson is only, but precisely, an Old Testament hero, of unambiguous fame.

Such a conclusion eliminates, we can observe now, the pseudo-problem of the "Christian tragedy."[27] *Samson Agonistes* is a pure tragedy, after the classical manner, on the life of an Old Testament hero, by a Puritan poet of the seventeenth century. Its ending, like that of a classical tragedy, allows for the possibility of divine order and of providential disposition of the actions which have passed; but it does no more than that, and, in particular, there is nothing especially Christian about it.[28] In addition, Samson is no more (though by no means any less either) than the hero of a classical tragedy (Oedipus of *Oedipus at Colonus* is certainly as pious as Samson).[29] Indeed, Milton seems to stress such an equivalence, though indirectly, when he has the chorus remark, apropos of God's dealings with his servants:

> 'Nor only doest degrade them, or remit
> To life obscured, which were a fair dismission,
> But throw'st them *lower than thou didst exalt them high*,
> Unseemly falls in human eye.'   [*SA* 687–90; emphasis added]

We recognize here, of course, a crucial element of the classical definition of tragedy, an element that became all-important in the Middle Ages; as worded by Chaucer's Monk, it goes:

> 'I wol biwaille, in manere of tragedie,
> The harm of hem that stoode in heigh degree,
> And fillen so that ther nas no remedie
> To brynge hem out of hir adversitee.'
>   [*The Monk's Tale* 1991–94, Robinson, p. 189]

Milton implies, then, that Samson is a tragic hero, like the tragic heroes of classical Greek drama, and he does so in a rhetoric which is at the same time also consonant with the Old Testament, especially with the Psalms (see *SA* 667–73 and Ps. 8:4). This implication, and the stress Milton lays on it, account importantly, I believe, for the painstaking way in which he has designed the imagery of the play to incriminate Samson in his enemies's flaws and wrongs.

After a brief but splendid analysis of the imagery of *Samson Agonistes*, showing the ways in which it suggests that Samson is like the Philistians and Dalilah, John Carey concludes:

> In *Samson Agonistes*, then, the imagery does not merely reinforce the drama's triumphant upward arc. On the contrary, it contributes meanings which threaten to invert this arc and bring the weak-minded, vengeful hero to the level of Dalila and the Philistines. In this way it makes a major contribution to the moral maturity of the work.[30]

This conclusion, as far as it goes, is correct; Carey is quite right to stress that the play on several occasions implies that Samson is the same as the Philistines or Dalilah, for this is the flaw, the tragic flaw, which Milton has designed for Samson's character. But, as we have learned, if Samson is the same as the Philistines, he is also different, and Carey's conclusion does not extend to this important feature of Milton's design. For example, he writes:

> The destructive and amoral power of the sea which, at the opening of the drama, was specifically associated with the Philistines, has now been transferred to Samson. His last bloody act of vengeance, which the surface voice of the drama invites us to applaud, is condemned, at a deeper level, by the progression of imagery.[31]

True enough. But the word *associated* is a problem. What exactly does it mean? In fact, it is too vague by far. All we learn of the Philistines is that they worship a "sea-idol" (*SA* 13). But we learn of Samson, as Carey rightly observes, that he becomes like the sea itself in its awesome destructive force (*SA* 960–64, 1647–51): hence—and I believe that this is Milton's point—the Philistines are destroyed, through Providence's design, by a force resembling, but also different from, the force which they idolatrously worship. So Providence has dualed Samson and the Philistines. Therefore, it is not enough to use *associated* and *transferred;* Milton's strategy with his imagery demands a more finely nuanced description. Samson is indeed flawed. The imagery tells us so, tells us that he is a weak-minded, superhuman force barely contained within his flesh. And so much leads precisely to his tragic downfall. But Samson is also—and the imagery tells us this, too—a Nazarite, separate unto God, and the physical embodiment of God's avenging wrath—and any conclusion less self-consciously dual will not do for Milton's singular achievement.

Notes

PREFACE

1 The text of Milton's poetry cited throughout this book is that of John Carey and Alastair Fowler, *The Complete Poems of John Milton* (London: Longman, 1968). I have also routinely consulted Merritt Y. Hughes, *Paradise Lost* (Indianapolis: Odyssey Press, 1962). I quote Milton's prose works from the Yale Edition (hereafter YE, followed by volume and page numbers): *The Complete Prose Works of John Milton*, ed. Don M. Wolfe (New Haven: Yale University Press, 1953–82). I have also consulted *The Works of John Milton*, ed. Frank A. Patterson (New York: Columbia University Press, 1931–38). The only other abbreviations I use are *CD* (for *Christian Doctrine*), *DD* (for *The Doctrine and Discipline of Divorce*), and the standard abbreviations for the poetic works—*PL* (for *Paradise Lost*), *PR* (for *Paradise Regained*), *SA* (for *Samson Agonistes*), and *C* for (*Comus*).

CHAPTER 1

1 It will perhaps be helpful to list the occurrences here in their order of appearance. *Sign* is used at 1.605, 672; 2.760, 831; 4.428, 429, 1011; 5.134, 194; 6.58, 776, 789; 7.341; 8.342, 514; 9.783, 1077; 10.1091, 1103; 11.182, 194, 351, 860; 12.175, 301, 442; *resign* at 3.688; 6.731; 10.148, 749; 11.66, 207; 12.301.

2 But, for comments on *part* and *partner*, see Anne Davidson Ferry, *Milton's Epic Voice: The Narrator in "Paradise Lost"* (Cambridge: Harvard University Press, 1967), pp. 100–01; see also Roland Mushat Frye, *God, Man, and Satan* (Princeton: Princeton University Press, 1960), pp. 55–56. A study devoted to *Dualities in Shakespeare* by Marion Bodwell Smith (Toronto:

University of Toronto Press, 1966), though very different from the present one, I have found useful occasionally, esp. pp. 15–52.

3 See Donald F. Bouchard, *Milton: A Structural Reading* (Montreal: Queen's University Press, 1974); and Herman Rapaport, *Milton and the Postmodern* (Lincoln: University of Nebraska Press, 1983). Rapaport, however, does notice part of the play on *impair* and *repair* in Milton's poetry (pp. 108–09).

4 See the helpful remarks on this line by Maureen Quilligan, *Milton's Spenser* (Ithaca: Cornell University Press, 1983); pp. 88–98.

5 See William G. Madsen, *From Shadowy Types to Truth: Studies in Milton's Symbolism* (New Haven: Yale University Press, 1968); Stanley E. Fish, *Surprised by Sin: The Reader in "Paradise Lost"* (Berkeley: University of California Press, 1971); and William Kerrigan, *The Sacred Complex: On the Psychogenesis of "Paradise Lost"* (Cambridge, Mass.: Harvard University Press, 1983).

6 An important step in this direction has been taken by John Hollander, *The Figure of Echo* (Berkeley: University of California Press, 1981).

7 See Ferdinand de Saussure, *Course in General Linguistics*, trans. Wade Baskin (New York: McGraw-Hill, 1966), pp. 120–21; also Jacques Derrida, *Writing and Difference*, trans. Alan Bass (Chicago: University of Chicago Press, 1978); idem, *Of Grammatology*, trans. Gayatri Chakravorty Spivak (Baltimore: Johns Hopkins University Press, 1974); idem, *Dissemination*, trans. Barbara Johnson (Chicago: University of Chicago Press, 1981); and Umberto Eco, *Semiotics and the Philosophy of Language* (Bloomington: Indiana University Press, 1984), esp. pp. 1–49. Consult also the provocative and helpful work of Michel Serres—for example, *The Parasite*, trans. Lawrence R. Schehr (Baltimore: Johns Hopkins University Press, 1982).

8 See the second edition of Chaucer's *Works*, by F. N. Robinson (Cambridge: Houghton-Mifflin, 1957), p. 396, line 637.

9 A preliminary list would include Boethius, *Philosophiae Consolatio*, III, m. 1, ed. L. Bieler (Corpus Christianorum Series Latina 94, 1:37–38); Guillaume de Lorris and Jean de Meun, *Le Roman de la Rose*, lines 21,543–52, ed. Félix Lecoy, 3 vols. (Paris: Champion, 1966–74), 3:148; William Langland, *Piers Plowman* B. X. 441–43, ed. George Kane and E. Talbot Donaldson (London: Athlone Press, 1975), p. 433; Edmund Spenser, *The Faerie Queene* 3.ix.2, ed. A. C. Hamilton (London: Longman, 1977), p. 383 (and see chapter 5 below); William Shakespeare, *The Merchant of Venice*, V.i.99, in *The Riverside Shakespeare*, ed. G. B. Evans (Boston: Houghton-Mifflin, 1974), vol. 1, p. 281. See also Robinson's note to *Troylus and Criseyde* 1.631 for further references (p. 816).

10 See further the helpful remarks by Michael Lieb, *The Dialectics of Creation: Patterns of Birth and Regeneration in "Paradise Lost"* (Amherst: University of Massachusetts Press, 1970), esp. pp. 7–8.

11 The theology of the image of God—its creation, ruin, reformation, and restoration—is extensive and complex, and the bibliography is correspondingly vast. In addition to Milton's own discussion in *CD* 1.18, YE 6:461–65, consult Robert Javelet, *Image et Ressemblance au douzième siècle*, 2 vols. (Paris: Editions Letouzey et Ané, 1967); and John E. Sullivan, *The Image of God: The Doctrine of St. Augustine and its Influence* (Dubuque, Iowa: Priory Press, 1963).

12 *Confessions* 10.29, trans. R. S. Pine-Coffin (Harmondsworth: Penguin, 1961), p. 233. See also *De Gratia et Libero Arbitrio*, 1, *Patrologia Latina* (ed. J.-P. Migne), 44:899.

13 *The City of God*, trans. Henny Bettenson (Harmondsworth: Penguin, 1972), pp. 575–76.

14 See *Confessions* 7.1–2, trans. Pine-Coffin, pp. 133–35; see also Steven Runciman, *The Medieval Manichee: A Study of the Christian Dualist Heresy* (1947; repr. Cambridge: Cambridge University Press, 1982), pp. 16–17.

15 "If accession to the logos and to the symbolic in general is salutary in that it provides the subject with an identity, the impossible coincidence of the (I), the subject of the enunciation, with the 'I', the subject of the utterance, begins the dialectic of the subject's alienations"—Anika Lemaire, *Jacques Lacan*, trans. David Macey (London: Routledge and Kegan Paul, 1977), p. 72). See also Jacques Lacan, *Ecrits* (Paris: Editions du Seuil, 1966), p. 843; and Jacques-Alain Miller, "Suture (elements of the logic of the signifier)," *Screen* 18, 4 (1977–78):24–34.

16 On the terms *chōrismós* and *méthexis*, see Ernst Cassirer, *The Individual and the Cosmos in Renaissance Philosophy*, trans. Mario Domandi (Philadelphia: University of Pennsylvania Press, 1963), pp. 22–23; see also the remarks by Paul Oskar Kristeller, *The Philosophy of Marsilio Ficino*, trans. Virginia Conant (Gloucester, Mass.: Peter Smith, 1964), pp. 126–30, 149–50; and idem, *Medieval Aspects of Renaissance Learning*, ed. and trans. Edward P. Mahoney, Duke Monographs in Medieval and Renaissance Studies, 1 (Durham: Duke University Press, 1974), pp. 76–77. On *perichōrēsis*, see Stephen Gersh, *From Iamblichus to Eriugena: A Study of the Prehistory and Evolution of the Pseudo-Dionysian Tradition* (Leiden: Brill, 1978), pp. 253–60.

17 See Arthur O. Lovejoy's description of "the natural genesis of both epistemological and psychophysical dualism," in *The Revolt Against Dualism: An Inquiry Concerning the Existence of Ideas* (New York: Norton, 1930), ch. 1, esp. p. 10.

18 See Frederick Copleston, *A History of Philosophy* (London: Burns, Oates, and Washbourne, 1958), 4:116–23.

19 Cf. J. H. Adamson, "The Creation," in W. B. Hunter, J. H. Adamson, C. A. Patrides, *Bright Essence* (Salt Lake City: University of Utah Press, 1971), pp. 81–102, esp. 100–01: "Surely it is obvious that the main move-

ment of mind in the seventeenth century was from Greek dualism, which had something of a late flowering in Descartes, to metaphysical monism and to the later idealists."

20 See Martin Heidegger, "The Question Concerning Technology" and "The Turning," trans. William Lovitt, in *The Question Concerning Technology and Other Essays* (New York: Harper and Row, 1977), pp. 3–49.

21 Cassirer, p. 134, cites Francesco Patrizzi: "Cognitio nihil est aliud, quam Coitio quaedam cum suo cognobili."

22 See Jacques Derrida, "Différance," trans. Alan Bass, in *Margins of Philosophy* (Chicago: University of Chicago Press, 1982), pp. 3–27.

23 Cf. Gilles Deleuze, *Nietzsche and Philosophy*, trans. Hugh Tomlinson (New York: Columbia University Press, 1983), pp. 47–49.

24 Cf. René Girard, *Violence and the Sacred* (Baltimore: Johns Hopkins University Press, 1972), pp. 56–63. My debt to Girard, as one would imagine, is considerable, but as sentences like this and others that follow suggest, my position on duality differs from his very much. See, further, on the phenomenon of twins, J. Rendel Harris, *The Cult of the Heavenly Twins* (Cambridge: Cambridge University Press, 1906); and Donald Ward, *The Divine Twins: An Indo-European Myth in Germanic Tradition*, Folklore Studies, 19 (Berkeley: University of California Press, 1968). Consult also Claude Levi-Strauss, *Structural Anthropology*, vol. 1, trans. Carol Jacobsen and Brooke Grundfest Schoepf (New York: Basic Books, 1963), pp. 206–31; vol. 2, trans. Monique Layton (New York: Basic Books, 1976), p. 166.

25 On the tradition of Eros and Anteros, see R. V. Merill, "Eros and Anteros," *Speculum* 19 (1944):265–84.

26 Cf. Cassirer, p. 135, on Ficino's "theodicy of art."

27 Madsen, pp. 86–89.

28 See Adamson, "Milton's Arianism," in *Bright Essence*, pp. 53–61, on the revival of Greek learning in the seventeenth century and the importance of Platonism and Neoplatonism to Milton and his contemporaries.

29 See *Confessions* 7.9, 20, trans. Pine-Coffin, pp. 144–46, 154–55.

30 John Calvin, Commentary on John 6:56, cited in Ronald S. Wallace, *Calvin's Doctrine of the Word and Sacrament*, Tyler, Tex.: Geneva Divinity School Press, 1953, (repr. 1982), p. 201.

31 I am aware of W. B. Hunter's conclusion in "Milton on the Incarnation," in *Bright Essence*, pp. 131–48, that "Milton conceived of the Incarnation as a somewhat less close union than orthodoxy generally has permitted," but I also think it very important not to forget his qualification of this conclusion: "It must be recognized, however, that he resolutely refused to speculate upon the final meaning of the Incarnation, preferring to accept it as a mystery" (p. 137).

32 See Rosemund Tuve's discussion of the figure in *Elizabethan and Meta-*

physical Imagery (Chicago: University of Chicago Press, 1947), pp. 130–32, esp. 131: "Many religious symbols would be catachretical if tradition had not taught us to remark compatible terms rather than dissonant suggestions (*agnus dei*)."

33 Cf. Sigurd Burckhardt, *Shakespearean Meanings* (Princeton: Princeton University Press, 1968), p. 241.

34 "The same, precisely, is *différance* (with an *a*) as the displaced and equivocal passage of one different thing to another, from one term of an opposition to the other. Thus one could reconsider all the pairs of opposites on which philosophy is constructed and on which our discourse lives, not in order to see opposition erase itself but to see what indicates that each of the terms must appear as the *différance* of the other, as the other different and deferred in the economy of the same (the intelligible as differing-deferring the sensible, as the sensible different and deferred" ("Différance," trans. Bass, p. 17).

35 Cf. Stanley Fish, "Things and Actions Indifferent: The Temptation of Plot in *Paradise Regained*," *Milton Studies* 17 (1983):163–86, esp. 183.

36 Moreover, Ramism, the principal movement in logic during the period, intensified the appeal, especially through its emphasis on classification by dichotomy. See Walter J. Ong, *Ramus, Method, and the Decay of Dialogue* (Cambridge, Mass.: Harvard University Press, 1958), pp. 199–200, 286; Jackson I. Cope, *The Metaphoric Structure of "Paradise Lost"* (Baltimore: Johns Hopkins University Press, 1962), pp. 32–35; E. J. Ashworth, *Language and Logic in the Post-Medieval Period* (Dordrecht: Reidel, 1974), p. 15; Lisa Jardine, "Humanism and the Teaching of Logic," in *The Cambridge History of Later Medieval Philosophy: From the Rediscovery of Aristotle to the Disintegration of Scholasticism* 1100–1600, ed. Norman Kretzmann, Anthony Kenny, Jan Pinborg, (assoc. ed.) Eleonore Stump (Cambridge: Cambridge University Press, 1982), pp. 797–807, esp. 802–04 on Ramus; and Wilbur Samuel Howell, *Logic and Rhetoric in England, 1500–1700* (New York: Russell and Russell, 1961), pp. 162 and 211–19, esp. 211, where he notes that Ramism was particularly strong at Christ College, Milton's college.

37 For a description of this phenomenon—Hegel's "Aufhebung"—see Bass's note 23 in his translation of Derrida, "Différance," p. 20: "*Aufhebung* literally means "lifting up," but it also contains the double meaning of conservation and negation. For Hegel, dialectics is a process of *Aufhebung*: every concept is to be negated and lifted up to a higher sphere in which it is thereby conserved."

38 *Religio Medici*, I, 34, quoted in Isabel Rivers, *Classical and Christian Ideas in English Renaissance Poetry* (London: George Allen and Unwin, 1979), p. 88; emphasis added.

39 "Man," lines 13–24, in ibid., p. 86.

40 Cassirer, pp. 46–72.

41 Ibid., p. 45; see also Kerrigan's helpful remarks, p. 136.

42 Cassirer, p. 39.

43 Ibid., p. 20.

44 See Rosalie L. Colie, *Paradoxa Epidemica: The Renaissance Tradition of Paradox* (Princeton: Princeton University Press, 1966; repr. 1976), esp. pp. 96–189.

45 On Milton's repudiation of dualism, see Arthur E. Barker, *Milton and the Puritan Dilemma 1641–1660* (Toronto: University of Toronto Press, 1942), pp. 318–19; see also Diane Kelsey McColley, *Milton's Eve* (Urbana: University of Illinois Press, 1983), pp. 9–11, 15, 27, 29–30, 81; Thomas Kranidas, *The Fierce Equation: A Study of Milton's Decorum* (The Hague: Mouton, 1965), pp. 69–71; and the important remarks by Kerrigan, pp. 200–201, 260.

46 See Cassirer, p. 51, who quotes "*Luca Pacioli*, the friend of Leonardo[:] proportion is not only the mother of knowledge; it is the 'mother and queen of art'."

47 See Edgar Wind, *Pagan Mysteries in the Renaissance* (Harmondsworth: Penguin, 1967), p. 202 and n. 42.

48 See Don Cameron Allen, *Doubt's Boundless Sea: Skepticism and Faith in the Renaissance* (Baltimore: Johns Hopkins University Press, 1964), p. 134.

49 Here I reveal and confirm my conviction, which I share with Kerrigan and Joseph A. Wittreich, among others, that Milton's is a prophetic voice and *Paradise Lost* a prophetic poem. See William Kerrigan, *The Prophetic Milton* (Charlottesville: University Press of Virginia, 1974), esp. pp. 17–124; and Joseph A. Wittreich, *Visionary Poetics: Milton's Tradition and His Legacy* (San Marino: Huntington Library and Art Gallery, 1979), pp. 3–8 and 79–87.

50 Milton's treatment of the issue of justification is found in *CD* 1.22, YE 6:485–94.

51 See Heidegger, *Being and Time*, trans. John Macquarrie and Edward Robinson (New York: Harper and Row, 1962), p. 56; also R. A. Shoaf, *Dante, Chaucer, and the Currency of the Word: Money, Images, and Reference in Late Medieval Poetry* (Norman, Oklahoma: Pilgrim Books, 1983), pp. 31–32.

52 On the dyad and duplicity and the duplicity of duplication, see Alastair Fowler's comments on Spenser's oppositions of one and two, in *Spenser and the Numbers of Time* (New York: Barnes and Noble, 1964), pp. 7–15.

53 For an introduction to the theory of accommodation, in the patristic, medieval, and Renaissance periods, with helpful bibliography, see Leland Ryken, *The Apocalyptic Vision in "Paradise Lost"* (Ithaca: Cornell University Press, 1970), pp. 7–24. For a more theoretical analysis of accommodation

in Milton which is also very stimulating, see John Guillory, *Poetic Authority* (New York: Columbia University Press, 1982), pp. 146–71.

54 I am indebted for this play with *pair* and its reflexes, in part to Lacan, *Ecrits*, p. 843, in part, as I will shortly demonstrate, to Edmund Spenser. I wish to cite here, since these words figure so prominently in my book, the etymological essay in *The American Heritage Dictionary* (first edition):

> perə-. To grant, allot (reciprocally, to get in return). Extended root of *per*-⁴ [from which, for example, REPAIR, SEPARATE, PARENT, PARCAE]. Zero-grade form **prə* (becoming **par-* in Latin) in: a. suffixed form **par-ti-* in Latin *pars* (stem *part-*), a share, part: PARCEL, PARCENER, PARSE, PART; BIPARTITE, COMPART, IMPART, REPARTEE; b. possibly suffixed form **par-tiō* in Latin *portiō*, a part . . . PORTION, PROPORTION; c. perhaps Latin *pār*, equal: PAIR, PAR, PARITY(2), PARLAY, PEER(2); COMPARE, HERB, PARIS, IMPARITY, NONPAREIL, PARI-MUTUEL. [p. 1534, col. 2]

55 On such echolalic structures in *Paradise Lost*, see also Hollander, pp. 26–51.

56 The text of Dante cited here and elsewhere is that prepared by Giorgio Petrocchi for the Società Dantesca Italiana, Edizione Nazionale, *La Commedia secondo l'antica vulgata*, 4 vols. (Milan: Mondadori, 1966–67); the translation which I use throughout is that by Charles S. Singleton, Bollingen Series, 80, 3 vols. (Princeton: Princeton University Press, 1970–75).

57 Ariosto, at canto 6, stanzas 26–53, of *Orlando Furioso*, ed. Lanfranco Caretti (Turin: Einaudi, 1966), pp. 120–37; Spenser, at *FQ* 1.ii.30–34, ed. Hamilton, pp. 50–52; Tasso, at canto 13, stanzas 40–50, of *Gerusalemme Liberata*, ed. Luigi Bonfigli (Bari: G. Laterza, 1930), pp. 304–06.

58 See Fowler ed., pp. 433–34, on such syntax—he calls it "double syntax"—in the poem. I should remark here that I cite Carey's and Fowler's respective parts of their edition separately, as each quotation warrants, throughout this book.

59 It should also be noted that the three attempts are almost certainly an echo, albeit distant, of Aeneas's three attempts to embrace Creusa (*Aeneid* 2.792–94) and Anchises (*Aeneid* 6.700–03). The evocation of vanity— *frustra* is Virgil's word (*Aeneid* 2.793, 6.701)—is even more telling when we remind ourselves that Satan is not "pius." What he essays, in the epic manner, is ultimately only more rhetoric for further seduction.

60 This verse of the Epistle to the Hebrews is as important to Dante as it is to Spenser. At *Purgatorio* 30.55–57, Dante has Beatrice exclaim: " 'Dante, perchè Virgilio se ne vada, / non pianger anco, non piangere an-

cora; / che pianger ti conven per altra *spada*'" ("Dante, because Virgil leaves you, do not weep yet, do not weep yet, for you must weep for another sword"; emphasis added). Then he continues the figure in the next canto, in which Beatrice is speaking again: "'O tu che se di la dal fiume sacro,' / volgendo suo parlare a me per punta, / che pur per taglio m'era paruto acro" ("O you who are on that side of the sacred river," she began again, turning against me the point of her speech, which even with the edge had seemed sharp to me). The sword, we can surmise, must have seemed a peculiarly apt symbol of duality, whether of language or of the body: two-sided, two-edged, often two-handed, sometimes double-guarded, its principal purpose, of course, was to cut into *two*. And as Spenser at least would also have known, one ancient theory of the origin of man and woman held that they were originally one but were subsequently cut into two—so Aristophanes, in Plato's *Symposium*, trans. B. Jowett (Indianapolis: Bobbs-Merrill, 1948), pp. 30–34. Add the phallic symbolism of the sword, and the case becomes even more compelling, for, as Lacan, among others, argues, the phallus is that which divides, distinguishes, signifies, even as the penis (the actual organ) unites; see *Ecrits*, pp. 685–95.

61 See Sir Thomas Browne, *Religio Medici* II, 6: "There are wonders in true affection, it is a body of Aenigmaes, mysteries and riddles, wherein two so become one, as they both become two."

62 Narcissus and narcissism are subjects of a, by now, vast bibliography; I have collected some of the basic texts in my *Dante, Chaucer, and the Currency of the Word*, p. 245, nn. 1 and 2. Deserving special mention are the seminal texts: Ovid *Meta.* 3.339–510—the text and translation of *The Metamorphoses* cited here and elsewhere is that of the Loeb Classical Library, edited by Frank Justus Miller (Cambridge, Mass.: Harvard University Press, 1916); Freud, "On Narcissism: An Introduction," in *The Standard Edition of the Complete Psychological Works of Sigmund Freud*, trans. and ed. James Strachey (London: Hogarth Press, 1957), vol. 14, pp. 73–102; Lacan, "Sur le narcissisme," *Le Séminaire* 1(1975):125–35; and idem, *Ecrits*, pp. 1–20.

63 See, further, the helpful remarks on narcissism by Kerrigan, *The Sacred Complex*, pp. 70–71.

64 See C. A. Patrides, *Milton and the Christian Tradition* (Oxford: Clarendon Press, 1966), pp. 32–36; and Adamson, "Milton and the Creation," in *Bright Essence*, pp. 81–102; also Hunter, "Milton's Arianism Reconsidered," in *Bright Essence*, pp. 29–51, esp. 49. Consult also Louis Martz, *Poet of Exile: A Study of Milton's Poetry* (New Haven: Yale University Press, 1980), p. 114.

65 "The time-honoured expression," as Patrides calls it (p. 35), is "bonum est *diffusivum* sui."

66 Cf. Lana Cable, "Coupling Logic and Milton's Doctrine of Divorce," *Milton Studies* 15 (1981): 143–59, esp. 158–59.
67 On this concept and its wide currency in the Renaissance, see Wind, p. 41.
68 Shoaf, pp. 28–29, 42–43.
69 *Copia* in Renaissance literature has recently received extensive and enlightening treatment; see Terence Cave, *The Cornucopian Text: Problems of Writing in the French Renaissance* (Oxford: Oxford University Press, 1979), esp. pp. 3–34. The word and its associations in medieval literature, Latin and vernacular, need similar attention.
70 Cf. the more thoroughgoing Derridean approach to this matter in Rapaport, pp. 26–27, 38–39.
71 Two useful studies on this paradox which is so essential to Christianity are Lovejoy, "Milton and the Paradox of the Fortunate Fall," in his collected *Essays in the History of Ideas* (Baltimore: Johns Hopkins University Press, 1948), pp. 277–95; and Earl Miner, "Felix Culpa in the Redemptive Order of *Paradise Lost*," *Philological Quarterly* 47 (1968): 43–54. See also the remarks in Colie, pp. 169–89; and the description of positions in McColley, p. 18, n. 3.
72 Cf. Fish, *Surprised by Sin*, pp. 88–91, on choice in reading *Paradise Lost*.
73 In this formulation, we can see the similarity and also the difference between Milton and his numerous contemporaries who sought, in a kind of paroxysm of Cartesian exactitude, an exact equivalency between word and thing—see Fish's excellent discussion of this matter, "Language in Paradise," in *Surprised by Sin*, pp. 107–31, esp. 117–18; consult also Richard F. Jones, "Science and Language in England of the Mid-Seventeenth Century," in *The Seventeenth Century* (Stanford: Stanford University Press, 1951), pp. 143–60. Their ideal of one word equals one thing Milton understands to be impossible of attainment; but the adjustment of the sign to its meaning is possible when the sign is repaired to the individual—and thus also the individual to the sign. Then, though there will be no equation of word and thing, the sign and the signified, in their state of repair, will nevertheless produce meaning and meaningfulness. That the risk of solipsism therefore exists is the inevitable—Nietzsche would say, tragic—consequence of subjectivity, the *part*ialness thereof, but if this state of affairs is not to be tragic, it will be because the part repaired, knowing its repair, will not mistake itself for the whole, to impose its Paradise on another. It will, in fact, be more humble than that. See also Shoaf, pp. 30–35.
74 His faith, in other words, issues in works. Milton, it will help to recall here, differed from other Protestants and Puritans on the issue of *sola fide*, justification by faith alone. For him, faith must be living—that is, productive of works: "We are justified, then, by faith, but a living faith, not a

dead one, and the only living faith is a faith which acts" (*CD* 1.22, YE 6:490). See further Maryann Cale McGuire, *Milton's Puritan Mask* (Athens: University of Georgia Press, 1983), pp. 87–88.

CHAPTER 2

1 *The Collected Poems of W. B. Yeats* (London: Macmillan, 1955), pp. 294–95.
2 Milton would certainly have known this connotation from his extensive reading of Italian, and especially of Dante; see Irene Samuel, *Dante and Milton: The "Commedia" and "Paradise Lost"* (Ithaca: Cornell University Press, 1966), p. 33.
3 Cf. *Inf.* 30.142–44 and *Purg.* 30.76–78; see also Shoaf, pp. 45–47, 50–51.
4 Cf. Derrida, *Of Grammatology*, pp. 144–45.
5 See Augustine's *Confessions* 7.7–14; also *The City of God* 11.9, 22;14.11; and the *Enchiridion* 4.14.
6 On these emphases and their significance, see Thomas M. Greene, *The Light in Troy: Imitation and Discovery in Renaissance Poetry* (New Haven: Yale University Press, 1982), pp. 4–7; see also Shoaf, pp. 31–32, 76–77.

CHAPTER 3

1 On this commonplace of medieval and Renaissance exegesis, see Jean Daniélou, *Primitive Christian Symbols*, trans. Donald Attwater (London: Burnes and Oates, 1961), pp. 29–41; see also Esther C. Quinn, *The Quest of Seth for the Oil of Life* (Chicago: University of Chicago Press, 1962), pp. 76–78. Consult also F. J. E. Raby, *A History of Secular Latin Poetry in the Middle Ages*, 2 vols., 2nd ed. (Oxford: Clarendon Press, 1957), 1:352.
2 Lest these remarks seem naive or rationalizing or worse, I would like to beg the reader's understanding to confess that they arise from my experience of the last months and weeks in the life of my friend, Russ Brantley (d. 1983). The dignity and the courage with which he faced and endured death by cancer were (and are) an inspiraton and a source of hope to all who knew him. He is to me now and will be for the rest of my life, I am sure, a living sign of what it is for a man to live significantly. And it is my hope that my brief remarks here can serve as a testimonial to that significance.
3 Cf. *PL* 11.286–88: "Whom thus the angel interrupted mild. / 'Lament not Eve, but patiently *resign* / What justly thou hast lost'" (emphasis added). The only way Eve can resign what she has lost *patiently* is to re-sign it to a new and different significance—which significance can then strengthen her patience.
4 Cf. the stimulating remarks on this subject by Leslie Brisman, *Milton's*

Poetry of Choice and Its Romantic Heirs (Ithaca: Cornell University Press, 1973), pp. 55–67.

5 The pattern I discern in Milton's text here may have been generated by his reading of Shakespeare's "The Phoenix and the Turtle" (see chapter 7 below for an extensive analysis of this lyric in relation to Milton's understanding of metaphor). At the end of the lyric, Shakespeare writes: "To this urn let those repair / That are either true or fair; / For these dead birds sigh a prayer" (quoted from the edition by Hallett Smith for *The Riverside Shakespeare*, vol. 2, pp. 1795–98). Though many other sources must have intervened, I find it difficult to imagine that Milton would have forgotten Shakespeare's rhyme repair / prayer.

6 For confirmation of this argument, note the description of Adam and Eve's post-lapsarian lust: "he on Eve / Began to cast *lascivious eyes*, she him / As wantonly repaid" (*PL* 9.1013–15; emphasis added).

7 Cf. these remarks on death with those by Marshall Grossman in "Milton's Dialectical Visions," *Modern Philology* 82 (1984), 23–39.

8 The ultimate paradigm of the phenomenon I am describing here, at least for Milton and his culture, is best illustrated by Jesus's parable of the seed (which is also, of course, a parable of his own life and death): "Truly, truly I say to you, unless a grain of wheat falls into the earth and dies, it remains alone; but if it dies, it bears much fruit" (John 12:24). The proximity of death and life appears as almost a causal nexus to naive perception: the seed appears to be buried, dead, to return only because of that burial to life.

9 Carey ed., p. 88.

10 A similar position is taken by J. E. Shaw, *A Variorum Commentary on The Poems of John Milton*, vol. 1 (New York: Columbia University Press, 1970), p. 366.

11 See R. A. Shoaf, *Word*, pp. 58–60 and 251, n. 13.

12 See H. F. Fletcher, *The Intellectual Development of John Milton*, 2 vols. (Urbana: University of Illinois Press, 1956), 1:73–88; 2:103.

13 A. Bartlett Giamatti also remarks on the possible relationship between Milton's sonnet and Dante's *Purgatorio*, canto 30; see *A Variorum Commentary*, 1:379–80.

14 Carey ed., p. 93.

15 On this disjunction of the real and the true in the figure of Master Adam, see further Shoaf, pp. 43–44.

16 See John Broadbent, *Some Graver Subject: An Essay on "Paradise Lost"* (New York: Schocken Books, 1967), pp. 151–52; Fowler ed., pp. 969–70, *ad PL* 10.832.

17 Cf. Roland Barthes, *S/Z* (Paris: Seuil, 1970), pp. 3–12; and Derrida, *Of Grammatology*, p. 158.

18 A deconstruction of Milton's poetry has recently appeared—namely, Herman Rapaport's *Milton and the Postmodern*. And just so, for example, at one point he writes: "And language? This expropriates, confiscates, enlists, transforms, rehabilitates, recognizes, reinstitutionalizes, exacerbates, dilates, alienates. Such activities are everywhere manifest in the poetic oeuvre, of course, whose aim is to expropriate and appropriate, to dismantle the legacy of feudalism and forge with that inheritance a new bourgeois tradition, one that is announced so clearly in *Paradise Lost*, whose 'Hail wedded love!' *ought to be rewritten as 'Vive les bourgeois'* (emphasis added).

19 I owe the terms *coinhere* and *coinherence* to Charles Williams, *The Figure of Beatrice* (London: Faber, 1943), pp. 92, 172, 195, 204, and 210.

20 And the dueling is necessary to the dualing, although it is not finally as important, since the dualing is the end of the writing. Here I reveal both my dependence on, and difference from, Harold Bloom, whose poetics of influence and the agon have moved me and so many of my generation. Particularly important to my reading of Milton are his texts *A Map of Misreading* (Oxford: Oxford University Press, 1975), pp. 125–59; *Poetry and Repression: Revisionism from Blake to Stevens* (New Haven: Yale University Press, 1976), pp. 1–27; and *Agon: Towards a Theory of Revision* (Oxford: Oxford University Press, 1982), pp. 16–71.

21 Cf. Kerrigan's different, but related, argument in *The Sacred Complex*, pp. 169–70.

22 Kerrigan, *The Prophetic Milton*, p. 185. Cf. also, in this regard, Milton's claim that "every true Christian . . . is a person dedicate to joy and peace, offering himself a lively sacrifice of praise and thanksgiving, and there is no Christian duty that is not to be season'd and set off with cheerfulness" (*DD* 1.7, YE 2:259).

23 In Fradubio's subjection by *Duessa*, for example; most especially perhaps in such lines as " 'Both seemde to win and both seemde won to be' " (*FQ* 1.ii.37), where the pun won/one betrays doubt's confusion of doubles—doubt is always between doubles.

24 Cf. Kerrigan, *The Sacred Complex*, pp. 180–82.

CHAPTER 4

1 Cf. Lieb, *Poetics of the Holy: A Reading of "Paradise Lost"* (Chapel Hill: University of North Carolina Press, 1981), pp. 43–63, esp. 60.

2 I am aware, as I write this chapter, of E. le Comte's *A Dictionary of Puns in Milton's English Poetry* (New York: Columbia University Press, 1981), which prints 210 pages of supposed puns. I should perhaps emphasize here that I am not questioning Milton's tendency to pun—although I am not always persuaded that what le Comte identifies as puns *are* such; rather, I am trying to describe and explain Milton's attitude to puns in the

light of duality in his poetry. See the very helpful, sensitive discussion of puns in Milton by Christopher Ricks, *Milton's Grand Style* (Oxford: Clarendon Press, 1963), pp. 66–75, esp. 72 on puns and silence.

3 "The Voice of the Shuttle," in *Beyond Formalism* (New Haven: Yale University Press, 1970), p. 347.

4 See *The Consolation of Philosophy*, trans. Richard Green (Indianapolis: Bobbs-Merrill, 1962), 5.6, pp. 115–19.

5 Thus, too, Aristotle: "It is metaphor that is in the highest degree instructive. . . It follows, then, for style and reasoning [enthymenes (*sic*)] alike, that in order to be lively . . . they must give us *rapid* information . . . What we like are [enthymemes] that convey information as fast as they are stated—so long as we did not have the knowledge in advance—or that our minds lag only a little behind" (*Rhetoric* 1401b14–25; emphasis added). Cited in Umberto Eco, *Semiotics and the Philosophy of Language* (Bloomington: Indiana University Press, 1984), p. 102.

6 Hartman, *Beyond Formalism*, p. 339.

7 In this argument, my debt to Fish is the greatest, as well as the clearest; see esp. pp. 88–91.

8 Both quotes are from "The Verse," Fowler ed., p. 457 (emphasis added).

9 William Perkins, "Of the Sacraments," in *A Golden Chain or the Description of Theology*, ed. Ian Breward, *The Work of William Perkins*, The Courtenay Library of Reformation Classics, 3 (Appleford: Sutton Courtenay Press, 1970), p. 215; emphasis added.

10 Cf. Kerrigan's excellent analysis, *The Sacred Complex*, p. 244.

11 See Fowler's note at p. 915, to *PL* 9.1018.

12 For helpful commentary on this phrase and the related passages, see Lars Engle, "Character in Poetic Narrative: Action and Individual in Chaucer and Milton" (Ph.D. diss., Yale University, 1984), p. 185 and n. 41.

13 So much is explicit when Milton writes of the fallen angels: "Their song was *partial* . . ." (*PL* 2.552; emphasis added).

14 See *PL* 3.169–70: " 'Son who art alone / My word, my wisdom' "; cf. 1 Cor. 1:24 and Col. 2:3. On the patristic convention of identifying the Son with Wisdom (*Sapientia*), see *The Oxford Dictionary of the Christian Church*, 2d ed. F. L. Cross and E. A. Livingstone (New York: Oxford University Press, 1974), p. 1493.

15 And also Christ:

> He sovran priest, stooping his regal head
> That dropped with odorous oil down his fair eyes,
> Poor fleshly tabernacle entered,
> His starry front low-roofed beneath the skies,
> *O what a mask was there, what a disguise!*
> ["The Passion," 15–19; emphasis added; Carey ed., p. 120]

Christ, too, had a role to play, that of man. On Milton's understanding of the *person* of Christ (and of the sense of *persona*), see Hunter, "Milton on the Incarnation," in *Bright Essence*, pp. 131–48, esp. 147.

CHAPTER 5

1 See Sonnet I, in John Carey, *Milton: Complete Shorter Poems* (London: Longman Group, 1968), p. 88 and the bibliography cited there.

2 For my use of *transuming*, I am indebted to, but not always dependent on, Harold Bloom, *A Map of Misreading*.

3 The best study to date of Milton's figure of the bird is Ferry, *Milton's Epic Voice*, pp. 20–43, esp. 27–34.

4 See the discussion of *even* in Sonnet VII in ch. 9 below.

5 Moreover, she figures significance itself. As Milton probably knew, the word for "nightingale" in Old French and Provençal, in various spellings, is *rosseignol* (Tobler-Lommatzsch vol. 8, p. 1492), the regular formation off late Latin **lusciniolus*, the "little bird of light"—itself symbolizing an important connection between Milton and the nightingale. One of the variant spellings of *rosseignol* is "ros*sign*on," and it is not inconceivable that Milton kept this visual pun in mind as he meditated on the nightingale, bird of signs, and his own poetic career.

6 For a recent helpful discussion of Milton's relation to Ovid, see Martz, pp. 203–44, esp. 232–36; consult also Don Cameron Allen, *Mysteriously Meant: The Rediscovery of Pagan Symbolism and Allegorical Interpretation in the Renaissance* (Baltimore: Johns Hopkins University Press, 1970), p. 295.

7 Roy J. Deferrari, M. Inviolata Barry, and Martin R. P. McGuire, *A Concordance of Ovid*, (Washington: Catholic University of America Press, 1939), lists twenty-one occurrences of *caecus* in the *Metamorphoses* alone, twenty-eight of *silentium* and *silere*, nine of *mutus*, and thirty-two of *nefandum* and *nefas*.

8 See, for example, Homer *Iliad* 1.459.

9 See Hartman, pp. 337–55, esp. 347 and 351.

10 Do we have here perhaps the single greatest difference between God and man? God does not need to destroy in order to create: he is first, and his primacy ensures the purity of his creation. Man, on the contrary, is always belated, and his creations seem always to involve destruction:

> The mind is the great poem of winter, the man,
> Who, to find what will suffice,
> Destroys romantic tenements
> Of rose and ice
>
> . . . .
>
> [T]he mind, to find what will suffice destroys
> Romantic tenements of rose and ice.
>
> [Wallace Stevens, "Man and Bottle"

My debt to Harold Bloom is again obvious; and yet, I would want to leave open the question of whether man and his mind can create *only* by destruction, though I do not deny that this is what man often does.

11 At *Thebaid* 5.435, Statius characterizes Orpheus thus: "et durae similem nihil Orphea Thracae" ("Orpheus, in nought resembling barbarous Thrace"). It seems unlikely that Milton would have forgotten this important distinction.

12 Saussure, pp. 120–21.

13 See Fowler's note to *PL* 5.40–41 and the bibliography cited there.

CHAPTER 6

1 CF. Michel Serres, *Hermes: Literature, Science, Philosophy*, ed. Josue V. Harari and David F. Bell (Baltimore: Johns Hopkins University Press, 1982), pp. 39–53.

2 Gilles Deleuze and Felix Guattari, *Anti-Oedipus: Capitalism and Schizophrenia*, trans. Robert Hurley, Mark Seem, and Helen R. Lane (New York: Viking Press, 1977), p. 210. Deleuze and Guattari's stimulating, often challenging remarks should be tempered nonetheless by comparison with Serres on the same issues; see *Hermes*, esp. pp. 45–51.

3 See Derrida, *Of Grammatology*, p. 267, on Rousseau and incest.

4 See, for example, Robert Burton, *The Anatomy of Melancholy*, ed. Holbrook Jackson (London: Dent, 1932; repr. 1977), pp. 143–44: "And from these melancholy dispositions, no man living is free, no Stoic, none so wise, none so happy, none so patient, so generous, so godly, so divine, that can vindicate himself; so well composed, but more or less, some time or other, he feels the smart of it. Melancholy in this sense *is the character of mortality*" (emphasis added).

5 For the present argument, I elect to exclude the Greek, Sophoclean fable to which I will refer in my discussion of *Paradise Regained*, ch. 11 below.

6 Alain of Lille, *AntiClaudianus*, 7.40; Jean de Meun, *Le Roman de la Rose*, lines 15,645–720; 21,165–84; Petrarch, *Trionfo d'Amore* 3.76; Dante, *Inferno* 30.38; *Purgatorio* 20.103; Chaucer, *Troylus and Criseyde* 4.1139; *The Physician's Tale*, line 14; Boccaccio, *Teseida* 6.42, 7.43; Shakespeare, *Venus and Adonis* (see n. 10 below).

7 Cf. Deleuze and Guattari, pp. 161–62.

8 And even then its guilt is problematic, as demonstrated profoundly and troublingly by Hannah Arendt in *Eichmann in Jerusalem: A Report on the Banality of Evil* (New York: Viking Press, 1964), esp. p. 276: "The trouble with Eichmann was precisely that so many were like him, and that the many were neither perverted nor sadistic, that they were, and still are, terribly and terrifyingly normal. This new type of criminal . . . commits

his crimes under circumstances that make it well-nigh impossible for him to know or to feel that he is doing wrong." See also Arendt's *The Life of the Mind*, 2 vols. (New York: Harcourt, Brace, Jovanovich, 1977–78), 1:6.

9 Or, as Shakespeare says, "Things growing to themselves are growth's abuse" (*Venus and Adonis*, ed. Hallett Smith, in *The Riverside Shakespeare*, ed. Evans, vol. 2, p. 1707).

10 See the prefatory essay by Hamilton, pp. 299–303, and the discussion of the bibliography there.

11 See his *Play of Double Senses: Spenser's "Faerie Queene"* (Englewood Cliffs, N.J.: Prentice-Hall, 1975), esp. p. 89.

12 Cf. the more sweeping remarks on the radical importance of incest in the *Faerie Queene* by Jonathan Goldberg, *Endlesse Worke: Spenser and the Structures of Discourse* (Baltimore: Johns Hopkins University Press, 1981), p. 117. See also Lieb, *The Dialectics of Creation*, pp. 162–64.

13 Consider, as a representative example, the following lines by Piere Vidal in *Lyrics of the Troubadours and Trouvères*, ed. and trans. Frederick Goldin (reprint, Gloucester, Mass.: Peter Smith, 1983), p. 255:

> E s'ieu sai ren dir ni faire,
> ilh n'aia .l grat, que sciensa
> m'a donat e conoissensa,
> per qu'ieu sui gais e chantaire.
> E tot quan fauc d'avinen
> ai del sieu bell cors plazen,
> neis quan de bon cor consire.
> [And if I can do or say a thing or two, / let the thanks be hers, for she / gave me the understanding and the craft, / because of her I am courtly, and a poet. / And everything I do that is fitting / I infer from her beautiful body, / and even these words of longing, rising from my heart.]

14 Quoted from J. E. Neale, *Queen Elizabeth* (New York: Harcourt, Brace, 1934), p. 385.

15 See "The Merchant's Tale," in *The Works*, ed. Robinson, IV E 1415–30, p. 117.

16 See Hamilton's note at p. 355 to *FQ* 3.vi.4.2.

17 See Carey's note at p. 196 to *C*406.

18 On the proper, see the famous essay by Derrida, "White Mythology: Metaphor in the Text of Philosophy," in *Margins*, trans. Bass, pp. 207–71, esp. 245–57; see also the stimulating remarks by Serres in *The Parasite*, trans. Schehr, pp. 177–81.

19 See, in this regard, the lines from Shakespeare's "The Phoenix and the Turtle" cited and discussed in ch. 7 below.

20 See, for example, *A Variorum Commentary on the Poems of John Milton: The*

Minor English Poems, vol. 2, ed. A. S. P. Woodhouse and Douglas Bush (New York: Columbia University Press, 1972), part 3, p. 948. On "Moneta Dei Sumus," and similar economic and commercial tropes as applied in the patristic and medieval periods to the relationship between man and God, see Martin Herz, *Sacrum Commercium: Eine begriffsgeschichtliche Studie zur Theologie der Römischen Liturgiesprache*, Münchener Theologische Studien 2, 15 (Munich, 1958); see also R. A. Shoaf *The Poem as Green Girdle: "Commercium" in "Sir Gawain and the Green Knight"*, Humanities Monograph Series of the University of Florida, 55 (Gainesville: University Presses of Florida, 1984), pp. 9–11 and nn. 7–10.

21 On the Renaissance continuation of this ancient and medieval tradition, see Charles Trinkaus, *In Our Image and Likeness: Humanity and Divinity in Italian Humanist Thought*, 2 vols. (Chicago: University of Chicago Press, 1970), 1:xxii, 180–83; 2:465, 476–78. See also Milton's own arguments in *CD* 1.12, YE 6:396, and *Tetrachordon*, YE 2:587.

22 See Augustine, *De Trinitate* 10.6 and 15.24, trans. A. W. Haddan, rev. W. G. T. Shedd, in *A Select Library of the Nicene and Post-Nicene Fathers of the Christian Church*, ed. Philip Schaff (Grand Rapids, Mich.: Eerdmans, 1956), pp. 138 and 223 respectively; see also *CD* 1.12, YE 6:394–95.

23 See Alain of Lille, *De Planctu Naturae*, prosa 4 (*Patrologia Latina* 210: 453; trans. Moffat (1972), p. 44); see also R. A. Shoaf, *Dante, Chaucer, and the Currency of the Word*, p. 117 and 258n.

24 See, among a variety of sources, Matt. 25:14–30 (the parable of the talents) and the Old English poems "The Wanderer," lines 108–10, and "The Seafarer," lines 64b–66, in *Seven Old English Poems*, ed. John C. Pope (Indianapolis: Bobbs-Merrill, 1966), pp. 32 and 35 respectively.

25 Cf. the very helpful remarks by Angus Fletcher, *The Transcendental Masque: An Essay on Milton's "Comus"* (Ithaca: Cornell University Press, 1971), pp. 212–13: "Chastity . . . is a ritually present, continuously rededicated ordering of the self. It is a cyclical rhythm, by which one lives and, more important, loves. In *Comus*, it is the double of charity and thus has no beginning or end. It is the perfect instance of Christian temperance for both Spenser and Milton, since they are able to conceive of "married chastity.""

26 See Carey's note at p. 204 to *C*557.

CHAPTER 7

1 In animal sacrifices subsequently eaten, this, of course, is physiologically the fact; the sacrificial meats make the recipients different. Cf. Girard, *Violence and the Sacred*, p. 266.

2 Or, in the words of Oswald Ducrot and Tzvetan Todorov, *Encyclopedic*

Dictionary of the Sciences of Language, trans. Catherine Porter (Baltimore: Johns Hopkins University Press, 1983): "The use of a word to designate an object or a property occurring in an existential relationship with the habitual reference of this same word. '*Bell, book* and *candle* shall not drive me back' (Shakespeare, *King John*)."

3 Again in the words of Ducrot and Todorov, "the use of a word to express a meaning resembling, yet differing from, its habitual meaning. 'Eye, *gazelle,* delicate *wanderer,* / *Drinker* of horizon's fluid line' (Spender)."

4 In these observations, I rely to a certain extent on Roman Jakobson, especially the essay "The Cardinal Dichotomy in Language," in *Language: An Enquiry into Its Meaning and Function,* ed. R. N. Anshen (New York: Harper, 1957), pp. 155–73; see also the excellent comments by Angus Fletcher, who cites this essay, in *Allegory: The Theory of a Symbolic Mode* (Ithaca: Cornell University Press, 1964), esp. pp. 160–62. I have been most influenced, however, though not always persuaded, by Umberto Eco; see especially *Semiotics and the Philosophy of Language,* pp. 114–17.

5 For similar formulations, see also *PL* 3.385–89; 6.719–22; 10.63–67.

6 This is a different—and for Milton, I think, superior—way of expressing Nicolas of Cusa's "copulative theology." Cf. Cassirer's formulation (p. 39): "Christ alone is the genuine *natura media* that embraces the finite and the infinite in one. And this unity is not accidental, but essential. It does not designate a merely actual 'conjunction' of things in themselves separate; rather, it signifies that an original and necessary connection of the two opposed moments is required. The required *natura media* must be so constituted that it includes both the higher and the lower in their totality. As the maximum of the lower and the minimum of the higher world, it must be capable of embracing the whole universe with all its possible forms, so that it may—to use Cusanus' term—'complicate' them within itself. Thus this nature becomes the actual connecting link of the universe, the 'bracket [*copula*] of the world.'"

7 See *CD* 1.5, YE 6:209.

8 Cf. the very useful remarks on these theories in Georgia B. Christopher, *Milton and the Science of the Saints* (Princeton: Princeton University Press, 1982), pp. 4, 21, 121–28, and 130–32.

9 Wallace trans., p. 197.

10 Ibid., p. 161.

11 Breward ed., p. 216; emphasis added.

12 Wallace ed., p. 165; emphasis added.

13 See John Freccero, "The Fig Tree and the Laurel: Petrarch's Poetics," *Diacritics* 5 (1975):34–39, esp. 35–36, but see also Eco's comments on such regress in *Semiotics and the Philosophy of Language,* pp. 25–35.

14 See "Two Songs from a Play, II," in *Collected Poems* (New York: Macmillan, 1933), p. 240.

15 In the *Letter to Can Grande*, p. 7, in which he calls the sense of the *Commedia* "polysemous" and goes on to illustrate this polysemous sense with the fourfold method and its terminology. See the convenient translation by Robert S. Haller, *Literary Criticism of Dante Alighieri* (Lincoln: University of Nebraska Press, 1973), p. 99.

16 The perhaps quintessentially Renaissance version of this argument would be fairly represented in the following meditation by Cusanus: "Oh Lord, how marvellous is thy face, which youths cannot conceive but as youthful, men but as manly, and the aged as aged! . . . Oh marvellous face, whose beauty all those who see it are insufficient to admire! The face of faces is veiled in all faces and seen in a riddle" (cited by Wind, p. 220). And Milton's version of this ecstasy we find, of course, in the three words, "human face divine" (*PL* 3.44).

CHAPTER 8

1 A "trope," of course, is literally a "turning"—see Shoaf, *Dante, Chaucer, and the Currency of the Word*, pp. 182 and 269, n. 14—and "verse" derives from "vertere" ("to turn the ground"), itself at the root of a crucial group of words in Christian apologetics; see Kenneth Burke, *The Rhetoric of Religion: Studies in Logology* (Berkeley: University of California Press, 1970), esp. pp. 62–65. Also recall at this point Spenser's play with *verse* and *reverse* in the speech of Despaire, *FQ* 1.ix.48 (see ch. 1 above).

2 See the quotation from *Of Education* cited in ch. 1 above: ". . . out of that knowledge to love Him, to imitate Him, to be like Him, as we may the nearest by possessing our souls of true virtue."

3 See also *PL* 9.494–503 and the remarks of John Hollander, p. 93.

4 Cf. Kerrigan's helpful remarks on this matter, *The Sacred Complex*, p. 188.

5 Cf. the very helpful remarks on Milton's originality in David Quint, *Origin and Originality in Renaissance Literature: Versions of the Source* (New Haven: Yale University Press, 1983), pp. 207–19.

6 My position on the vexed issue of Milton's supposed Arianism is basically, with certain variations in emphasis, that of Hunter, as argued in "Milton's Arianism Reconsidered," in *Bright Essence*, pp. 29–51, and as supported, though with qualifications, by Adamson, "Milton's Arianism," in ibid., pp. 53–61; both essays are responses to Maurice Kelley's *This Great Argument: A Study of Milton's "De Doctrina Christiana" as a Gloss upon "Paradise Lost,"* Princeton Studies in English, 22 (Princeton: Princeton University Press, 1941), esp. pp. 118–22.

7 See Hunter, p. 29; also Kerrigan, *The Sacred Complex*, p. 151.

8 "For to Adam, formed out of the dust, God was Creator rather than Father; but he was in a real sense Father of the Son, whom he made of his own substance. It does not follow, however, that the Son is of the same

essence as the Father. Indeed, if he were, it would be quite incorrect to call him Son. For a real son is not of the same age as his father, still less of the same numerical essence: otherwise father and son would be one person" (*CD* 1.5, YE 6:209).

9 Cf. Christopher, who notes at p. 4 that Luther, too, "seiz[ed] upon the naïve analogy that Father and Son are related as 'speaker' and 'speech'."

10 See Fowler ed., p. 810.

CHAPTER 9

1 Carey edits the sonnet at pp. 146–48 of his edition and provides a brief summary of scholarship. Consult further the recent essay by William A. Schullenberger, "The Power of the Copula in Sonnet VII," *Milton Studies* 15 (1981):201–12, esp. 209–10. I would like to thank here my colleague Leslie Moore, for first drawing my attention to the importance of Sonnet 7 in the context of Milton's similes.

2 See Carey ed., p. 147.

3 Ibid., p. 148.

4 See, for example, *PL* 2.8; 4.95; or, even better, 1.40: "He trusted to have *equalled* the *most High*" (emphasis added; see also 1.248–49).

5 On this much debated (too much debated?) issue, see Quint, pp. 213–14; also Joseph A. Wittreich, *The Romantics on Milton* (Cleveland: Case Western Reserve University Press, 1970), pp. 5–8.

6 See 1 Cor. 7:31, and consult Shoaf, *Dante, Chaucer, and the Currency of the Word*, pp. 238–39.

7 Though, of course, they can be singular (unique because dual, not single)—see the discussion of Christ's singularity in *Paradise Regained*, ch. 11 below.

8 For a very different approach to this problematic not concerned, at least directly, with Milton, see Gayatri Chakravorty Spivak, "Displacement and the Discourse of Woman," in Mark Krupnick, ed., *Displacement: Derrida and After* (Bloomington: Indiana University Press, 1983), pp. 169–95.

9 For helpful comments on this passage, see, among the many studies, Kelsey, pp. 74–85, esp. 75, and Quilligan, pp. 227–29; both writers, and especially Kelsey, cite ample bibliography in their discussions.

10 Cf. Quilligan, p. 228.

11 Obviously I am speaking here from within the assumption of Plato which Milton would have shared: an image is inferior to reality or, more precisely, to the truth. It is not admissible, however, to infer viciousness from inferiority—viciousness results from the element of will (that is, malice)—and, just so, Milton will espouse the belief that this world as image,

like Scripture as image, is a trustworthy medium for rising to the truth; see, for example, *PL* 5.574–76 and *CD* 1.30, YE 6:574–92, esp. 580–82.

12 Jacques Derrida, *Of Grammatology*, trans. Spivak, p. 144, emphasis added.

13 Ibid., p. 145.

14 Such imposition, I have argued elsewhere, is the error of Pandarus as he coins Criseyde for Troylus's currency; see my study of the extensive coinage imagery in *Troylus and Criseyde* in *Dante, Chaucer, and the Currency of the Word*, pp. 101–57, esp. 107–09.

15 Consult the fascinating, provocative discussions of this matter by Hannah Arendt, especially in "Ideology and Terror: A Novel Form of Government," *The Origins of Totalitarianism* (New York: World Publishing Co., 1958), pp. 460–79, esp. 476; also idem, *The Human Condition* (Chicago: University of Chicago Press, 1958), pp. 324–35.

16 *Meta.* 7.20–21; see also Fowler's note at p. 842 to *PL* 8.609–11.

17 See Fowler's note at p. 909 to *PL* 9.908–10.

18 See also *PL* 9.915–16.

19 C. Iulius Hyginus, *Historicus et Mythographus*, ed. F. Serra (Pisa: Giardini, 1976), p. 55; trans. Mary Grant, *The Myths of Hyginus*, University of Kansas Publications, Humanistic Studies, 34 (Lawrence: University of Kansas Press, 1960), p. 28.

20 Apollonius Rhodius *Argonautica* 3.191, ed. and trans. R. C. Seaton, Loeb Classical Library (New York: Putnam, 1912), p. 207.

21 Ibid., 2.1146; Seaton ed., pp. 179–81.

22 For a convenient summary of the lore surrounding Hermes, see the introduction by Harari and Bell to Serres, *Hermes*, xxx–xxxvii.

23 For a convenient summary of the information on the *Argo*, see H. J. Rose, *A Handbook of Greek Mythology* (London: Methuen, 1928), pp. 196–205, esp. 198.

CHAPTER 10

1 Hence, too, Milton's introduction of the serpent:
        close the serpent sly
     Insinuating, wove with Gordian twine
     His braided train, and of his fatal guile
     Gave proof unheeded.   [*PL* 4.347–50]
Where the serpent is, there proof is; proof and the serpent/Satan are inseparable. Indeed, as we know, proof is almost always "sly," "insinuating," "woven," "braided"—so the fallen intellect must go, making "intricate seem straight" (*PL* 9.632).

2 Hence Satan's total misunderstanding of such proof: "'And do they only stand / By ignorance, is that their happy state, / The proof of their obe-

dience and their faith'?" (*PL* 4.518–20). Ignorant himself of innocence, he can imagine proof only as experience, cannot imagine it as fruition, improvement. Thus he thinks that they are suffering (experiencing) ignorance when, in fact, they are innocent and suffering nothing, and when their proof (of obedience) is only fruit. He, on the contrary, only experiences (suffers), and when he "improve[s]" (*PL* 9.54), it is only "in meditated fraud and malice, bent / On man's destruction" (*PL* 9.55–56)—in other words, in anti-fruit, destruction.

3 All of which is implicit, of course, in Satan's cry: " 'Which way I fly is hell; my self am hell' " (*PL* 4.75): whatever Satan *does*, he *is* Hell (and, of course, what he is, he does)—the same damn thing over and over again, for all eternity.

4 The famous exclamation " 'Death, thou shalt die'," figures prominently in the theology of the redemption—and redemption, of course, is the way Christ transforms mortal change into change-to-fruition; see Shoaf, *Dante, Chaucer, and the Currency of the Word*, pp. 220–21 and 274, nn. 18–20, for further discussion of this matter.

5 Cf. Lieb, *The Dialectics of Creation*, pp. 219–20.

CHAPTER 11

1 Cf. W. H. Auden, "New Year's Letter":
But all his [Mephistopheles] tactics are dictated
By problems he himself created,
For as the great schismatic who
First split creation into two
He did what it could never do,
Inspired it with the wish to be
Diversity in unity . . .
He knows the bored will not unmask him
But that he's lost if someone ask him
To come the hell in off the links
And say exactly what he thinks
[*Collected Longer Poems* (Random House, 1969), pp. 96–97]

2 A good starting point on this issue is Carey's introduction to his edition of the poem, pp. 418–20; see also his notes to, for example, *PR* 1.89–91, 204–205, 356, 410–20; 2. 245–59, 327–28.

3 To this conclusion, a significant corollary attaches. Whether Satan doubts the human Jesus or the title "Son of God" (cf. Carey, p. 445, *ad* 1.356) makes no difference—it is the fact that *he*, Satan himself (*PR* 1.100–05), doubts and consequently tries or tests Jesus and/or the title which makes the difference, which marks the absolute, pure difference of Jesus and the

title as applied to Jesus. Whichever he doubts, that he doubts either one proves both—that Jesus is the perfect man who is the singular Son of God by merit; his failed doubting (doubling) makes both man and title singular.

4   See ch. 1 above, nn. 64 and 65.

5   See Carey's note at p. 498 to *PR* 4.184.

6   See R. A. Shoaf, *Dante, Chaucer, and the Currency of the Word*, pp. 182–84, 207–08, and 269–70, n. 14, on the dialectic of appropriation and expropriation.

7   Cf. the thoroughgoing Girardian reading of Milton's poetry by Donald F. Bouchard, *Milton: A structural reading* (Montreal: Queen's University Press, 1974); the point of greatest similarity (also greatest difference) between his argument and mine regards this necessity of the manhood of Christ—cf. pp. 165–66 with my remarks on the Incarnation earlier in the chapter. See also Rapaport, pp. 186–88.

8   The paraphrase, in brackets, is Carey's, p. 517, of *PR* 4.560–61.

9   On this difficult matter, see Carey's introduction, p. 424, and his lengthy note at p. 517 to *PR* 4.560–61.

10 Cf. Carey's note at p. 518 to *PR* 4.572–75.

11 Cf. the similar conclusions concerning Sophocles' Oedipus reached by Serres in *Hermes*, pp. 46–48. And we can point out that, in Sophocles play, Oedipus is precisely the victim of identity—he is, for example, identical with his mother's husband.

CHAPTER 12

1   See Carey's note at pp. 328–29 to the title.

2   I find further support for this position in Carey's conjecture that "if M. believed in this (incorrect) etymology it would be a possible starting-point for his idea of a second encounter with Dalila. No such encounter occurs in *Judges*, where he resists her three times by lying, then falls" (p. 329). See further on Samson's name Mary Ann Radzinowicz, *Toward "Samson Agonistes"* (Princeton: Princeton University Press, 1978), p. 99.

3   See Carey's note at p. 345 to *SA* 31.

4   *SA* 951–53; Carey ed., p. 338.

5   Carey ed., p. 338.

6   See *The Works* VII 3163–64 [B2 *4353–54], Robinson ed., p. 203.

7   See Carey's note at p. 396 to *SA* 1635–38.

8   Cf. Adam with Samson in this regard, especially at *PL* 9.998–99, and see ch. 8 above.

9   Carey ed., p. 341, lines 1–9.

10 See Radzinowicz, p. 359 and n. 18, and the bibliography she cites there.

11 See Jacques Derrida, "Play: From the Pharmakon to the Letter and from Blindness to the Supplement," in *Disseminations*, trans. Barbara Johnson, pp. 156–71, esp. 168–69.

13 For these remarks, I depend to a large extent on arguments put forward by Stanley Cavell in "The Avoidance of Love: A Reading of *King Lear*," in *Must We Mean What We Say?* (New York: Scribner's, 1969), pp. 267–353.

13 Consult Hannah Arendt, *The Life of the Mind*, vol. 2, *Willing* (New York: Harcourt, Brace, Jovanovich, 1977–78), pp. 125–46, esp. 144, on the Scotist formula, "Amo: volo ut sis"; see also Shoaf, *Dante, Chaucer, and the Currency of the Word*, pp. 64 and 251 n. 20.

14 I know that "Samson" does not mean "son of the same"; I simply wish to posit the possibility that Milton might have heard, even as we can hear, the potential for the phrase in the name.

15 See Carey ed., p. 335.

16 See Carey's note at p. 355 to *SA* 305.

17 Thus, Samson falls short of the ancient heroic ideal of "fortitudo et sapientia"—the just and true combination of strength and wisdom in the hero. On the topos of "fortitudo et sapientia," see E. R. Curtius, *European Literature and the Latin Middle Ages*, trans. Willard R. Trask (London: Routledge and Kegan Paul, 1954), pp. 173–78. See also Robert E. Kaske, "*Sapientia et Fortitudo* as the Controlling Theme of *Beowulf*," *Studies in Philology* 55 (1958): 423–56, repr. in *An Anthology of Beowulf Criticism*, ed. L. E. Nicholson (Notre Dame: University of Notre Dame Press, 1963), pp. 169–210.

18 Carey's note at p. 346 to *SA* 52.

19 The best brief introduction to this issue for the general reader is the study by Gustaf Aulén, *Christus Victor: An Historical Study of the Three Main Types of Atonement*, trans. A. G. Hebert (New York: Macmillan, 1969), pp. 49, 56, and 73.

20 This, of course, is the sense predominant in *The Canterbury Tales*; see, for example, *The Works, The Miller's Prologue* I A 3119, 3127, Robinson ed., 47. In this sense, if Samson has repaid himself like Samson, he has "bought" himself "back" ("redemptio") for himself—his life, if you will, has repaid his name, buying himself back for his name.

21 See Carey's note at p. 379 to *SA* 1092.

22 Obviously I must concede at this point that I am assuming that Milton here means *single* in the sense of "singular"; see again "Milton's Numbers."

23 I depend for this argument, and especially for the last sentence, on Alasdair MacIntyre, *After Virtue: A Study in Moral Theory* (Notre Dame: University of Notre Dame Press, 1981), especially chapters 1 and 2.

24 See *The Book of Beasts*, ed. and trans. T. H. White (New York: G. P. Putnam, 1954), pp. 125–28, esp. 126.

25 See Carey ed., p. 329, for the various senses of "Agonistes."

26 Ibid., p. 334.

27 On this issue, see Carey's helpful summary of scholarship at pp. 334–35. Cf. also Radzinowicz, pp. 88–90.

28 See the examples of endings from classical tragedies cited in Carey's note at p. 399 to *SA* 1745–48.

29 Consider, for example, his opening speech in the play, lines 1–13, in Sophocles, *Oedipus at Colonus*, trans. F. Storr, Loeb Classical Library (London: Heinemann, 1912), p. 147; see also line 1763, p. 305.

30 Carey ed., p. 341.

31 Ibid., p. 338.

Index

Abdiel, 117, 131, 148
accommodation, 15, 196n53
ad-serere ("assert"), 58
"Adam Unparadized," Draft IV, 37
Adam: as part, 15–16; 26, 30–39, 42,
    45, 47–50, 53–54; and puns, 60–62;
    66–67, 69, 71, 80, 97, 100, 103,
    108–109, 115–20; and imperfection,
    120–21; 131; and growth, 134; 134–
    43; and Medea, 138–43; 149; and
    birth, 150–52; 156, 167, 183, 201n6,
    209n8, 213n8
Adamo, Maestro, 51–52, 201n15
adjustment, 15–17, 133, 199n73
Adonis, 87–88, 90, 93
Adversary, the, 44, 114–25, 131, 166
advocate, 12–13, 40, 53
agon, 162, 168; agonistes, 185, 215n25
Alain of Lille, 87, 97, 205n6, 207n23
all, 26; all/ill, 67
ambiguity, 106, 108–09, 116, 158,
    166–67
Ambrose, St., 50
Anteros, 6, 194n25
apart, 16, 29, 44, 68, 85–86, 119, 129
Apollonius Rhodius, 142, 211nn20–21
apple, 31–32, 35, 41, 62, 69–70, 109,
    116, 140
appropriate, 100, 109, 112, 162, 213n6
approve, 147–49
Arachne, 74, 76
arbitrariness, 29, 31, 38–39, 43–45,
    69

arbitrium, 31
Areopagitica, 2, 35, 117, 158
Argo, 75, 143, 211n23
Arianism, 194n28, 198n64, 209n6
Aristophanes, 198n60
Artegall, 92–94
Arthur, 17–23, 94
as, 13–14, 16, 38, 62, 81, 101, 115–
    16, 121–22, 126, 128–29, 137, 155–
    56, 168–69
assimilation (and metaphor), 102–03
association, 102
Athena, 74, 76
atone, 4–5, 45, 214n19
attempting (and temptation), 122
Auden, W. H., 212n1
Aufhebung, 102, 195n37
Augustine, St., 3, 4, 7, 31, 36–37, 50,
    200n5, 207n22
author, 39, 81, 129–30, 147, 173–74
authority, 66, 114–27, 133–34, 146,
    149
autothanatography, 5
avarice (avaritia, avaritia sui), 38, 51,
    90, 94, 109, 185

Baroque, 11
Beatrice, 50, 197–98n60
Beelzebub, 16, 115
Belphoebe, 94
between (between-ness), 8, 41
bird, 74, 80, 99–100, 204n3
birth, 152–53

217